7/20

JUNGLE PARADISE, ALMOST

Jungle Paradise, Almost

Our Adventures in Costa Rica

Skip and Chipper Carey

VANTAGE PRESS
New York

To the late Dr. Chester S. Eastep, retired professor and dean, Shippensburg University, Shippensburg, Pennsylvania. "Chet" was responsible for our travels to Costa Rica. His invitation led us there; his hospitality kept us returning. His promise to God while adrift on the ocean led to the completion of the church in Nosara. He was a good citizen, a mentor to Skip, and a very loyal friend. Sadly, Chet succumbed to cancer in 1993 before the completion of the Nosara church, but his beloved wife, Martha, maintained the momentum that led to the fulfillment of his promise.

Contents

Preface

"Someone should write a book about this place." We heard that statement so frequently from folks who visited us in Costa Rica that we finally began to think seriously about it. We agreed; it *should* be written. Chipper wanted to, but Skip was highly reluctant. "It's a huge commitment," he complained. "It'll take up all our free time. It'll change our lifestyle. You have no idea how much work it is to write a book."

But Chipper persisted. She wanted to do something that she could consider a real accomplishment, something "important." This could be it. "We've got to do it," she stated emphatically.

Chipper had always kept a log of happenings and anecdotes during our visits to Costa Rica—sketchy at first, then more complete as the idea of a book took hold of her. When she became committed to writing the book, she began organizing her notes. In 1995 she began handwriting a rough draft. That did it. Skip succumbed to her pressure and began rewriting her script as he typed it on the word processor of his little Macintosh. (He's a very slow typist.) Hence, the book you read here is mostly from Chipper's point of view, rewritten by Skip. Chapter 3, however, the lost-at-sea adventure, was written by Skip from his own point of view. Other than that, when you read an *I,* it refers to Chipper. (We've used nicknames most of our lives—Chipper's given name is Eileen; Skip's is Albert.) Our marriage has survived four children and ten grandchildren, plus four stepgrandchildren added during the writing, so working together on this book probably wasn't too large a risk to our marriage.

We'd discussed whether to write our book as fiction or nonfiction and never really made a decision before we began writing. It turned out to be a moot point, since we found we couldn't fictionalize, given what we thought to be so much interesting truth. The "truth" we present here is of course our perception of reality, as it must be, but as true as we could make it.

The book is dedicated to Chet Eastep, but his wife, Martha, is certainly our leading character. Without them we would never have had all the enriching experiences that formed the basis of our narrative. Martha holds the book together; she provided a center around which we could build. Without her there would be no book. Some of our anecdotes about her may be amusing or emotional, but through it all we loved her, and still do.

We certainly hope to have offended no one, and we offer our apologies to anyone who does feel offended, for we are only telling it as we see it or saw it. Where we didn't observe an incident ourselves, we tried to portray it as something we heard or were told, but still as accurately as we could.

Finally, we confess that we have great affection for Costa Rica, the pueblos of Nosara and Esperanza, and the adjacent "gringo" development where we lived, called Beaches of Nosara, including the people we describe herein, even the "character" types, with all their foibles and eccentricities. Many of these characters are the salt of the earth; they lend spice to our lives and color to what would otherwise be a less vivid landscape. We hope you enjoy them and the Nosara scene as much as we have.

Acknowledgments

Several individuals were instrumental in the production of this book. Our Elderhostel instructor Bud Angst (Atlantic City, New Jersey, course title, *Writing for Money*) encouraged us to "go ahead and write it," to "get down to work," and to "begin at the beginning," words that we needed to hear at the time. Going far beyond the call of duty, he read several of our beginning chapters in order to start us on the right track.

Helen Ritchey, Skip's sister and an avid reader, found the many errors in our early drafts and made suggestions for improved expression, always careful to "let it be our book." She helped take the embarrassment out of our dumb mistakes.

Evelyn Minshull, another Elderhostel instructor (Clarion, Pennsylvania, course title, *Creative Writing*) and a well-published author, helped us improve the color and descriptiveness of our writing. She, too, read a couple of chapters and offered much-needed constructive criticism. In fact, her whole class provided encouragement that helped motivate us to continue.

Maxine MacKay's manuscript, *Never in Nosara,* added much to the chapters about herself and the Horselady of Nosara; like Martha, they are wonderfully interesting women.

Finally, we must credit many friends and acquaintances in Elderhostel classes, travel groups, and otherwise who said, "Oh, please let us know when it comes out! We want a copy." How could we quit with support—or pressure—like that?

JUNGLE PARADISE, ALMOST

Prologue

I'm too young to be a widow, I thought as Martha raced the "jeep" along the rough jungle road. We were trying to locate a boat, someone to help, anything to aid us in getting our husbands back from that awful windswept ocean. Darkness was approaching and they were nowhere in sight. They should have been—they *promised to be*—back by noon.

How could a day that had begun so beautifully have gone so wrong? Here we were in one of the loveliest spots in the world, having a grand vacation with friends; then our husbands went fishing. The Pacific had been calm, the sky clear and blue, when they shoved off around 7:00 A.M. that Sunday. Pablo, the local Costa Rican fisherman, was an old hand at fishing these waters. He must have put to sea in his little boat just that way hundreds of times. Why would something go wrong now?

I was deep in my thoughts of denial when the jeep skidded in the loose dirt at the edge of the road, rudely bringing me back to the present. "Holy cow, Martha!" I cried. "Don't kill us now, before we can get someone to rescue them!"

Martha was in her midsixties, some twenty years older than I, very energetic, and prone to become hyper in times of stress. Right now she seemed to be floating about three inches above the seat of the jeep and had a wild look in her eye. I knew I had to talk her down, or we really could wreck. If we didn't get help for our husbands, it was entirely possible that no one would.

But let me go back to the beginning and explain how we got ourselves into this situation.

1

1981, the Beaches of Nosara

Chet and Martha Eastep had traveled the world looking for the perfect winter retirement location. They had finally settled on a spot far out in the jungles of Costa Rica near a village called Bocas de Nosara, meaning "the mouth of the Nosara," where the river by that name runs into the Pacific Ocean. The Easteps were old friends and wanted us to visit. In fact, they gave a great sales pitch, making it sound like paradise. We just *had* to visit, they said.

The travel brochures said Costa Rica was a small country, about the size of West Virginia, known for its scenic beauty. About one acre in twelve is national park land or nature reserve, displaying a great diversity of tropical habitats from sea level to forested mountains reaching above twelve thousand feet of altitude. They also said the people were warm, friendly and welcoming to visitors, which made it a perfect place for vacationing or retirement. Of course brochures always say those things. It did sound awfully good, but perfect? We gave in and decided to see for ourselves.

It was 1981, a very cold winter in Pennsylvania, with the thermometer standing at eight degrees Fahrenheit as we left the house. We picked up our friend Mel Checkum in Shippensburg and headed for Washington National Airport in the early-morning darkness. Our heavy winter coats felt good as we rushed from building to car and then car to building. However, the coats became a bother by the time we reached Miami and connected with our LLACSA (Costa Rica's national airlines) flight to Aeropuerto Juan Santamaria in San José, Costa Rica. Here it was in the high eighties, and we were carrying our heavy coats along with our luggage and sweating profusely. Customs and immigration were very interesting as well as confusing to greenhorns such as we. One customs officer checked suspicious-looking packages in my suitcase and found unmarked cereal packages, cake mixes, and soup envelopes that we had removed from the boxes in order to save space and weight. (We had prior orders from Martha to bring oatmeal and peanut butter with us or she wouldn't let us in the door.) We tried to make sense of the signs as we progressed, a sort of crash course in Spanish, but to little avail.

Feeling somewhat vulnerable, we chose a taxi and kept repeating "Hotel Amstel," until the driver nodded his understanding . . . we hoped. The Easteps had told us that the Amstel was the hotel to patronize. Young "Ticos"—a term Costa Ricans apply to themselves—carried our bags to the taxi, just boys off the street probably, trying to earn some tips. As we loaded the taxi, Mel tossed in a bottle of Scotch whiskey we had purchased at the duty-free shop for the Easteps, our hosts.

The ride to the hotel was fascinating in the newness and strangeness of the countryside. There were so many trees in blossom! Never had we seen trees with orange blossoms, large trees at that. There were also pink, white, and purple blossoms, plus huge tropical trees and palms. Could this be true in January? It was an exhilarating new experience as we sat perspiring in the taxi holding our heavy woolen coats and laughing at ourselves. Happily, the hotel had a lockup where we could stash our winter gear as we progressed to our even warmer destination.

Less happily, we found that we had left our bottle of Scotch in the taxi. We got the hotel desk clerk to call the taxi company, but no luck. The hotel staff seemed truly helpful, though, and we were satisfied with their effort, at least.

The rest of the day was spent trying to get our dollars changed to colones. The smallest task at one of their nationalized banks seemed to take hours. Stand in this line and receive a slip of paper entitling you to stand in another line. That line gets you an official statement of what you will receive when you take the statement to the next line. The system is maddening, but more brothers-in-law and cousins get jobs this way, we were told. We received about eight strange-looking colones to the dollar.

We stopped at a grocery store called the Automercado on our way back to the hotel and bought another bottle of Scotch, finding that it was cheaper here than in the duty-free shop. Another myth disproved, another lesson learned.

Rising next morning at 5:30, we trekked off to the Alfaro Ltd. bus station to catch the 6:30 A.M. daily to Nicoya. The people were friendly and helpful in a quiet, modest way and directed us to the ticket window and the proper bus. We could only say, "Nicoya," and they would take it from there. Again we felt vulnerable, but no one seemed in any way threatening.

4

The bus ride itself was something else. It was packed with humanity, plus a few other creatures. The folks looked pretty countrified, although many appeared to be dressed in their best. There was obviously the blood of Indians flowing in their veins, but a few had lighter, more European complexions. We could see they loved their children by the way they handled them and the bright and frilly way they dressed the little girls, who were beautiful and adorable, with flashing, ingenuous smiles and alluring dark eyes. The aforementioned "other creatures" included a couple of chickens being hand-carried, we supposed, to relatives and two small pigs. Mostly the animals were quiet except for outbursts of squeals and cackles when the bus hit an exceptionally large pothole, of which there were many.

At some point the driver's assistant collected some more money to cover the second leg of the journey. We had no idea how much he wanted, so we held up numerous types of bills like hands of cards. He would shake his head and explain something in Spanish, which we didn't understand, and proceed to collect from others. We got out larger and larger denominations. Someone finally concluded that he was having trouble making proper change. The fare was very small, and he carefully chose the right coins once we scaled down to reasonable denominations. Fare was very inexpensive, just a few dollars.

We were impressed by the mountainous scenery sporting coffee plantations on the slopes. Later we glimpsed the Gulf of Nicoya, the large indentation on the southwest coast on the map of Costa Rica, with the Nicoya Peninsula positioned between it and the Pacific Ocean. As we reached lower altitudes we began to see sugarcane, cotton, and rice fields, banana patches, some coconut and orange trees, and herds of what looked like Brahma or zebu cattle. The cattle, sometimes in large herds, were handled by vaqueros (cowboys) who reminded us of pictures we'd seen in *National Geographic*. At one stop I said, "Skip, look!" There was a big, floppy-eared cow tied to a huge tree, like the rain tree in the shampoo commercial. An aging vaquero was milking her as her calf nudged at him from behind, as if to say, "Hey, that's mine!"

Martha and Chet met us at the bus station in Nicoya, their familiar smiles a welcome sight after so much strangeness. They took us to lunch at the Princess restaurant, which was nice but not quite up to its name. We had rice and chicken (*arroz con pollo*) and chatted happily about our trip.

5

Chet announced that he and Martha had to do some business at the bank, so we waited in the park across the street. It seemed to take forever, but we strolled around, looking at the flowers and birds. There really were orchids growing in the trees, and anis, like grackles but with parrotlike bills, chattering among the blossoms. Skip bought a couple *refrescas* from a nearby vendor to quench our thirst. *Refrescas* are colorful exotic fruit drinks, made in a blender with a multitude of tropical fruits blended with sugar and ice. They had strange names like *tamarindo*, mango, *mora*, *anona*, *naranjo*, and *banano*, some of which translate easily and some of which do not. To us, coming from a nasty winter only the day before and now standing in ninety-degree heat, these drinks were nothing short of marvelous.

Finally, after about two hours, Chet and Martha emerged from the Banco de Nicoya and the final leg of our trip to Nosara began. Chet was driving their 1976 Toyota Land Cruiser, a jeeplike four-wheel-drive rough-terrain vehicle. Skip tied our suitcases on top along with cans of diesel fuel and a large sack of rice. Martha, Skip, and I rode in the rear along with sacks of groceries and various other supplies. Mel rode in front with Chet.

After a few kilometers of paved road, we hit the dirt and gravel on which we would travel for the next two hours. The terrain was rough and hilly, nearly mountainous, and small rivers broke through to the ocean at intervals. These had to be forded for the most part, since only a few bridges had been installed over the worst crossings. I held my breath at a couple of these where the approach was down a steep gravel hill into a winding ford and up an equally steep opposite slope. Now the brakes were wet, and the occasional cow, horse, dog, chicken, or pig had to be dodged, since stopping was a long-range proposition.

With less than an hour to go, as we were eating dust, breathing dust, and accumulating dust on our sweat-drenched bodies and clothing, we had a flat tire. Stopping on top of a hill, atilt on the berm of the gravel road, we searched for the jack among the bags and packages. Of course there was none to be found. Nothing to do but wait for a passing vehicle, and we hadn't seen many. This lent new meaning to the word *rural*!

Skip, who had wandered up the road, called, ''Look here!'' There on a fence post was the largest lizard I had ever seen.

Chet said, ''That's just an iguana. There are a lot of those hereabout. And that's not really a large one.''

I thought it amazingly large, probably eighteen inches long, colored in tones of brown and dull green. It looked prehistoric, like a small dinosaur. The fence post itself was unique in that it had sprouted leaves. I checked the adjacent ones, finding that they also had green leaves growing from their tops. "Wow!" I said "Living fenceposts."

Before long a rural-looking Tico came walking along the road. To our surprise, Chet seemed to know him. It turned out to be Jesus, the brother of Chet's caretaker. Jesus spoke only Spanish but could see our problem, and went to the nearest farm for help. While he was gone, a taxi came along and stopped. The driver spoke no English either, but saw the problem and dug out his jack. Jesus came back with the farmer from nearby, and the group managed to get the tire changed with much friendly chatter. Chet offered money to everyone and was cheerfully refused by all. Jesus accepted a ride to Nosara, and we were on our way again. Martha said, "Just another jungle experience." Skip and I were impressed by the helpfulness and good humor of the Ticos.

We forded eighteen streams between Nicoya and Nosara, most rather small, since this was the dry season. Still, some were pretty scary because the approaches were so steep.

Finally we passed through a small village that Martha said was the pueblo of Esperanza, which translates to "Hope" in English. Martha became tour guide, with, "There's our soccer field, and there's the school. Franco's girls go there, Yorleni and Cecilia. They're so dear. You'll love them." Franco was their hired caretaker, whom Chet had taught some English.

Frankly, it looked pretty third-world to us. Many of the houses were palm-thatched shacks, supported by poles hacked by machete from the jungle. The schoolhouse was made of rough boards painted green, with a corrugated sheet metal roof. Everything was dusty due to lack of rain. But all that paled in significance when people turned and smiled and waved. Their smiles were beautiful and genuine, and they appeared clean and healthy. They seemed glad to see Chet and Martha.

Everyone seemed to recognize the jeep, as we learned it was called. Martha said, "These people are all our friends." Indeed, that seemed to be the truth, for everyone along this section smiled and waved.

Just past the village we came to a gate on the right-hand side of the road. Chet said, "Here we are," as he shifted into low gear and drove the jeep up the cactus-lined driveway past a sign reading: CASA DE LAS FLORES (House of the flowers). "These buildings were part of the old

7

Casa de las Flores, the Easteps' home in the jungle near Nosara, Guanacaste, Costa Rica. The decks are new, but the buildings were once the old
Hotel Pacifico.

Hotel Pacifico,'' he continued, indicating the house, which was built upon
posts. "It was moved here just before we bought it. We added the two
guest *cabinas* in back and the kitchen between the two main rooms.''

Martha led us to the farther *cabina*, as we carried our luggage. It
was a fairly typical bedroom except there was no glass, only screen from
about seven feet high to the roofline. The windows were also covered
with nothing but screen but had shutters for the sake of privacy and
security. The temperature was in the high eighties, so privacy had to take
a backseat to ventilation. We soon found this to be true at night as well,
although the temperature dropped to the midseventies. Toward morning,
we would pull up a sheet, but never close the shutters except for high
wind or a moment's privacy.

Travel-weary as we were, it was off to bed early. Those warm,
balmy breezes seemed to evaporate our tiredness as they wafted through
the screens. The jungle sounds serenaded us rapidly into slumber.

We awoke to strange cries and bird songs at daybreak, eager to
explore our surroundings. As I straightened the sheets, I discovered I had

been sleeping with a scorpion. "Skip!" I yelled, "There's a scorpion in my bed!"

He replied, "We just got here. You don't know what a scorpion looks like." But he came running and verified it.

Strangely, the scorpion was nearly white, so we concluded that they must be able to change colors to match their background, like chameleons. We had only seen them before on television nature programs. This one bore a great similarity to a crayfish or baby lobster, only flatter, and with a tail that curled up toward its back, ending in a wicked-looking stinger. When the scorpion is riled, we learned, this large, curved stinger is thrust forward over its head, but we smashed this one in order *not* to learn by experience. Actually, Skip gave the sheet a quick shake, which flipped the scorpion right at me. I demonstrated my youthful reflexes by jumping and screaming at the same time, while he pounced on it with his size 11 sandals.

We told Martha about our adventure at breakfast, to which she responded, "Don't tell anyone or they won't want to visit us."

I said, "Martha! You mean to say you've seen these before?"

She replied, "Oh, yes, but not that many." From that remark we learned that: (1) Martha needed company pretty badly, and (2) keep your eyes open.

Later we drove to the ocean and hiked south along the beach past cliffs and pelican roosts to what Martha called Pooka Beach. There we searched for pooka shells, which are small, white ovals with holes in the centers. They can be strung as necklaces or bracelets and result in an attractive, though primitive-looking, piece of jewelry. We also were introduced to sea jade, a greenish shell fragment worn down by the waves.

A little farther on we reached the tip of the projection called Punta Guiones. Most maps show this point as the most noticeable projection on the coastline of Costa Rica west of the Gulf of Nicoya. This trek must be taken at low tide, and even then it is a rugged walk over rock shelves and loose pebbles. The lovely scenery made the exertion worthwhile, though, with the placid blue Pacific surrounding us on three sides and the rugged cliff walls of Punta Guiones at our backs. There were nearly always birds of some type flying or gliding on the drafts caused by the warm land protruding into the sea. Pelicans were numerous, but the magnificent frigatebirds caught our imagination most, with their size and regal manner of soaring.

On the long, hot return walk we were treated to a troop of howler monkeys drowsing in the trees adjacent to the beach. We envied their image of total relaxation as they sprawled lengthwise on tree limbs with their humanlike legs and hands simply dangling. Lovely as the adventure had been, we were happy to get back to la Casa de las Flores, shower, and gather on the back deck for happy hour.

Next morning, again timed to low tide, we parked the jeep near the Hotel Playas de Nosara (Beaches of Nosara) and walked north on Pelada Beach to what Martha called Hidden Beach. There a section of the cliff had broken away from the hill and created a gap that the ocean tides were ever enlarging. Entering this notch by wading, we found a cave entrance on the landward side. Caves are always fascinating, so we carefully explored, finding bats clinging to the ceiling and lobsters and spiny sea urchins in the clear tidal sluice that sucked in and out of the cave as if it were breathing.

Across from the cave entrance, on top of the segment of cliff that had broken away, was a tropical tree being used as a roost by the pelicans. The face of the cliff was white with guano, and the birds came and went, feeding at sea and returning for rest. Skip wondered how many small fish had given their lives and bones to whitewash that cliff so thickly.

The return walk on Pelada Beach was beautiful, with the surf shooting up through fissures in the rocks like it does through the blowholes in Hawaii. It was, however, a dangerous beach for swimming, due to the broken rock shelves and the constant banging of the powerful surf, but these were the very features that gave Playa Pelada such a potent and primitive aspect.

There was a break in the rocks at the south end of the beach next to Punta Pelada, the promontory upon which the Hotel Playas de Nosara was located. This break allowed the native fishermen access to the ocean, but there was no bay or harbor. They had to push their boats out through the surf, a difficult task unless the surf was exceptionally mild at the moment.

Tired and thirsty, we piled into the jeep and headed for Casa de las Flores. We had proceeded less than a kilometer when the jeep ground, literally, to a halt. The engine was still running, but the jeep wouldn't move. Skip guessed the problem was in the transmission or driveline, but we were stopped on a rough gravel road with no tools. Luckily, Ted Hill, a physician from Vancouver, came by and hauled us home in his little Amigo truck. We sat in the bed of the truck, eating even more dust than usual, until we arrived home. Dr. Hill arranged for Frank Dupla, a character who seemed to have stepped right out of the movie *Casablanca*, to have his Tico mechanic repair the jeep. It turned out that the transmission mounting bolts had shaken loose due to the extreme roughness of the roads. Chet was overcharged "two prices," as he said, for the repairs, but as usual he paid it in his patient, courtly manner. Martha commented, "Just another day in Nosara."

There was a bit of the old pioneer spirit of helpfulness in Nosara in those days, since people who spoke English were such a small minority and there were so few services available. Accordingly, Dr. Hill refused any kind of payment except a cold drink; however, Martha said he and his wife had the habit of occasionally dropping in for a visit just before dinnertime.

Life seemed to me like it must have been in the states fifty or so years ago. The electricity was on only from 7:00 A.M. until noon and again from 4:00 until 10:00 P.M. Martha required us to play games after dinner until as late as possible, and then we would all rush to get our teeth brushed and hop into bed before the lights went out.

Folks would race to the grocery store on the day the truck arrived from San José to buy fresh vegetables and fruit, although Chet kept a nice grove of banana stalks and citrus trees. People shared tools and helped one another repair things. Madeline Moore gave the news of the day over the CB radio at 7:30 each morning, some of it gleaned from short-wave Radio Free America and some from local gossip.

The next morning Chet drove Skip up the mountain to visit Ramon and Wilda Valentine. Wilda was a dedicated music teacher who had come from the States as an "old maiden-lady" on a teacher's pension, bent on teaching local kids to play instruments. She had accomplished part of her dream, but on a more romantic note, she had met and married Ramon, a retired ferryboat captain from Puerto Rico. They lived here full-time in a beautiful Spanish-style white stucco house with red roof tiles, her cherished baby grand piano gracing the living room. Wilda was enjoying the romantic life she had only dreamed about back home. Their hilltop vista of the jungle and ocean was stunning.

The purpose of Chet's visit to the Valentines was to borrow Ramon's fishing tackle in order to take Skip and Mel fishing the next day. Chet was trying to be a gracious host and so far was doing just great!

2

Lost at Sea: Chipper's Point of View

Sunday was beautiful. The sea was calm and pure cobalt blue. Martha and I drove the three men, Chet, Mel, and Skip, to the launching beach adjacent to Punta Pelada about 6:30 A.M. and watched as they made ready to go fishing. There they were met by Pablo, a local fisherman who had been engaged to take them out in his thirteen-foot aluminum boat. He carried two crude hand-carved wooden paddles as emergency backup for his 9.6-horsepower Japanese-built outboard motor and an old life preserver for each passenger. That was it, except for a rum bottle filled with water for himself, a small tackle box, and Ramon's two fishing rods. They expected to fish until about 10:00 or 11:00 A.M., when Martha and I were instructed to pick them up for lunch.

Off they went, pushing the little boat out through the surf and jumping in. Pablo jerked on the starter rope a couple of times, and the engine coughed, took hold, and powered them away on that lovely blue sea. Martha and I watched until they were well out, then crawled back into the jeep and drove home to CASA DE LAS FLORES.

Sometime after ten we returned to the landing to wait for our fishermen to return. It was pleasant but had become quite breezy during the morning. The boat was nowhere in sight. Still, it was early, so we enjoyed the beach, strolling and chatting, occasionally looking out to sea for the boat. We searched the horizon more and more thoroughly as time passed, becoming increasingly uneasy. Finally Martha said, "Well, I'm getting worried. They should be in by now."

I replied, "Yeah, me, too. It's not like them to be late."

A friend of Martha's, Fiona Frazier, joined us on the beach, listening as we told her of our situation. She kept us company as she peeled oranges and chatted. I didn't say anything at the moment, but I recall being intrigued by the skill with which she peeled those oranges. Fiona was a full-time resident, knowledgeable of local lore like peeling oranges, fishermen, the ocean, and such. Her husband, John, also was a fisherman as well as a builder. She agreed that she would be worried in our situation.

12

We drove the short distance to the hotel on the point, where we could see better and get some other opinions. Friends there said, "Oh, they're just catching some fish. You know how fishermen are. Give them some time. They'll be back when they get hungry." We certainly wanted to agree, but this wasn't like Chet and Skip. We tried to stay calm, but our fears were not allayed. A cold, nagging ball kept growing in the pit of my stomach.

Fiona told us of someone who had a boat and motor, so we took off in the jeep. Martha was getting hyper and driving too fast on the rough mountain roads, talking a mile a minute and not concentrating very well. I hated the thought of crashing over the side and never knowing what had happened to my husband or being able to help get him back. I snapped, "Martha, slow down! You're going to kill us!"

That trip was in vain; no one was at home, and the boat was gone. We returned to the hotel and asked someone to call the Costa Rican Coast Guard on the radiophone, the only means of communication with the outside. John Frazier made the call, reporting that the Coast Guard couldn't help us today but would try to dispatch a cutter to the area tomorrow—not very reassuring.

Finally, late in the day, Gene Talboy, a full-time resident builder, offered to call the U.S. embassy for us. It, of course, was in San José, but they promised to do everything possible, although by now it was too late in the day to do anything. We scanned the horizon under a windy but still beautiful sunset. Costa Rican sunsets over the Pacific are among the greatest in the world, but Martha and I weren't enjoying this one.

There was nothing to do but go home and try to rest. Easier said than done. My mental neurons were firing on their own, nonstop. I was going over in my mind what life would be like without Skip. Our youngest son was a college freshman, and our two older sons had recently married. Our daughter, who is next to youngest, was soon to be married. They all still needed a father, and then there were those college expenses. What was going to happen to my life?

Martha talked a little about trying to go on without Chet, which certainly didn't cheer me up. I wasn't ready to be resigned to Skip's demise. Martha and I decided to sleep in the same bed that night for comfort and support, but it seemed that all we did was toss and turn. Martha and I had been acquainted for nearly fourteen years but had never become truly close. She was the wife of my husband's dean, his boss,

13

so to speak, so I held her in some awe; however, this experience was certainly erasing barriers and drawing us closer.

We awoke Monday morning to a bright, windy day, but that tight ball of fear was tormenting the pit of my stomach again. We forced some coffee and breakfast down, though it didn't sit well, and took off for the hotel. We learned that the hotel lights, which were normally shut off at 10:00 P.M., had been kept on all night, in case our men might have been able to see them. We certainly appreciated that.

No one had yet sighted our men. John Frazier was at the hotel and told us that he had kept a number of his Tico construction workers on the beaches most of the night making bonfires at various points to guide the men to shore, in case they were close enough to see. Some carried flashlights and torches and had walked the beaches all night. That comforted us and brought a few tears of gratitude but didn't change the situation. It was frightening to think that they might have been searching for bodies or other signs of disaster.

This was the day we had planned to fly home and Martha had other guests arriving, so we had to go back and prepare the rooms. That meant packing Skip's and Mel's things and changing the beds. Dear God, that seemed so final. I just broke down and cried.

With that sad task completed, we pulled ourselves together and drove back to the hotel to find word that the U.S. embassy had called. They had informed Howard Air Force Base in Panama, and a rescue plane was on its way to search for our guys. At last, a glimmer of hope! Martha and I cried again and hugged each other. Our friends cautioned us that ocean searches were like looking for a needle in a haystack, but all we had left to us was hope and prayer.

We finally remembered that this was to have been our day to fly to San José and then home tomorrow. That wasn't going to happen, it seemed, so we called the airlines to cancel our reservations. I also called Laurie, our daughter, and told her the truth. It sounded harsh: "Your dad is lost at sea. We won't be home as planned. They are searching for them." I tried to cushion it a little, but that was basically how it was; she must have felt awful.

Martha was about to call four guests who were in San José prepared to fly out to Nosara the following morning, to tell them they should just go back home. I said, "Martha, you can't do that! They're your friends, and they would want to be with you at a time like this. You can't just send them home without even seeing them."

14

She thought for a moment, consternation written all over her face, and then agreed: "Yes, that's how I'd feel. I'll just have to let them come on out, whatever happens."

By late morning we spotted the search plane, a large twin-engine camouflaged military craft, flying a grid pattern up the coast, then out, then down the coast and so on. But what could they do if they did find the men? They couldn't pick them up, could they? We would just have to wait and see, and that was terribly difficult to do.

At about eleven-thirty Monday morning we received word by the telephone at the hotel that our fishermen had been spotted and appeared to be well. All four were in the boat, waving their orange life jackets. What wonderful news! However, the search plane had run low on fuel and had to return to base for refueling, so they were still out there somewhere, floating around.

Time passed endlessly without another word until about 7:00 P.M., just after full dark at that latitude, when a second call came in. The search plane had returned and relocated them, but attempts to drop survival gear and a life raft had failed. The wind had blown it all out of their reach. The search plane was giving up its rescue efforts for the night and returning to base. What a downer! They would be out for another night. Would they be able to relocate the men in the morning, or would they just disappear in the darkness?

A little while later another call came in. As the plane was leaving the area, it had spotted a British ship and led it to them. They were now thought to be aboard. Hallelujah! How relieved can a person be? Martha and I hugged each other and received hugs from others, this time with tears of joy.

Martha said, "Now I'll be able to eat!"

But as we ate with Martha's friends at the hotel restaurant, folks began to admit how hopeless they had thought our situation to be. They hadn't told Martha and me, but many of them had feared we had almost no chance of ever seeing our husbands again. We began to realize how lucky we were.

We began to relax and breathe a little more easily. We still didn't know how the men would get back to Nosara, but that was a comparatively minor concern. We slept much better that night, no longer worrying about what to do if we never saw our husbands again, also because we were exhausted from the stress of the ordeal.

15

The next morning we received word that our husbands were on the bus to Nicoya from Puntarenas, the small port city on the Gulf of Nicoya where the British ship had deposited our men. We also met Martha's four guests at the airstrip in Nosara and took them back to the house to get them settled in. One of the newly arrived guests, Glenn Lytle, volunteered to drive the two hours or more to pick them up. He found them eating a hearty dinner at the same restaurant we had patronized on our incoming trip.

They arrived home a little after four o'clock Tuesday, wearing white ship's coveralls, looking very tired, burnt, and weather-beaten. It was a tearful reunion; Martha was in Chet's arms and I was in Skip's. But Mel had no one to embrace, so Louise Lytle, thoughtful as always, took care of that task. Louise was departmental secretary for all three men back at Shippensburg University, which seemed at this moment so far away. We posed for a picture, Martha and I with tears streaming down our faces, the four men in their white coveralls, including Pablo the guide, fishing rods and all.

That evening at supper we all gratefully held hands around the dinner table as Chet tried to say grace, but he choked up after a stammered opening. Martha picked up in the awkward silence with her usual Girl Scout blessing ("for food, for raiment, for friendship and fellowship, we thank Thee, O Lord, amen") and we ate a relieved, albeit emotional dinner.

The next morning we arose shortly after five, snatched a quick bite of breakfast, and dashed to the Nosara airstrip for the half-hour flight to San José and the trip home to Pennsylvania. At the airstrip, a level patch of gravel frequented by cattle and pigs that had to be chased away when a flight was due, a few Ticos moseyed by to eye these lucky gringos. One old-timer said something to Mel that he seemed to partially understand, since he had studied some Spanish long ago. I heard Mel say, *"Gracias a Dios,"* which I understood to be "Thanks to God." I guess we all felt that way.

As for Skip and me, we had cemented our relationship with Chet and Martha, learned to love Costa Rica, and learned a few lessons about ourselves. We weren't yet sure what those lessons were, only that something important had happened and that we would always be a little changed by it. I do believe that we have appreciated each other a bit more ever since.

16

3

Lost at Sea: Skip's Story

Chipper and I agreed that I should write down my recollections as soon as I found time after returning home to Shippensburg, before they became vague or distorted. This chapter is taken from that original handwritten account.

It was a gorgeous day for fishing. Chet, Mel, and I helped Pablo float his little boat out through the smooth breakers alongside Punta Pelada. Chet, my old department head and dean, was about seventy, white-haired and balding but still tall and distinguished-looking. Mel was a professor of education, short and jovial, with thick, wavy salt-and-pepper hair and long mustache. I was in my late forties, medium height and still fit, but turning gray. We were all longtime colleagues at Shippensburg University in Pennsylvania. Pablo was a small, trim, well-weathered man of the sea.

The motor started nicely and we were soon trolling, taking turns with the two rods that we had borrowed from Ramon. Mel caught the first fish, a type of tuna about fifteen inches long. Then I caught a large creval jack, which Pablo called a *jurel* in Spanish (pronounced "hooREL"). It was a deep-bodied, strong fish but has dark meat and thus is not a top choice for eating. Chet caught one like it, then I caught a Spanish mackerel, and so it went for an hour or two. Sometimes there were several fish following the one on the line. We were enjoying all this immensely when the motor coughed and jerked. We shot apprehensive looks at one another, but I told myself that Pablo did this nearly every day and he was still here. Yeah—that's what I told myself when I focused on the fact that there were only rough paddles and no real oars, water, or flares.

We saw a migration of sea turtles, probably Ridley's, when the motor sputtered and quit. Pablo tried but couldn't get it going. We also noticed that now the wind was growing stronger and the boat was bobbing a lot more.

17

Just then one of the turtles swam directly at the boat, and Mel asked, "Is he going to ram us?" before the turtle ducked gracefully under us and out the other side.

Pablo removed the spark plug and held his cigarette lighter under the electrodes to clean and warm it, but to no avail. To do this he had to pull the motor up and remove the cover, which was not easy, due to the bobbing of the boat. After replacing it, he then yanked at the starter rope so long that he tired his arm. Following a short rest he repeated the process until the starter rope broke. This I could handle, so I removed the recoil unit with Pablo's pliers and reknotted the rope a bit shorter. Pablo resumed yanking, but no luck.

We sat for a while trying to think of something to do. Fishing had lost its appeal. For me that's a pretty dire statement. Chet queried, "Skip, is there anything you could do to fix that motor?"

I said, "I don't think so. I don't know anything about that engine, and I don't have any tools, other than Pablo's pliers and knife. Worse yet, this boat is beginning to bounce like a bucking horse." And it was.

A little later Pablo gave another try at fixing the engine. As he leaned over to heave the motor up, the boat lurched, dumping him overboard. Mel, being nearest, made a fast grab and caught Pablo's shirt. I quickly hopped into the stern and helped drag him back on board. He was soaked and sputtering. That experience dissuaded us from much more effort at starting the motor.

Pablo dug out a long coil of light rope to which he tied the small anchor from the usual short anchor line. He motioned for me to climb forward and tie the rope to the bow. There seemed to be about eighty feet of line, maybe more. It reached bottom, but with not much to spare. I could feel it dragging on the bottom. I think this rig is called a sea anchor, with the purpose of keeping our bow to the wind. Staying nose to the wind was very important, since it kept our little thirteen-foot aluminum boat facing the relentless oncoming waves. We expected it to upset or fill with water in a moment if we turned crosswise to the waves. But despite the anchor it was obvious that we were still being blown farther from shore.

The day remained bright and sparkling, but the wind and waves were becoming worrisome. We were bobbing pretty energetically, riding up the face of a wave and then dropping into the next trough. For a while I watched constantly to see if we would be swamped by each wave as it loomed above us, but I soon realized the futility of that. We came to trust

18

the buoyancy of the little boat, even to marvel at the way it never failed to ride up the next wave.

We should have been back at the landing by now and knew our wives would be anxious. We didn't talk much about that, but I knew Chet was as concerned about Martha being frightened as I was about Chipper. Mel was a widower, but I guessed he was probably thinking about his late wife. His daughter would be the one most likely to worry about him, but she would not be aware of our situation for some time. Same thing for my three sons and daughter. We were so isolated that even the news media wouldn't catch on for quite a while. We were all wandering about in our own thoughts, I suppose; at least I was.

The wind was still increasing. We guessed it had reached at least light gale level, thirty- or forty-mile-an-hour winds. Now when we dropped into a pocket between waves, we couldn't see land; there was nothing but sky and walls of gray water around us. But we would bob up the next wall like a cork, and then we could see the forested hills of Costa Rica again. I crept forward to check the bowline to which the anchor was tied; it was hanging free, off the bottom. Apparently we were drifting over deeper water now, farther from shore, but our sea anchor was keeping our bow to the wind and waves. The only way we were taking water was by windblown spray and the occasional splash. We began to bail for something useful to do, nothing desperate yet, but we did feel so awfully helpless. We watched for ships and planes, but nothing promising ever came within sight. Once we saw a large ship, barely in view on the horizon; otherwise, we were very alone on a very large ocean in a very small boat.

Toward sunset the winds slackened somewhat, so we pulled our anchor and tried to paddle toward shore. Pablo and I kept paddling for several hours, probably four hours, more or less. Oars might have done the job, but Pablo's homemade paddles couldn't give us enough boost to make any serious headway. My paddling left something to be desired, too, since it was getting too dark to see where we were heading. Apparently I was repeatedly pulling us off course, for Pablo would signal me to guide left or right as he deemed necessary. He was working on the left side and I on the right, so it was difficult to steer a straight course. Finally the stars brightened enough that I could make out the Belt of Orion over my right shoulder and use it as a guide to keep us aimed toward shore. To this day I can't see Orion's belt without recalling that ominous night at sea.

Pablo and I pulled on those rustic oars until our arms ached. At one point something caught my attention in the water, and I called to my companions to look. At every stroke of my paddle, myriad tiny phosphors swirled in glowing formation around it. We were all fascinated by this phenomenon and discussed the science surrounding it for a short while but soon fell back to musing about our predicament.

At another point we saw lights, probably the hotel, and thought we could hear the surf breaking onshore. But then the wind picked up again and it all faded into the background. We gave up paddling in despair, reset the sea anchor, and tried to position ourselves to rest as best we could. It was a pretty low moment.

Thank goodness we were in the tropics "enjoying" warm wind and water, for even there we chilled when the sea sprays would soak us during the night. There was no way to get comfortable in the small rowboat. Water sloshed in the bottom, requiring occasional bailing, permitting no one to lie there. We all sat on wooden seat boards. Mel and I, sitting on the middle seat, had no place to lean. Chet sat in the bow and could lean against the converging sides but bounced a lot and took a lot of spray. Pablo sat in the stern and, being smaller, could curl up and brace his feet against the motor for some moments of rest. But we all would doze fitfully and then get doused into chilled wakefulness by spray and wind. Sometimes a wave would seem to reach up and slap us, leaving us shaking and chattering—damned uncomfortable, to say the least. Chet and Mel were probably worse off than Pablo and me, since we were a bit younger and in better physical shape and had at least benefited from the exercise of paddling. I felt some sympathy for them. Also, by now I was developing some faith in the boat and had less fear of capsizing.

Now and then I had to admire the beauty of the night sky. We were located eight or nine degrees north of the equator, so the constellations appeared a bit different in perspective from our usual view in Pennsylvania at forty-odd degrees north. The polestar was lower in the sky, along with the Big Dipper, but most of the constellations were still familiar and observable. There were some strange ones to the south with which I wasn't familiar, but there was no one with me who could name them.

I guess we were all waiting and watching for dawn. I could readily identify with the early humanoids getting caught up in sun worship and orienting all their structures to face the east. It was easy to understand a great fear that the sun might not rise. What a catastrophe that would be. I could comprehend how prayer might have evolved even before organized religion. I also wondered what my shipmates might be thinking, but none of us seemed to want to do any philosophizing out loud or share inner thoughts. As I look back, this seems strange, because Chet was a great philosopher and often talked long and seriously about his somewhat mystical views of the cosmos. Mel was a lighthearted, outgoing Welshman but didn't say much beyond his own observations of the moment while in this predicament. That seemed to be true for us all, however strange.

What a relief to see the first gleams of dawn; it had seemed to come so slowly! It sneaked over the horizon just as the Big Dipper reached its zenith. Even so, we were very slow to warm, taking a couple of hours to absorb enough slanting rays to ease the long chill of the night. The wind had abated somewhat toward morning, but only to a stiff breeze. At least it wasn't gale-force any longer.

We were now twenty-four hours out, without food or water. (Pablo had finished his rum bottle of water before noon yesterday.) But that was not our preoccupation. We seemed focused solely on watching and listening for rescue efforts. By midmorning we felt better again, our spirits lifted by the bright sunshine and its warmth after the long, cold, dark night. We talked a little more now, pondering how we might be rescued, how they might go about it, who would make the effort. We concluded that Chipper and Martha would leave no stone unturned to effect our rescue and that Chet had some friends in the area who would certainly help. Still, how would they locate us? We were now pretty far out and a mere speck, fast becoming a *very* small speck on a very large ocean. We never solved that persistent question in our minds: *How would they retrieve us if they did find us?*

Pablo began to fillet one of our fish, then cut it into strips and laid them out to dry in the sun on the seat and sides of the boat, throwing the remainder into the water. He repeated the process with a couple more fish; then we threw the rest overboard. It wasn't long before we spotted several sharks swimming around us, apparently foraging for the remains of the fish. They stayed only a short while, then went on their mysterious way. We were impressed with their speed in the water.

Sometime later I shouted, "Look!" A large, shining gray stingray shot out of the water about fifty feet away, did a full flip, and reentered headfirst. Very obligingly, it repeated the performance for those who had missed the first show. We guessed it was about three feet across its "wingspread" and cleared the surface three feet or more. I have since

21

seen them about that size washed up on shore, victims of the purse seiners who fish for shrimp up and down the local coastline, truly a wasteful practice. A big ray Chipper and I found had a stinger about the size of my little finger. Vultures were the cleanup crew, a really ugly sanitation department.

Sometime between ten and eleven that morning, we spotted a plane cruising up the coastline, a sight that elated us. Mel asked, "Do you think they're looking for us?"

We all agreed they must be; it was a moderately large military craft wearing camouflage paint. What else would it be doing here? We immediately directed our attention to assessing what we could do to assist in our own location and rescue. I said, "Let's polish our reel faces; they're chrome. Then we can flash them at the plane." That was done immediately and produced a blinding flash that should be seen for miles. Next we tied the brightest orange life preservers to each of the fishing rods and waved them back and forth.

By this time the search plane had been up the coast, turned out some distance away from the shoreline, and headed back south. We desperately hoped they weren't quitting the search. All eyes focused intently, almost breathlessly, on the plane. Slowly it disappeared from our view, eight hungry eyes straining intently. We glanced briefly at one another, avoiding eye contact for fear of letting our deep disappointment be seen.

Then we saw it returning! It was farther out to sea this time and heading back up the coast on a pass that would bring it closer to our position. We cheered, realizing that they were forming a search grid pattern. Now we began aiming the shining reel faces at the plane and waving the life jackets for dear life. One more pass, turn, pass, and they spotted us, making a forty-five-degree turn directly toward our position. No matter: we kept waving and shining frantically, taking no chances that they might miss us. It flew directly to us, circled twice, and flew off southward. That was that. We looked at one another in stunned silence. There was that question again: *How are they going to pick us up?*

We began to speculate once more after the silence and isolation that had reclaimed us for a while. Maybe they were sending the Coast Guard, if Costa Rica had one. Maybe they had radioed to shore and notified our wives. I felt a strong wave of emotion to think that maybe now Chipper would know I was safe. I had thought a lot about her during our quiet moments. I felt deeply about her and was able to identify with what I supposed she was feeling. But the unspoken code in the boat seemed to be that we keep emotion submerged. No one spoke of feelings or of loved ones. Despair would show on a face only at pivotal moments and then only briefly. If emotion showed on a face, the others would not look beyond a quick glance, as if to allow privacy.

We learned later that the search plane had run low on fuel and had been forced to return to base before continuing its rescue operations. Not knowing that, we had only conjecture to sustain us. For a while we diligently scanned the horizon, expecting to see a boat appear at any moment. Our enthusiasm for that gradually lagged, although we still slowly scanned most of the time. The wind was growing again. We had endured a strong breeze most of the time, but now it was more like a light gale. We bailed more regularly, using an old coffee can that Pablo carried for that purpose. We also used that same can as a latrine, but not often, due to the dehydration that was making itself felt. Nonetheless, we greatly appreciated that old coffee can.

I had regularly applied lip balm, which I always carry in my pocket. Now, Monday afternoon, I realized that Mel, sitting nearest me, was becoming badly burnt, cracking and beginning to peel. So I passed the lip balm around. We applied it to our cheekbones and noses as well as our lips. Mel admitted later that he had nibbled it a bit, due to hunger. No wonder we were burning; Chet was the only one of us wearing a hat, and that was due to doctor's orders because of skin cancer. We all wore short-sleeved shirts. I tried to scratch my head, only to find that I could hardly get my fingers through my hair, it was so stiff with salt. I patted my head and it sounded like potato chips crunching. My pants and shirt were stiff with salt, too. I said, "Hey, guys, look," and we all marveled at how our hours of exposure had crept up on us. We discussed our level of thirst, all wishing we had some water, but agreed that our attention was fastened to one thought: rescue. Food and drink would certainly have been welcome but were not yet foremost in our awareness. That seemed strange for us well-fed Americans accustomed to eating too well and too regularly.

As for Pablo, we couldn't know what he was feeling. He was more stoic than the rest of us, and we weren't doing badly in the stoicism department ourselves. We regretted that Pablo, who spoke only Spanish, couldn't participate in our discussions, desultory though they were.

Past midafternoon we spied a large, colorful ship cruising northward out on the shipping lanes. At least we presumed they were the shipping lanes, since we had seen a ship about that far out during the prior day and again earlier this same day. They were still too far away to discern our little speck in the huge expanse of the great Pacific Ocean. We learned later that a Costa Rican Coast Guard vessel had been dispatched that morning to locate us but had broken down about halfway from its base in Puntarenas. Ironically, the only other Coast Guard boat had been sent to tow it in.

By now, the day was waning. It was still quite windy, blowing spray off the tops of the waves, which I estimated to be six or eight feet high. The sun was still bright, but the angle was lowering; the sea spray was beginning to feel cool again on our sunburnt skin. The faces of all in the boat were beginning to look more drawn and worried again, and we still held eye contact only briefly. No one wanted to disclose the growing dread in the backs of our minds. Morale was pretty low: Doubt: 5, Optimism: 1.

Then we saw it. Our rescue plane was returning. Joy filled our hearts! They seemed to know precisely where we were; how, we couldn't figure, since we had been drifting and blowing all afternoon. Maybe they had charts of the direction and speed of the wind and currents. However they relocated us, we were certainly glad they did. It was getting late in the day.

The winds and seas were slowly getting worse again, as they do in this part of the world. Chet said the winds were called the *Guanacastes,* after the westernmost province of Costa Rica, which we were visiting. They are strong, unpredictable winds often rising in the late afternoon or evening and blowing most of the night, often easing in the middle of the night or next morning. Sometimes they blow for several days, intermittently or constantly, and then disappear just as unpredictably. We just happened to go fishing as one spell of Guanacaste winds had begun. Now the rescue plane was circling as we bobbed on the steep waves like a cork, still wondering how they could possibly rescue us under these circumstances.

Something dropped from the plane. We looked hard, every eye intent. It was a large splotch of orange dye marker, maybe ten or fifteen feet in diameter, floating with us about forty or fifty feet away. It slithered up over a wave and into the next trough, then back up another, just as we were doing. They dropped another and then a smoke marker. The plane made very low passes to do all this. How I truly wished we could communicate with them. We could have seen their faces except the windows were hidden from our view, due to the configuration of the craft.

Then came a large package that opened as it fell, and miraculously there was a large, beautiful, self-inflating life raft, with a supply of good-looking stuff inside. We tried desperately to get our sea anchor aboard and paddle to this large, safe-looking raft, but the winds just blew it past us at a distance of twenty or thirty feet and then out of reach. In what seemed like the blink of an eye it was gone. Just like that, it was gone!

We learned later that the raft was loaded with survival gear; a sun canopy, sea rations, coveralls, a water distillation kit, flares—the works. We looked at each other blankly as if to say, "What the hell happened here?" The plane circled overhead once more, still very low, and then headed off southward.

We were stunned. Our would-be rescuers were gone, totally gone, and here we were, no better off than before. Worse than before! It was nearly sunset and we were thirstier and hungrier and more tired and stiffer and . . . damn, this was discouraging! I turned to look at Chet. I just knew the disappointment that I had kept hidden so well was showing on my face this time. He looked just as disappointed, and worst of all, I could see his heart fall when he looked at me. His wonderful physical presence seemed to wilt; he appeared to age before my eyes. I had to avert my gaze.

This was the lowest point of our ordeal. At that moment, we felt we were facing death. Chet told me later that I had read him correctly, that he was depending on my strength to buoy him and the look I threw him at that moment had pulled the rug from under him. I regretted it, but as a counselor I know that feelings are our truth, and that's the way it was. Everyone now grew morbidly quiet as we scanned slowly and dispiritedly the seemingly endless sky and sea for the help we so desperately wanted and needed before nightfall. And darkness was rapidly approaching.

Suddenly Mel said, "Look there!" The search plane was returning, aimed directly at us again. Mel wondered aloud, "But what can they do?" That summed it up for us all. What *could* they do? Pablo seemed to cast his opinion by turning his back on the plane and curling up on the stern seat next to his defunct engine. He had caught some spray again and said, "*Frío, muy frío*," meaning he was cold, very cold.

The plane dropped flares along the way and then passed low over us. It circled and then returned on the same path by which it had arrived, leaving us puzzling about its actions. I looked down the line of flares and asked, "Isn't that a light down that way? Look the way the plane went."

Then the plane returned on the same flight path, but the light was still there. Mel cried, "That's a ship!"

Sure enough, there was a big yellow ship coming toward us on the line the plane was drawing in the sky and by flares in the water. Oh, what a beautiful sight! Hope leaped again that we would not have to spend another night on the dark ocean. Surely they would be able to get us off the water.

The plane flew by us again, tilting its wings right and left in salute, and we waved good-bye as it disappeared. The ship came within a couple of hundred yards and stopped, turning broadside, the captain apparently afraid of coming too close to our delicate craft.

Now it was up to us. We pulled up our anchor as fast as we could. Pablo and I situated ourselves in the stern and manned the paddles. We seemed to move so slowly in the blowing waves! It seemed incredible that so large a ship was waiting just for us! It was dark now, so the ship lit great floodlights to guide us in. What a sight!

Thank goodness the ship was more or less downwind, because even so it seemed to take us forever to reach it. When we did get there, the approach was dangerous. The crew lowered a hydraulic stairway, but the ship was rocking and we were bobbing beneath it like some kind of mad amusement park ride. It looked awfully easy to drop off a wave and drift under the ship as it wallowed. The crew was shouting encouragement and threw a line when we bobbed close enough. We caught the line on the second try and tied it fast to the bow where the anchor was tied. A couple of men stood on the bottom step, which appeared to be bobbing up and down about six feet, sometimes in the waves, sometimes well up in the air. They dragged our boat up to the step they occupied.

I heaved Chet up toward them, everything bounding in opposite directions. Chet was stiff and awkward from sitting so long, but the men grabbed him and bodily hoisted him up the stairs, others coming down to help. I hung onto Mel as he crawled across the wet board seats, slipping on the curved bottom of the boat, banging into this and that, and being tossed around until he reached the crew.

The trick was to push and grab as the boat rose and the stairway fell. In this manner we all made it to the stairs and up into the ship. It was very difficult to walk. We staggered like drunks. It was now thirty-six hours since we had first crawled into that little boat, and we had not walked in all that time. We were so very stiff, and besides, the ship was rolling with a motion new to us. They asked us what language we spoke and if anyone spoke English. They were obviously pleased when we said we did.

Pablo was reluctant to leave his boat, which surprised us all at first, but then we realized his boat was the sole means of livelihood for a very poor man. The problem was taken to the captain, who ordered the boat hauled aboard. It was tied to lines, winched straight up, and then swung in onto the deck, a bit battered but intact. We were taken to a room and given seats and small glasses of water, then butter sandwiches, by the purser, Danny Setchell, a warm, humorous, outgoing man, seemingly glad for the diversion we provided.

The captain appeared, whom Danny introduced as Captain Rosie, from Edinburgh, Scotland, in charge of this ship, HMV *Samaria*. Of all things, we were being rescued by the Good Samaritan! It was a Cunard Lines freighter out of Liverpool commissioned to United Fruit in Los Angeles to haul bananas from Central and South America. It listed, to my recollection, over forty thousand tons displacement. The captain interviewed us with regard to our nationality, what we were doing "out there," our destination, and such. He said he would drop us off at the next port of call, which was Acapulco, or else at Los Angeles, his destination. He was carrying a refrigerated load of bananas, very perishable.

We were happy to be rescued, we explained, *very* appreciative, but we wondered if he could possibly drop us in Costa Rica. Besides, there was the matter of Pablo's boat. He would never be able to get it home from Acapulco or LA. Captain Rosie frowned and said that would be out of his way—actually seven hours back to Puntarenas and then seven more to return to this spot, fourteen hours lost not counting rescue time or unloading time in Puntarenas Harbor. Also, Puntarenas was located some distance up the Gulf of Nicoya and a bit shallow and would be tricky for a freighter the size of this one. But he would radio headquarters and let us know his decision.

Chet, the only one of us carrying a wallet, asked Captain Rosie if he could pay him anything. The captain replied, "You couldn't begin to afford it." After all, we had informed him that we were college professors. He mentioned that Cunard Lines carried rescue insurance by Lloyd's of London. Additionally, he informed us that the rules of rescue allowed him to claim any property picked up at sea during a rescue and to drop any rescued persons at his convenience. His inclination was to drop us at Acapulco. We were then led off to cabins with showers and told we could clean up and rest a bit. They gave us white ship's coveralls and left us alone.

I stood my salty clothes in the corner and enjoyed the best shower of my life. Then I gave my clothes a quick rinse and wrung them out. At least now they were flexible. Plopping on the bunk, I closed my eyes, only seeming to drift and rock and roll. It felt like only a few minutes before someone shook me and requested my presence in the crew's lounge. He told me that we were on our way to Puntarenas. Happy news!

I donned the white coveralls and was led through various passage-ways to a lively-sounding lounge filled with British accents and the smell of beer and stronger stuff. Soon my companions appeared, also in formal white and presumably with nothing else on except a soggy pair of sneak-ers. We all looked groggy, but these guys were dying for relief from the boredom of one another, it seemed, and craved our conversation. They plied us with drinks and snacks, although we couldn't take too much alcohol in our present state. They were truly gracious hosts and lively conversationalists. We chatted back and forth of home, families, careers, and the like, obviously enjoying one another's company. We begged off around one-thirty and tried to rest, but I still had that rotating, floating, and rocking sensation.

We were wakened about 2:00 A.M. and told to appear on deck ready for disembarkation. We slid into our life jackets and located our posses-sions. I had earlier noticed that the mate, who had eyed our fishing rods, now had them stowed in a dark corner. Unsure of what to do, I told the purser they were borrowed and we would like to return them. Danny said, "He has the legal right to keep them, but that doesn't make it the right thing to do. Go ahead and sneak them off at the last minute." I gave him a subvocal blessing, along with a handshake and a brief, "Thanks, Danny," and off I went. It was dark and shadowy on deck, as it was the middle of the night, so I had little trouble accomplishing my mission without attracting attention, but I saw the mate eye me as I went over the side and down the rope ladder, rods in hand.

The captain had informed us that there was still a light gale blowing, so he wasn't taking his ship all the way into the harbor. He had radioed the Coast Guard, and they were to pick us up in the middle of the gulf.

Due to the heaving of the two vessels side by side, he deemed it safer to have us use a rope ladder than the hydraulic stairway. However, from our point of view, that rope ladder was awfully wriggly, not to mention a long way down to the deck of the little cutter, and I was carrying those precious fishing rods in the bargain. Mel came next, and he was still pretty weak (it turned out he had walking pneumonia from the adventure), so I had to lift him off that swinging rope ladder onto the deck. I was doing some wobbling, too, due to the rocking of the cutter. Chet came next and told me that the captain said he would make only one try to lower Pablo's boat, since it was risky under such windy circumstances.

So when the boat was lowered I bounded from one end to the other, untying lines for all I was worth. No problem: it was unfastened almost before it hit the deck, though it was somewhat buckled in the middle from rough handling. We were relieved to have it, anyway.

Pablo slithered down the ladder, and we were on our way to land! Pablo had a big bag over his shoulder filled with clothes from the ship's crew. They had also taken up a collection of their remaining Central American money to give to Pablo: truly they were Good Samaritans, touchingly displaying a tradition of the sea.

It was a brief cruise into port, where we were taken to Immigration, Puntarenas being Costa Rica's major port of entry. We were escorted into a very modest facility lit by a few bare bulbs and staffed by a few sleepy-looking people. We had to wait for a doctor to come and examine us for communicable diseases. They asked some questions in order to determine our status as immigrants from the sea with no papers except for Chet's driver's license. Actually, this period is a bit blurry in my memory, since it was between 3:00 and 4:00 A.M. and we hadn't been getting our usual quota of beauty rest. I'm sure we dozed a little as we waited in hard chairs for each step in the process. It seemed a long time, whatever we went through there, and I remember them calling a taxi for us.

I believe we stopped by Pablo's daughter's house so he could tell her to have his boat picked up. We then went to a restaurant near the bus station for breakfast because the bus for Nicoya would be leaving around six, and that was about all we had time for.

Breakfast picked us up a bit. We tried to order ham and eggs but wound up with rice and eggs and delicious coffee. We have become used to this type of confused service over the years and believe it due partly to language and partly to their practice of substituting whatever is available for what isn't at the moment.

The local people certainly eyed us at the bus station, dressed as we were in our impeccable white coveralls, all blistered, and carrying fishing

Return from the sea. From left: Mel Checkum, Chipper and Skip Carey (the authors), Martha and Chet Eastep, and Pablo, the local fisherman whose motor quit while they were fishing. The British banana freighter MV *Samaria* rescued them off a windy sea just at dark their second day out. They returned the following day.

rods. We dozed off and on as we bounced along in the bus, but there were the usual chickens and a pig or two on board to serenade us. At the rest stop along the road we were again the subject of much scrutiny as small clusters of folks glanced or stared and discussed those lucky ones who came back from the sea. We heard later that some Tico fishermen had been lost in the same windstorm and were still out there. We decided it was a good thing to be Americans and to pay taxes to support an embassy and armed services. Later Chipper said, ''I'll never again complain about paying my taxes.'' Maybe.

Toward noon we arrived in Nicoya and made our way to the same restaurant at which we had eaten on our way in from San José. We again ordered *arroz con pollo*, rice with chicken, a very common dish and our first full meal since Saturday evening. It was now Tuesday afternoon, and it felt good to replenish our bodies with food and drink, though we were still groggy and feeling vulnerable. It was here, stuffing ourselves, that our friends found us. Glenn Lytle, our department secretary's husband, from Shippensburg, and John Frazier of Nosara had driven Chet's jeep here to pick us up. After the long, hot, dusty, bumpy ride back to Nosara, we were finally in the arms of our wives for a wonderful, tearful reunion. We have a photograph of the four of us in our white coveralls, plus Chipper and Martha and the fishing rods, taken just after we arrived home at Casa de las Flores. No doubt about it: we were very lucky even to be alive—a very humbling experience.

Afterward, we learned some of the details of our rescue. Gene Talboy of Nosara had been instrumental in contacting the U.S. embassy in San José, which had started the ball rolling. From that point on our rescue was engineered by Col. Bob McGarity, U.S. Military Command at the embassy, via contact with Howard Air Force Base in Panama. The plane was dispatched after the Coast Guard cutter had failed, and then it had run low on fuel. After refueling it had returned to relocate us and dropped fifteen thousand dollars' worth of equipment, only to have it blown away before we could reach it. The plane then led the HMV *Samaria* to us at a point about thirty miles west and twelve miles north of Nosara, our point of departure.

Chet told me later in a quiet moment that while in the boat he had made a promise to God that if he were spared, he would build a church for the people of Nosara. He said, "Skip, I was really afraid I was going to die. It especially hit me the moment you looked at me when the plane left us the second time. You were my strength throughout the ordeal, and when I saw you look like you were giving up, it shook me. I made a bargain at that point, and I'm going to keep it, somehow."

I felt bad that I had let Chet down, but they had been honest feelings. All I could say was, "Well, maybe some good will come from the experience, Chet. Lord knows it was a unique ordeal, one which you would surely never sign up for."

Everyone we met wanted to talk with us about our "boat trip," but for us it was not easy. I know I felt myself tense up when anyone directed attention to it, and Chipper has already mentioned how Chet broke into tears while trying to say grace the evening of our return. He told me later that he didn't like to talk about it because of the stress it created. I asked Mel about it one time, and he agreed.

Still, people were inquisitive for whatever reason. Most were sympathetic; some seemed awed. One colleague back at the university laughed heartily, as though it were a big joke, which I admit I didn't appreciate.

My brother Harry, an adventurer himself, said, "Now how will I ever beat that?" I was invited to tell my story at our university Counseling Center meeting, which I did. It was interesting to observe the different ways people reacted to our experience.

Martha and Chipper had already rearranged our homeward flight schedule, soon after they'd learned we were returning from the sea, so Chipper and I flew out the next morning, two days late.

Looking back, I can see that we hadn't talked through our experience enough to come to grips with it. I say that as a counseling psychologist. I was, at that time, a professor of counseling at Shippensburg University. Chet had been a psychologist and department head when I was hired and then was our dean until he retired. Mel was a professor of education, nearing retirement.

We were the object of much curiosity on campus and were interviewed for the student newspaper, the local biweekly, and the alumni newsletter. I was asked to discuss the emotional reactions of people facing death at our department meeting. Martha's charitable sorority had us tell our story at a picnic the following summer. We had to wear our white ship's coveralls, too.

Chet secretly told me he hated to talk about the ordeal. He confided, "Skip, I haven't been as in control of my emotions since that experience. I'm always afraid I'll break down. You saw what happened that night at the table." Yes, I could identify with that. I became very uneasy myself at such times, which added to the normal stress of being in front of a group.

We'd been left with a vulnerable feeling that took a long time to gradually ameliorate. My approach was to make light of it or answer briefly. Chet would sometimes drift off into philosophizing. Mel would answer briefly and then kind of drift off into thoughtful silence or change the subject. Mel died a couple years following our experience, and Chet died twelve years afterward. But some of the scenes and feelings of that brief period remain brightly alive today in *my* mind's eye.

Pablo went back to fishing and, as of this date, can still be seen around Nosara. I regret being unable to fully share recollections and feelings with Pablo. We couldn't communicate in the boat, and my Spanish is still not up to comprehending his old-fashioned rural Guanacaste dialect. I can speak with younger Ticos, but most of the old folks seem to speak a different tongue, and Pablo is in that category. We still share a nonverbal bond, though, when we bump into each other, similar to that of old war buddies, I suppose. I do know I'm always glad to see him, and he seems to share the pleasure.

4

1983, Our Return to Nosara

Two years after our misadventure there, we decided to return to Costa Rica. After all, we had enjoyed most of the prior visit, and now we were ready for more excitement. Getting away from the winter weather was also alluring, but a deeper motive was to reassure Chet and Martha that we were neither afraid nor harboring any ill will because of the near-tragedy we had experienced.

Mel Checkum decided to accompany us again, and Martha had also invited Harry Sweely and his daughter, Jill. Harry was a colleague, a professor of psychology, and Jill was a teenager at the time.

There were a few problems getting away this time, since our alarm clock had failed, due to a momentary power outage. Mel had overslept, too, and then Jill became sick during the ride to Washington National Airport. But we made it to San José okay and were at the Hotel Amstel by 3:00 P.M.

Again we were impressed with how lovely the weather was here, compared to the brutal Pennsylvania winter we'd left only that morning. This time we had left our winter coats behind, remembering how silly we had felt on our prior visit, carrying winter coats on our arms in Miami and Costa Rica.

Harry asked, "Why in the world do we stay up north and endure those punishing winters? Some people have this kind of weather all year round."

The next morning we breakfasted and hit the streets. The weather was indeed very pleasant in the Central Valley, where San José is located. Low temperatures are usually in the upper sixties, and highs reach the upper eighties.

Jill wore short shorts on the streets and received some exaggerated stares. We learned later that shorts were considered improper attire, although in years to come they would be barely noticed. Skirts or dresses were expected. Shorts or even slacks drew critical stares from both men and women, especially the elders.

With no regular air service to Nosara, we decided to charter a flight for the five of us. We had to taxi back to Aeropeurto Juan Santamaria, about half an hour, board a twin-engine Piper, and fly thirty or forty minutes to Nosara. We enjoyed seeing the mountains and valleys along the way. We crossed the Gulf of Nicoya and could see the Pacific Ocean. Here and there were cattle grazing and fields of sugarcane.

As we approached the Nosara airstrip we watched people run out and chase cattle and pigs off the graveled area. Landing was a rough, dusty affair. Some visitors never returned after one landing experience, especially if the infamous Guanacaste winds were howling and the plane was overloaded as usual. The pilots reminded us of the famous Alaskan bush pilots we had read about. This was routine for them, but not for us.

What an airport! The pilot hopped out, helped his passengers down, and handed the baggage to the owners. The passengers then carried their luggage toward a tiny thatch-roofed building, over dirt and gravel and weeds, then through an opening in a barbwire fence.

We learned that the little ramshackle building also served as post office, constabulary, and lockup, as well as airport. There was a crack where letters were dropped into a brown paper bag waiting inside. Sometimes they missed, we were told, and could be lost forever. Election results were posted here, too. But all this was only charming in Costa Rica, since there were also parrots in the large mango tree hanging over the ''air terminal,'' a few chickens in the street, and beautiful smiles to greet us. Every sunburnt face seemed to smile genuinely. The arrival of an airplane was no mean event; numerous folks showed up just for the excitement.

Thankfully, there is usually someone to greet arrivals. In our case, Chet and Martha were there, reliable as always, dropping off prior guests and collecting the new batch. They hugged us as Martha chattered gaily and Chet smiled patiently, introducing us to the departing group and waving good-bye as the outgoers climbed on board the little plane. We ducked behind the tiny weathered building as the plane revved its engine, dust and gravel particles flying past like shrapnel under the bright tropical sun. We loaded our bags on the luggage rack of the jeep; then everyone seemed to talk at once during the sweaty, dirty, jarring ride to Casa de las Flores. Natives watched and waved and smiled as we rode by, seven of us crammed into the Land Cruiser, grimy and mopping sweat.

Harry commented on the post office, leading Martha to explain that the mail arrived from Nicoya by the daily bus. She related a story that ''a rat chewed a hole in the bag'' as an explanation for late or lost mail.

We were very glad to arrive at Casa de las Flores and change into shorts and sandals. After the travel from the States, then out to the jungle into tropical heat, our energy was sapped. Chet said, "It'll take you a couple of days to get acclimated. Just go easy and drink lots of water. Wear a hat, too. Maybe take a siesta. That'll get you ready for happy hour." Sounded like good advice to us!

Martha and Chet were certainly great hosts. They made everyone feel at home, from catering to dietary needs or whims to supplying forgotten items of clothing and toilet articles. Martha is a fine cook and an entertaining hostess, a natural people person. A bundle of energy, she plans each day from menus to social activities.

Like a radio station, Martha deplores "downtime." Beach time is scheduled according to the tide chart, with low tide being preferred in order to bask in the tide pools. Happy hour is called about four-thirty. Everyone gathers with a cold drink on the back deck to chat quietly and watch the birds and other wildlife. There is often a troop of howler monkeys, a coatimundi, an armadillo, or a pair of squirrels onstage for our entertainment as the bats usher in twilight.

Dinner is eaten at sunset on the open porch. Grace is said while we hold hands around the table, with the distant roar of the surf providing auditory background during quiet moments. Dishes are done at astonishing speed in order to get to the game room without loss of time. A few minutes of sitting and chatting are allowed after cleanup, but soon Martha says, "Wellll . . . ," meaningfully drawn out. Everyone soon knows what that means: *get to the game room.* Ignore it, and she will fidget for a few minutes and repeat the, "Welll . . . ." Ignore *that* and you will soon learn that this is a serious issue. You *will* wind up playing games.

The game room is essentially a screened room behind the main house, containing table and chairs for up to eight people to play cards or Scrabble or Rummy Cube or Triominos or Zonk (a dice game) . . . the list goes on and on. The day is a disappointment to Martha if she doesn't get to play her games. Sometimes she gets so hyper during the evening's games that she has to sit and rock awhile to "calm myself," as she says. She does love her games, and they do take the place of television, which is conspicuously absent, as is a telephone.

On occasion, young Ticos from the adjoining native pueblo join in the games. They speak only Spanish, which makes the games a bit more interesting. Martha teaches them how to play some of the games when she has no guests on hand. This way she is never without evening games. The problem is that they have young, bright minds and soon become sharper at the games than she is. Besides, some of the young boys have a bit of the devil in them and can cheat Martha before she knows what's happened, laughing cheerfully while they do it. They laugh and giggle, which usually results in everyone else laughing, too.

One game night Mel got angry with us, accusing us of changing the rules when he made a play. We all laughed, but he was serious. This was so uncharacteristic that I later commented to Skip that something must be wrong with Mel. He was a cheerful, loquacious Welshman, never known to be grumpy. Skip said, "Well, we can keep an eye on him, but maybe he's just tired or getting too much sun." We then dropped the subject.

Bedtime follows games around 9:30 or 10:00 P.M. The gringo development in these days had their own generators which were shut down at 10:00 P.M., so we had to remember to quit playing in time to get to bed before we were plunged into darkness. This was due to more than one consideration. As we were located literally in the jungle, it was reassuring to be able to check the sheets before hopping in the sack. Remember the scorpion? There were also tarantulas and other less formidable, but nonetheless annoying, visitors to the bedchamber. One night we heard something flying about the room and decided to ignore it, since it was probably one of the cheeky wrens that regularly gleaned the insects from the screens surrounding the top of our exterior walls. The next morning we found a huge flying grasshopper warming its belly on the night-light. We photographed and measured it: four and one-half inches long. I'd like to see the wrens eat that one.

Mornings were glorious. Sunrise was around six o'clock. As it is so near the equator, the days and nights are about equal. This surprised us. I guess we expected long days, but the seasonal variation is small, so days begin and end close to six. The spring and fall equinoxes create two "longest" days of the year, while summer and winter, irrelevant terms here, may vary fifteen minutes from the average day.

As it was January, the dry season had begun, and every morning was bright and nearly cloudless. Before rising, we could lie in bed and listen to the jungle sounds. There was the sweetest bird-song I'd ever heard, sometimes followed by the most raucous noise imaginable from a flock of jungle fowl, called *chachalakas*. If there happened to be a troop of howler monkeys in the neighborhood, it became a veritable din of jungle music.

This was the time Skip loved to stroll quietly through Chet's garden paths with his camera, clicking on a trogan or motmot bird here, a new hibiscus or bird-of-paradise bloom there. And then Martha's breakfasts were wonderful, with Costa Rican coffee and fresh fruit: papaya, mango, watermelon, cantaloupe . . . . Mmm!

Martha tried to get us to the beach nearly every day, missing only when some special happening occurred. The *playas* (beaches) here are absolutely beautiful. The sand is light and fine, reaching up to a hundred yards in width from the jungle to the water at low tide. The water is warm except when the Guanacaste winds stir it too long, and the waves roll in with long, even swells. We frequent the beach called Playa Guiones, named for Punta Guiones, the long point of land seen on maps, jutting into the Pacific as you follow the coastline northwest from the Gulf of Nicoya.

The gringo development fronting on Playa Guiones is called Playas de Nosara, but that is just to simplify its connection to Bocas de Nosara, the nearest village of any size and the location of the airport. Playa Guiones is a cresent about five miles long with rugged promontories at each end, creating wonderful vistas from the beach. Ships can occasionally be seen plying an offshore lane, and shrimp seiners work the waters at times.

Some days produce practically no activity. We love those days when we have the beach totally to ourselves, although such times are not frequent. Skip and I have been known to enjoy skinny-dipping and pretending we were enjoying the Garden of Eden at these quiet times. The tide pools, areas of water trapped behind rock reefs that become quiet due to protection from the surf, are like our own giant honeymoon spa.

Every day is a bit different at the beach. High tides can reach clear to the jungle when they are at their peak. We learned from Martha's tide charts that there are high high tides, mean high tides, and low high tides. Low tides vary the same. So when there was a low low tide during the day we made a special effort to get to the beach, since the tide pools would be at their lowest. This also meant they would be quite still, undisturbed by the surf. Snorkeling is great then, with every part of the pool bottom visible and fewer places for the reef fish, eels, octopi, rays and shellfish to hide or be hidden. And the beach at low low tide is at its widest, a choice time for the young Ticos to enjoy a quick pickup game of *futbol* (soccer).

Some days a new batch of shells miraculously appears or your favorite strip of sand is washed away, leaving gravel in its place. A small river, trapped above the sandy beach one day, breaks through and is running right into the ocean the next. Or a run of *sardinas* numbering in the millions may appear, followed by schools of game fish. On such days the word spreads miraculously and Ticos gather from all about, seining the minnows and using them for bait to catch large snook or jacks or snapper, off which they and their neighbors dine for days. The great ocean is a constantly changing source of wonder here.

Martha and her guests use the tide pools as a large swimming pool and social center. They float, bob, and swim while gossiping and planning get-togethers, such as card or bingo nights, dinners or beach parties. Once or twice a season they are chased out of the water by jellyfish or too many sting rays, but rarely. They then reconvene on the beach to sunbathe and continue the gabfest. Searching for shells while strolling the beach is a regular activity. Some of the residents have fine shell collections.

One particular time Chet accompanied us to the beach. He ordinarily preferred to work at his flower gardening and landscaping projects, but this time he gave in to our pleas and was glad he did. We took a walk up the beach and came upon two young Belgian couples, also strolling. One of the women was enjoying the freedom of going topless, and kind of hung back, though the guys would have appreciated her presence "up-close and personal." (Incidentally, the Ticos discourage nudity.) Chet graciously invited them to the *casa* for drinks and *bocas*. (*Bocas* are finger foods in Costa Rica, a common choice for party refreshments, similar to *tapas* in Spain and possibly related.) This was a common practice of Chet's, which often resulted in meeting interesting people. I said, "At least this way you guys can see what she looks like with a shirt on, and maybe you'll even notice the men."

One of the Belgian men worked for the State Department, and the other was a businessman. When we first began conversing, we thought they said they were Persians, which produced some awkward moments discussing carpets. Skip and the guys were so mesmerized with the topless exhibit that they were ready to believe in flying carpets and weren't concentrating very well.

One of Martha's social activities that week was a kite-flying contest, held at what she called Baker's Beach. The Bakers had a house at one beach-access point where the Nosara Civic Association had located a picnic table and barbecue pit under a palm tree. Martha posted a notice at the hotel and told everyone she saw at the tide pools or Zambrana's store to spread the word. Then on kite day she made a general announcement over the CB. A couple of dozen people showed up to create a graceful scene of colorful blotches against the flawless blue sky over the Pacific Ocean. Since there were few gringo children, it was interesting to watch so many adults at play. We enjoyed being part of it, and Martha was in her glory, exhibiting her early elementary-school teaching skills to perfection.

It seemed so brief a time before our week was up and it was time to catch the bus for San José. Oh, those Tico buses! They stop anywhere someone chooses to stand along the dirt road, their national highway. So we caught the bus in front of the Casa de las Flores, pushing our way into the large but already crowded vehicle. No matter how you prepare your mind, it is always a dirty, rough, crowded, tiring ride. However, it is invariably an interesting window on the Costa Rican culture.

Buses loom large in the lives of the Ticos. Few country folks, or urbanites for that matter, have automobiles, so the bus lines connect the whole country together. Many city dwellers return to their rural homes on weekends or at least on holidays, mostly by bus. As mentioned earlier, parcels are sent by bus, along with the mail and even occasional livestock. The driver may stop to receive a soda or piece of fruit from his cousin or aunt. He may stop while someone leaves the bus to run into an isolated *ranchito* to pick up a parcel or drop off some medicine. But this is only the surface; look more closely.

There are no route numbers or color codes or letters and no maps in the stations. Schedules consist only of approximate times of departure from this or that village or in the city, from locations known as the Coca-Cola or the Alfaro Terminal or this or that plaza.

However, the people love to render assistance. If one of them speaks a little English, he or she is only too proud to demonstrate and practice on you. Their warmth is wonderful. At any rate, we learned to look for the small destination card in the right corner of the bus windshield. Of course, we found that we first had to know where we were going, especially if there was an intermediate stop or a change of buses.

Once you are on your way there is a new world of communication, of which we were initially unaware. The buzzers or bells that signal the driver when you want off are generally disconnected. Apparently they add to the ambient noise, which is considerable, or maybe they had just shaken loose. The signal that works is a sharp whistle. If you can't whistle, just look agitated, yell, or stand up and someone will whistle for you. At least that worked for us and for some others we observed.

Some drivers christen their buses after their *novias*, or sweethearts, or perhaps a child or mother. This name is often painted on the bus with great multicolored decorative complexity, like a tattoo, and can be quite beautiful. Many buses are decorated by locally well-known artists. Their murals are usually lovely or at least interesting and imaginative.

I suppose that bus decorating must be an artistic specialty here. Apparently it is a great honor to be chosen to drive a bus in Costa Rica, confering a sort of minor stardom. The driver will normally be assisted by a sort of conductor who will collect the fares, make change, handle baggage, and do whatever needs to be done. If someone is eating or is feeding a baby, the conductor will wait until it is convenient to collect.

It is common to eat and drink on a Tico bus, since the journeys can be pretty long. The ride from San José to Nicoya, the main leg of the trip to Nosara, takes about six hours or so, seven being not uncommon. As a result, people often carry snacks and drinks, since the temperatures are typically warm or hot. Some peel fruit and feed children. I hate to eat oranges in such a situation, but numerous mothers do so while dressed in their best clothes. Just traveling with several children under such conditions seems a terrible chore to me, but they do it regularly. After all, they have little choice: ride the bus or stay home. And they even look clean and composed in the process.

Any empty seat can be yours for the taking, but you may have to crawl past someone to a window seat or you may have to stand. And more people may enter and stand, and more and more, until they are nearly hanging out the door. We are told the law limits the capacity to the number of seats, but the driver rarely lets anyone stand at roadside. He wouldn't want his own mother left in the dust, would he? We rode one bus where people hit the deck as we approached a traffic checkpoint, trying to make it look as if no one were standing. It seemed to work, too.

Some rules of Tico busmanship:

1 A clean bus reflects well on the nation; throw all trash out the windows.
2 If you can't whistle, yell, "*parada*," roughly meaning "this is my stop."

3 Try to get to the door before the bus actually stops. If you feel macho, hit the ground running while the bus is still in motion. I think this is to impress the opposite sex, and it does establish you as a true Tico busman.

4 Carry a wet washcloth in a plastic bag in your purse or pocket. This will come in handy if you eat an orange or, worse, a mango—also in case someone next to you happens to be eating these luscious tropical fruits.

5 A bus being listed *"directo"* doesn't mean it won't stop before its final destination; it may or it may not. Generally, it is a through bus, but don't count on it letting you off or digging out your baggage before its final destination.

Getting back to our ride to San José: As you may suspect, we were filthy, and so were our bags. It was definitely cooler here on the Central Plateau, but that only meant that the sweat had dried and with it the dirt. Upon our arrival, the hotel bag boys looked askance at us but then laughed and took our bags anyway. No doubt they were accustomed to tourists arriving from the jungle looking as we did, whether they approved or not. They probably had a good chuckle after depositing us in our rooms.

We showered and changed and happily set off for dinner. Martha and Chet had recommended the Swiss Chalet Restaurant, not far from our hotel. We all received nice dinners and enjoyed the evening, retiring early with the hope of visiting the Irazu Volcano the next day.

By morning I was sick as a dog and so was Mel. By chance we two had ordered mushrooms with our dinners at the Chalet. We told the others to go on to the volcano without us, but as it turned out, it was too cloudy on top, so the trip was canceled. Mel and I were well enough to fly home the following day on schedule, but we felt the effects of the food poisoning for a week afterward.

Several months later Mel had a serious stroke, was hospitalized, and then spent more long months in a rehabilitation center. Within a couple of years he was dead. We still occasionally mention the night he became angry playing cards and wonder if there was any connection. His name comes up when we discuss the lost-at-sea incident, too. We miss our friend the jovial, philosophical little Welshman, Mel Checkum.

5

The Ticos

Twenty-five years ago, when Chet and Martha first ventured into this part of Costa Rica, the Ticos lived in rather isolated simplicity compared with today. They were much less consumer-oriented due to the lack of both money and goods. Of necessity, they lived off the land and sea. Television was still in the future, and radios were a sign of wealth.

Transportation generally meant walking. A fortunate few had the use of riding horses, while ox carts were the trucks of the time. These ox carts became the symbol of Costa Rica, and the *boyeros* were—and to some degree still are—the proud drivers of some of the most beautifully painted vehicles in the world. We suspected that the bus drivers who had their buses painted so intricately had been inspired by the ox carts. Nowadays they are seen only occasionally and tourists go wild over them, nearly wrecking their cars to get photos.

The Nosara Civic Association has hired a *boyero* to haul trash from the beach with his ox cart, and this lent some color and authenticity to the local scene. On a mail run to Nosara Pueblo we noticed a team of oxen tied in front of a bar. Skip walked down the street from the post office to sneak a photo of them, but the owner noticed him. Was he going to object? No. He hurried out to his team and posed with them, positioning them properly for the picture. Such is the pride of the Tico *boyero*.

Guanacaste is the "wild west state" of Costa Rica, so it should be no surprise to see *vaqueros* herding cattle down the road or on the beach. Yes, they do herd cattle on the beach if it happens to be convenient. It is a magnificent sight while lazing on the beach or floating in a tide pool, upon hearing the whips crack like pistol shots along with the whistling of the vaqueros, to look up and see a large herd of those gentle-looking Brahma-type cattle moving toward you. This practice still occurs. They do leave some manure on the sand, but the next high tide cleans it away nicely.

Only a few of the Tico couples we know are married. Only since the church was completed, about 1994, has there been a full-time priest locally, and it seems that the local men have used this as an excuse not to marry officially. At least they joke about it in that vein.

Some couples stay together for years, but many are temporary arrangements, some very brief. They tell us that an adolescent girl feels pressured to prove her womanhood by bearing a child, and almost invariably this is the case. The machismo of the young men is pronounced. They joke and brag about their conquests and behave very dominantly toward women.

"Women's work" is anathema to men, although they may work vigorously at their "men's jobs." Women work extremely hard, according to our observations, although generalities do not hold in every case.

We constantly commented on how clean they were and despite so few conveniences. Showers were usually taken outside, with clothing on. Baths were done the same way, dipping water from a bucket or steel oil drum with a tin can and pouring it over oneself. There was little privacy, though nudity practically never occurred. One of our neighbor women even wore underwear under her swimsuit. Laundry may be hung on barbwire fences and often was, but the family would be clean when it arrived at the fiesta, church, or school benefit dance. Typically, Mother did it all, with the help of the daughters, who began to learn at a very early age.

Nosara followed the pattern of the rest of the world in its trend toward modern living, it seems. First they got electricity, then televisions, then blue jeans; in a word, they Westernized. Now they ride bicycles and wish for motorcycles, which some who have gotten steady jobs with builders or with hotels have already obtained. They twist the arms of gringo friends to bring small electric appliances from the States, where they are much cheaper. In short, they are rapidly becoming a consumer-oriented society, which brings sadness as well as smiles for them as well as for us.

Some of the faces we saw on the road and in town reminded us of pictures of Indians we had seen in *National Geographic*. One anthropologist stated in the *Tico Times*, the biweekly English-language newspaper from San José, that well over 90 percent of the nation's population probably have some Native American blood flowing in their veins. Others claimed that much of the population was really of European descent. Our observations tend to the former, though there may be some truth in both due to much intermixing. And a beautiful mix it is in many cases. Some of the young women are world-class gorgeous. Rarely does one see obesity or bad teeth, although we fear the benefits of Westernization may change this for the worse. McDonald's is literally a landmark in the city, and ice-cream shops now abound there, along with Pizza Huts and Burger Kings.

On our first visit with Chet and Martha they took us up on the mountain and showed us the work of the "grave robbers" or, more accurately, artifact thieves. These were illegitimate digs into the old burying grounds of the Indians, possibly ancestors of some of the current residents.

It was common ten years ago for traveling artifact salesmen to stop by the homes of "wealthy *Norteamericanos*," unfolding their wares from an old blanket or bandanna. Many current residents still display such artifacts on their shelves. Even today these dealers occasionally pop in on motorcycles with "old" pottery of questionable authenticity. Such relics, whatever their origin, include urns, three-legged stools, whistles in the shape of birds or toads, and medallions in the shape of serpents or crosses. (The three-legged stool with concave seat is actually a *metate* once used by the Indians to grind grain by crushing it with a rolling-pin type of implement.) These artifacts always appear ancient, whether they truly are or not. Some say they bury reproductions in the ground for a few weeks or months to achieve the desired ancient look.

We still see an older Tico now and then pounding grain with a large mortar-and-pestle system. The mortar looks like a large wastebasket made from a piece of log. The pestle is a limb about five feet long, some three or four inches in diameter at the butt end, and tapered to about two inches at the handle end. He pours some grain into the mortar and uses the pestle as a tamper, pounding the grain to flour. This will probably be the last generation to use such relics.

Some still use outdoor wood-fired ovens in the country, and many cook on open fires built on elevated hearths. Large amounts of beans and rice are consumed that have been simmered slowly on these hearths. We often watch the wood smoke float over the village of Esperanza at suppertime. It smells good and creates a homey atmosphere. I get hungry for beans and rice just thinking about it. Usually the male population is playing soccer while mothers and sisters are preparing the food. They play loudly and happily, though with great energy. It is a fine thing to watch.

45

Some families still live in the thatch-roofed *ranchitos*, eating and living outdoors for the most part and sleeping within. Old folks, as well as some of the young couples just getting started, generally occupy *ranchitos*. Those with enough means now have homes built from concrete blocks and corrugated steel roofing. In the late 1980s the German government subsidized low-interest loans for housing, and we watched Esperanza move from a dozen or so *ranchitos* to two or three dozen solid homes. The government money provided materials, and the people provided the labor. Then payments were small, seeming like low rent. The Ticos in these new houses must be much drier and more comfortable than before, especially during the rainy season, but of course some of the quaintness is gone.

By chance, we were able to watch a young neighbor, Manuel, build a *ranchito* so he could go into housekeeping with his *novia*, Josafina. The first we realized this was happening was when Manuel and Gerardo, his half brother, came dragging a long pole down the hill from the jungle past our house. They had cut it with Grandpa Roman's axe, were drenched with sweat, and stopped to rest and talk a moment with us. We brought out some cold water and learned what was going on.

The construction was simple, mixing a few new items with the traditional. A forked pole was placed at each corner and the center of each end. A longer, more slender pole was cut and dropped into each fork, creating gable rooflines and forms for walls. Smaller pieces were tied or wired to this framework until they were ready for thatching the roof and covering the sides. Sides were covered with boards, corrugated roofing, palm thatch, or even polyethylene, whatever was available and within the budget. Palm thatch is made by cutting fronds from the wild oil palms. This entails climbing a limbless trunk some fifteen or twenty feet with a machete in your belt (or else having someone toss it to you after you make the climb) and then hacking off perhaps a dozen of the huge fronds from each tree. I say huge because many of them are fifteen feet long and six inches through the base where they are cut. A *ranchito* requires many of these, so the boys usually get a gang of friends and neighbors together for a cutting party.

Each frond then has to be split lengthwise, since the leaves that hang from both sides of the center rib must always point downward on the roof. They are then tied to the framework, rib side up, leaves pointing downward, starting from the bottom edge of the roof. When complete, it makes an attractive and fairly watertight roof. The main problem is that the thatch must be replaced every two years. Those rainy seasons are pretty hard on a roof, sometimes seeming as if the clouds had literally burst. We don't envy those who live in *ranchitos* during the rainy season, since even if the roof doesn't leak, the floors are dirt and everything must be very damp.

The enviable part of their lives is the climate, which negates the need for coats and boots. They are accustomed to standing in the rain bareheaded, perhaps waiting for a bus, chatting amiably as water courses down their faces and bodies.

And they live with a profusion of beautiful flowers and plants: hibiscus, pink and yellow shower trees, white frangipani, orange flame trees, multicolored crotons, red pagoda plants, orchids, the list goes on and on. The variety of fruit is wonderful: bananas, oranges, lemons, grapefruit, mangoes, plantains, melons, star fruit, bullock hearts, *guanabana*, and so on. Just when you think you've tried them all, someone says, "Here, try this! I bet you've never seen it before."

Tico homes out here in the jungle are often surrounded by animals. There are almost always pigs and chickens. Some of the pigs are tied by a hind leg to a tree. A neighbor, Simona, keeps hers that way. We occasionally hauled pig feed from Nosara for her.

Many Ticos have skinny flea-bitten dogs, which they pretty much let shift for themselves. They do not buy dog food. Dogs get little attention and know to stay out of the way. A few are aggressive in defending their boundaries, but generally not those around the village. They sniff out whatever food they can find, and that includes a broad spectrum. They will make their rounds of anyplace where they have located a tidbit and are constantly searching for new sources. Chet had to train Martha not to toss them scraps. She has a soft heart, especially when she sees their ribs showing.

Tico dogs are not trained to obey, and nights can be a cacophony of barking and yowling, calls and responses. Skip says he has fantasies about sneaking out with his machete to seek vengeance. Apparently he is not alone in his fantasies, because one Alfredo, the village carpenter, was arrested a few years back for poisoning numerous local canines. He was actually jailed in Nicoya for several months. Skip says that some nights, especially at full moon, he would be willing to pay Alfredo's bail and even buy the poison for a little peace and quiet.

Esperanza has an elementary school, grades one through six. It is of frame construction, with large screened windows (no glass), a concrete floor, and a corrugated tin roof. It is rather shoddy in appearance, painted a dull green, but is surrounded by red hibiscus and has a couple of large mango trees for shade and, yes, snacks! The village soccer field is just across a dusty lane, the federal highway. Most children attend six grades, at the end of which time they are pronounced literate. This allows Costa Rica to claim a 96 percent literacy rate. Kids who wanted to go to high school, or *colegio* (co-LAY-he-o), as they call it, had to board in Nicoya until March 1997. At that time a new *colegio* opened in Nosara, much to the pride and happiness of the surrounding community. This is highly important, even if it turns out to be less adequate than the school in Nicoya. Many children just couldn't abide the long separation from their families that was required in order to attend school in Nicoya, not to mention the expense. The family is of extreme importance in Costa Rica, despite their problems with paternal responsibility. To our knowledge, this tends to be true in most Spanish-speaking cultures.

Nosara is about six or seven kilometers, approximately four miles, up the coast from Esperanza. Those are tough miles on foot or bicycle, due to the rough, very dusty conditions. It is a winding road over a hill and through the jungle. Cars, trucks, and buses, while far from being like city traffic, zip by pretty frequently, creating terrible dust clouds and some real danger. Wrecks are becoming more common as population and tourism increase.

Nosara is the business and cultural center for this area. It has numerous small bars and restaurants, the Catholic church, and several *sodas* (small stores serving the function of our minimarts, except these are generally only the size of one tiny room).

There is a barbershop, although families and neighbors often do this job themselves. A story is told of the barber whose shop sits adjacent to the soccer field at the center of town. His shop was arranged so he could watch the games. Naturally, one time he became excited and chopped the customer's hair pretty badly. The customer said he didn't care about the bad haircut but resented the nicks in his ears. Tico humor.

Nosara also has a dressmaker's shop, a supermarket and a butcher shop. The current butcher has a freezer, but Martha used to buy her meat from Melo (MAY-lo), a butcher outside town. She had to be there on a specific day, since Melo didn't have a freezer. We would arrive on Thursday at 9:00 A.M., and Melo would be in his shack hacking away at the fresh, bright red beef, while his helper was sweating over the hand-cranked hamburger grinder. They were doing their best to be sanitary without benefit of running water or even screens. The shop was a roofed area with a couple of walls and a rough counter board in front. As the day heated up, the smell grew stronger and the flies accumulated. They would brush at them ineffectively, but in all honesty, there were fewer than could have been expected. The trick for Martha was to get the meat wrapped and into the ice chest as quickly as possible, then home to the freezer. Needless to say, we never ate rare meat.

Bocas de Nosara is the full name for the village, which translates to "mouth of the Nosara River." It is situated in a bend of the Rio Nosara. Some of the youngsters have to cross the river to get to school, which makes it difficult during the rainy season, from May to December.

One of the Peace Corps workers tried to get a walking bridge built to solve this problem. She succeeded in getting foundations and uprights constructed at each end, but the project became stuck there for some reason. The bases have been sitting there for several years now, monuments to good intentions. Sometimes children are ferried across in a boat.

The most recent Peace Corps worker, who had hitched a ride with us once or twice, involved herself in teaching, mostly English. She is still living in Nosara as far as we know, involved with a tall Tico named Carlos who had been working in the hardware store behind Harold's supermarket, the SuperNosara. The SuperNosara had closed, along with the attached hardware store, so we were concerned about the welfare of the pretty young Peace Corps teacher and her husband. Then a new hardware store opened and there was Carlos, so we presumed things were okay.

The SuperNosara reopened in a different location under new management. (Incidentally, *supermarket* doesn't mean "large"; it means "self-service," from what we have seen.) Harold apparently got squeezed out by Super La Paloma, farther out of town, but better stocked and better-managed.

There is ambulance service in Nosara. The vehicle was purchased after a long fund drive, including tapping the gringos and holding fiestas and dances. It is a four-wheel-drive Toyota Land Cruiser, probably well over ten years old, with bald tires. It is a very durable vehicle but very likely rides like a covered wagon, painful to those under physical stress. Skip and I agree that we don't want to learn firsthand just how uncomfortable it really is.

A medical doctor serves the area at a clinic just down the street from the airport/post office. He was present one day per week, but the village had pressed for two days of service. Now there is a full-time doctor assigned to the Nosara Clinic, and the building itself is being expanded. Lines are long when the clinic is open, and they move at bureaucratic speed, just like the banks. One of the local wags nodded toward the queue at the clinic and quipped with a smirk, *"Las tortugas"* (the turtles). We pity the mothers with ill children and, indeed, all those who must wait so long. Still it is far better than no treatment at all, and they have grown up with the system. The only option is to travel to Nicoya to the hospital and still have to wait in a line there.

The medical service is covered under Costa Rica's Social Security system, so it is indeed bureaucratic, but free. Every employer pays Social Security on every employee, and this is strictly enforced down to each cook, maid, and gardener. The "enforcers" occasionally drop in for a visit, making on-site checks on employees and employers. We wonder if this represents concern for workers or is just another demonstration of the Spanish tendency to create employment for family members. At least this seems to have more benefit for the country folks than some other forms of their nepotism.

Many Ticos are quite artistic and good craftspeople. One Nosaran named Antonio is locally famous for his carvings. His wife sketches the designs, and he executes them in one or another of the beautiful woods found in Costa Rica. We purchased one of an eagle snatching a rabbit. It was really a design intended for a chair back, as most of his carvings decorate furniture, cabinets, or doors. We have seen a solid entry door made from one slab of mahogany-type wood, about two meters high by one meter wide, with a large jaguar carved in relief on the face. It was extremely well done, a beautiful thing to behold.

Antonio is not the only carver in the area, although we think he may be the best. Our friends George and Beverly Baumunk have a lovely home on the hill behind the Eastep property that is decorated with many of Antonio's carvings of indigenous flora and fauna on doors and furniture. It reminds us of African carving in its accuracy, which attests to the familiarity of the carvers with their subjects. To achieve such living grace and beauty in their works these craftsmen must have spent much time watching and studying local mammals, plants, birds, and fish. The tropical woods of Costa Rica make an ideal medium for the carvers, being both workable and beautiful. Antonio once tired of carving and joined a local fishermen's cooperative. They somehow obtained a U.S. AID grant to build a large fishing boat and begin a commercial venture.

50

We weren't there during the time of construction and launching, but we heard they worked very hard on the boat, Antonio having been the head craftsman. By the time we arrived back in Nosara the boat had been launched, capsized, and dragged back onto the beach. They replaced it upon the crude wooden-wheeled, ox-drawn vehicle from which it had been launched.

The *Princess de Nosara*, sunk on her maiden voyage, now sits near the launching spot on Pelada Beach between Olga's Bar and the Hotel Nosara, another failed U.S. AID attempt. In all fairness, it was probably too much to expect that these men, so inexperienced at boatbuilding, could succeed on their first attempt.

Antonio nearly died from diabetes after that. Once a large, robust man with curly black hair and beard, he suddenly looked small and vulnerable. His sensitive eyes appeared sad. He is now recovering and has returned to his true calling: wood carving.

One thing we haven't mentioned directly is poverty. People often ask if there is much poverty in Costa Rica. There is poverty, but as someone explained to us, at this latitude it is ''soft poverty.'' The climate, along with family support being a requirement in this culture, plus gifts from the sea and wild mangoes and bananas all help to temper its effect. According to North American money standards, poverty would be described as extensive, but many of the Ticos themselves, even the poorer ones, would resent being classified as impoverished. It would hurt their pride, which is considerable. They generally want to be treated as equals, even when required to do servile tasks. Also, the gentle, friendly, and helpful Tico nature helps to cushion the effects of poverty.

6

The Early Years in Paradise

Nosara began evolving into the modern age in the early 1970s when a gringo named Alan Hutchinson began to buy up land for development. He produced a slick brochure and advertised in the *New York Times*. A few takers showed up, and Alan would meet them in San José and fly them to the new gravel strip in Nosara. He would wine and dine them in the old Hotel Pacifico. Chet and Martha later wound up with parts of that building as their house, the Casa de las Flores. Buyers were promised swimming pools, a golf course, good roads, and many things that failed to materialize. But Nosara fit the dreams of some, with its tropical charm like something out of old movies such as *Casablanca* or *Key Largo*.

Among the earliest of those who built there were Gordon Mills and his wife, Charlotte, reputedly the heirs to a fortune from the beginnings of automated vending machines. I'm not sure about that, but I do know that Charlotte was a lady with class, who could easily have been royalty. Tales are told of Gordon Mills shipping his household goods by sea, barging them ashore since there were no good docking areas, and then having them hauled to his house by ox cart. Nowadays trucks can reach Nosara, but in the ''pioneer'' days of the early seventies, there was no passable road to Nicoya, which is the provincial capital and main connection with the rest of the country. Ox carts could reach Nicoya, but that could take a couple of days, and they hauled relatively small loads.

The Millses built their house on a lower knob, as opposed to a hill house. They were still located on top of a hill with a grand view, but they didn't have to climb the mountain, as did those like the Baumunks who later built far up on the high hills. The two houses are only a half-mile or so apart as the crow flies but nearly three hard miles by rough dirt road. Both houses have stupendous views of the Pacific, spreading from Punta Guiones to the hotel, which is located on Punta Pelada. But the Baumunks have that ''halfway to Hawaii'' view that motivates them to drive the mountain road every day. Probably the mountain road was even less passable when Gordon and Charlotte selected their site.

The Mills house was designed by Mrs. van Wilpe, the architect who became involved with the project's development in its early days. Her husband was the engineer who designed the roads and their drainage system, so we presume they were a team. His roads and culverts still work, and the houses she designed still stand, tributes to good work.

Mrs. van Wilpe's houses, designed specifically for the tropical climate, were very interesting to us. They generally have red tile roofs, off-white stucco exterior and local wood trim, often with some carving. All were situated with an eye to the view and with some means of catching the Pacific breezes. Some have whole walls that could be opened to the breeze, working like large entry doors or like overhead garage doors. All have high ceilings of the open beam type, meaning open to the underside of the roof, with screens at the ends to allow a constant flow of air.

Invariably these homes were then landscaped with bougainvillaeas, hibiscus, and other flowers, with banana and papaya stalks added by the owners. Each owner seemed to live out a fantasy by creating a little tropical paradise of his or her own design. Remember, though, there were no fans or refrigerators unless you carted in a generator. These pioneers worked their way through bottled-gas lights and stoves, to cooperative electric generators, to public power in the last thirty years. I think they loved the whole process.

Some of the participants, such as Mary Yost, stayed at the old Hotel Pacifico and were treated like family. They enjoyed family-style meals that included the *mesa tipico* (the typical table), consisting of black beans and rice, fried plantain, sometimes lobster or fish or chicken or *biftec*. Usually there were fruits: papaya, mangoes, melons, bananas, etc. Always there was coffee and rum.

A common dessert was flan, a pudding similar to butterscotch in flavor that is again becoming available in the States. (Skip's older sister tells us that flan was common in the United States at one time, probably an import from England.) Sometimes they had *sopa de mariscos,* a seafood soup full of various types of crustaceans, shells and all. The old-timers still talk fondly of those days, getting that faraway look in their eyes as they reminisce. It truly was more special in those days to be in the exotic Costa Rican jungle after difficult traveling and before many others knew about or could afford to reach such a special place.

One of the early characters we have been told about was "Big Jim." The image I got was that of a tall, macho type who slouched around the hotel with underarm sweat stains, smoked cigarettes, and eyed the Ticas (the *a* denotes the feminine). He drank a legendary mix of tomato juice, turtle eggs, and rum. Big Jim became totally smitten by a beautiful newly hired waitress. They say the air sizzled with the sexual tension between them. Apparently the Tico men resented Big Jim's interest in their women, for Jim returned home one day to find his house burned to the ground. Jim was one of the few gringos who had sold out back home to live full-time in Nosara, and it must have been quite a blow to him to feel trapped in a foreign place and have his welcome run out. Shortly thereafter he committed suicide with a handgun. Paradise is hard to take full-time, it seems, especially for younger folks.

The old hotel had separate rooms built *ranchito*-style on the edge of the cliff at the end of Punta Pelada, where the new hotel stands. Each room had a balcony that hung out over the edge where you could sit and watch the ocean with, seemingly, nothing between you and the water. The elevation, sixty feet or so, allowed you to see a good distance out to sea. Nowadays you might see a cruise ship lit up like a Christmas tree at night passing up or down the coast or several dozen surfers from around the world plying the waves, but back then there wasn't much to see other than an occasional small fishing boat. Certainly that was part of the charm of the place.

We already mentioned that the old hotel was dismantled and sold in the midseventies and Chet and Martha bought parts of it. However, before their sections were ready for occupancy they arrived in Nosara and needed a place to stay. Alan Hutchinson's assistant, a young man named Jim Rodingen, arranged for them to stay in a modest bungalow less than a mile away while their residence was being moved into place at its current location. This bungalow had windows with shutters but no glass or screen, not an uncommon arrangement then. Martha was unhappy with the delay but had to play along. The next morning, Martha awoke early to ponder the day and looked up to find a horse's head hanging over her. It had stuck its head entirely inside the window above her bed. Chet had to calm her, but then that was the pattern of their relationship.

Before long they moved into their jungle home. Martha had purchased a set of dishes and some other utensils from a departing resident, the beginning of her new household in paradise. But the unaccustomed lack of conveniences along with the irregularity of the water supply and power, plus the absence of familiar faces, became daunting to her, and she decided to throw in the towel. She simply could not handle the daily problems of living in the jungle and was ready to leave. Chet could not change her mind. She immediately began negotiating to sell her newly acquired kitchen goods.

It so happened that Charlotte Mills heard about Martha's precipitate actions and soon appeared on the Eastep doorstep, advising Martha to give it a chance, a trial period. "Nosara needs people like you," Charlotte said. "*We* need people like you. At least give it a month before you decide to leave."

That did it. Martha gave it a chance and became an avid promoter of the Playas de Nosara development. Truth is, she promoted Nosara so compulsively that she invited people she later wished she hadn't. But she absolutely did need company and did her best to always have someone visiting.

Chet bought some stock in the new hotel and was soon elected president of the board of directors. He and Martha found themselves taking in overflow guests from the hotel, hiring staff, and even driving employees home after late evenings. Martha even filled in for the cook in emergency situations. Our friend Glenn Lytle installed gas lighting in the hotel on his first visit there with Louise. We helped by cleaning up trash once while Chet was taking care of some business at the hotel in the earlier days. Looking back, it has the aura of the "good old days," when everyone pitched in and looked out for each other.

The development residents formed a civic association and pooled their resources to drill wells and upgrade to large electrical generators. The water they found was excellent, and they gradually got most of the bugs out of the electrical system, though never all of them. Life became easier as the years went by and the development grew. However, life in the jungle is not fully predictable; each day still brings another surprise. We wouldn't wish it any other way.

Skip, who spent countless hours listening to Chet, says he has some understanding of Chet's dream that culminated in his and Martha's move to Nosara. Chet was a veteran of "the Big War," WW II. He was taken away to the training camps just as the involvement between himself and Martha was at its most romantic. They became engaged; he went to glider pilot training camp. They married during his first short furlough. Quickly he was whisked away again for more training and sent to the South Seas as a cryptographic officer for army intelligence. He spent a long time on a tropical island, desperately lonely for his beloved Martha, dreaming of a better world. Somehow the tropical climate, beaches, and flowers fused with visions of Martha, romance, and happier times.

When they found Nosara, Skip says it must have been like *déja vu* for Chet. Nosara was Chet's dream finally come true, although Martha had never dreamed it. She needed people from home and lots of action. Maybe that's why Chet would sit dreamily and contentedly on the back deck with his Scotch on the rocks, listening to his tapes of the big-band music of the forties while Martha would bustle about caring for guests and arranging social activities.

Skip identified with Chet's feelings so much that he seemed to actually feel the same pangs of melancholy reminiscence that Chet felt when he was in his dreamy moods. Skip still can't hear Glenn Miller music without thinking of Chet in the jungle and of happy hour at Casa de las Flores. Chet seemed to become more and more vulnerable to those recollections as he aged and started declining, listening to those big-band sounds out there in the jungles of Nosara.

7
Five Years Later, 1988

We were in a quandary in 1988 as the time approached to leave for Costa Rica. Our daughter, Laurel, was expecting her second child, and she had had a difficult time with her first birthing. We set a late departure date in order to accommodate this event, hoping to be of assistance by taking care of Carey, Laurel's first child, as well as be in on the big event. Our airline tickets were dated February 29, a week after the expected delivery date, but even that day arrived with no action.

Our decision was to leave anyway. We held not only our tickets to Miami and San José, but Martha had also purchased tickets for us to ride the new Hotel Nosara shuttle bus, now regularly scheduled between San José and Nosara. These were to be awaiting us at the desk of the Hotel Bougainvillea, where we also held reservations. We could wait no longer; off we went.

A sales rep for Grove Manufacturing Company in Greencastle, Pennsylvania, sat beside me on the plane. He either liked me or was desperate to talk to someone, because he talked my leg off the whole way. I could have endured that, but he had the flu, coughing and blowing, all the while leaning close to me. I caught it; symptoms were evident before we reached Nosara.

The Hotel Bougainvillea turned out to be beautiful, much nicer than the old Amstel. It was clean and airy, had a beautifully landscaped pool and hot tub, was efficiently operated, and had a lovely restaurant. The lobby and restaurant had huge colorful tapestries on the walls, made to order at a nearby factory. The gardens were brimming with hibiscus, bougainvillea, honeysuckle and other tropical blooms. Fresh bouquets of flowers were placed here and there throughout the public areas. The hotel was a bit farther from the center of town but still within walking distance; it was worth the extra walk.

We met another couple there who were headed to the Easteps', so next morning we boarded the little bus sent from the hotel in Nosara and were on our way. The bus was a brand-new Korean-built machine, driven by a handsome young Tico named Ernesto. Ernesto had his pretty young wife and small baby with him. However, the throttle was sticking and the air-conditioning didn't work. The driver became sleepy when he wasn't scaring us to death by driving too fast and passing on curves, and the dust was still terrible once we left the paved road west of Nicoya. Nevertheless, we safely debarked eight hours later at Casa de las Flores.

Martha came running to tell us the big news: We had a new grandson named Luke Aaron Anspach, born the first day of March. Both mother and child were well. The message had been telephoned to the Hotel Nosara, and they had sent the message posthaste to Martha via messenger on a motorbike. What a relief! We later learned it had been another difficult birth, and the final one for Laurel to endure.

Chet assessed my sniffles and sneezing, saying they would fade in less than a week here in the tropics. He was right. With the hot weather, low humidity, and salt water of the tide pools, I recovered rapidly. We also got super quantities of vitamin C from the constant diet of fresh fruit and vegetables, along with plenty of rest and little stress. It's hard to beat. We were glad to be back.

Later that week, Martha received word that we were invited to a party and tennis court warming at a neighbor's home. Greg Maxwell, a "love boat" cruise director, had built a new tennis court and wanted to show it off. Of course we accepted, and the six of us got our drinks together and arrived at midmorning for the festivities. Greg had a large pig roasted for lunch and had organized a tennis tournament, which we all enjoyed, whether playing or watching. Skip and I were delighted to learn that this was the place where Martha and Chet had stayed the time the horse looked in the window to greet them at daybreak. We all agreed: this was better than February in Pennsylvania.

Martha's other guests soon departed, carried off by the hotel bus from the front gate. We soon jumped into our swimsuits and headed for the beach. It was a typical bright, sunny day, but the water seemed rougher and cooler than normal, probably due to some weather change way out on the ocean. We tried to enjoy the waves, but the undertow was strong and made us uneasy, so we strolled the beach and then returned to Casa de las Flores. Guests were arriving for dinner anyway, and we had to prepare chicken and rice, salad, and pie.

Just as we finished Martha's delicious mango pie, Franco, the Tico caretaker, emerged from the darkness looking distraught. He said there was a "big problem" at the beach. Several families had gathered that day for a beach picnic. Someone's girlfriend had gotten into trouble in the rough water near the reef that creates the tide pools (*our* tide pools!), and Franco's friend had attempted to rescue her. He'd come too close to the rocks and had been thrown onto them by a wave, disappearing in the turbulent water.

By now, they had gotten the girl out but couldn't find Franco's friend. Franco looked terribly agitated, near tears, but try as we might, we couldn't think of anything to do in the dark with the tide rising and covering the beach. A blanket of despair seemed to cloud our evening. We couldn't enjoy Martha's games that night.

Franco returned to inform us the next morning that the young Tico had been found with a gash in his head, drowned, adding that it wasn't the close friend he had believed it to be but another acquaintance. Once more, we faced the fact that life here was lived a little closer to the edge.

The following Tuesday, Jack and Helen Hargleroad arrived from State College, Pennsylvania. Jack had retired as director of medical services at Penn State University and before that had been a general practitioner in Shippensburg. He and Helen had wanted to see howler monkeys while visiting Costa Rica, but although they had toured the country for a week, they had seen none as yet. As if on cue, a whole tribe of howlers showed up to perform for us during our happy hour that evening on the back deck.

Contrary to our childhood lore, these monkeys never eat bananas. They gorge themselves on new shoots and blossoms of selected trees, making their rounds on a schedule known only to themselves. They follow paths through the trees as we follow paths and roads on the ground, often returning to their favorite trees by the same route until those particular varieties are no longer in season. This time they passed right over our heads, dropping leaves and twigs on us as they munched along. One or another of us would move this way or that in order to avoid being the target of excrement. The babies are very endearing as they cling to their mothers' fur or try their climbing and jumping skills while their mothers placidly continue foraging. The Hargleroads were delighted.

At seven o'clock Martha said, "Wellll . . . " We all knew we were expected to head for the game room. That night the women beat the men at Pennies from Heaven, Martha's favorite card game, delighting her greatly.

Grocery day was fascinating in its surprises. We met people and learned the news. Our guests enjoyed shopping and observing the natives. It took the place of a small community's newspaper or a trip to the mall.

One grocery day we returned with thirteen people in and on the jeep, plus large sacks of rice and sugar, bags of groceries, melons, and other purchases. People rode on top, on the running boards, even hanging on the ladder on the back, not to mention the crowd inside. Skip sat in the back where two seats lined the sides facing each other, with a small Tico boy on his lap. The boy became fascinated with Skip's hairy legs and began pulling and stroking the hair gently with his fingers. Ticos are generally not very hairy, and he was apparently enjoying a new experience. Skip was delighted and couldn't wait to tell us all about it. Our passengers thanked us profusely and offered to pay when they were dropped off, Chet graciously refusing, as usual.

The very last passengers lived beyond Casa de las Flores, so gentlemanly Chet offered to take them on home. We proceeded through Esperanza, made a left through the stream, and climbed the trail up into the hills. It was only a couple of miles, but it was low gear most of the way.

When we dropped them off at a little farm, the patriarch came from the *ranchito* to thank us repeatedly, earnestly uttering some other Spanish phrases, unintelligible to us. We tried to leave, but he was pretty insistent about whatever it was he was trying to say. We questioned one another about it and listened again and again. Finally Chet said, "Naranjos. That's oranges. I believe he's trying to give us oranges." With repetitions and signs we confirmed that, but as it was late in the day, they didn't have any picked.

Next we had to decipher their question: "When do you want the oranges?"

Chet said, "Mañana."

The man said, "Mañana?"

Chet said, "Mañana, mañana," trying to convey, "Sometime, anytime."

The man said, "Mañana, mañana?"

Chet said, "Mañana, mañana, mañana."

The man's face lit up: "Ah!"

I do believe he understood. He smiled and shook Chet's hand and off we went. In a couple of days a large burlap sack of oranges showed up on our doorstep. We gradually learned that "*mañana*", aside from meaning "morning," means "anytime after today" or "sometime later."

60

Chet, Martha, Skip, and I were set to go on a trip that Sunday morning, while the Hargleroads were to manage Casa de las Flores. The Guanacaste winds began to blow on Saturday night. They had eased a bit by Sunday morning, so we decided to leave as planned. As it was the middle of the dry season, there were the usual field fires here and there, which seem common to many third-world countries. Some are set purposely to clear the fields of unwanted vegetation and insects, such as ticks, and may help to keep snakes away. Some are the result of carelessness with the outdoor cook fires that are so common. When the high winds lend their power to the flames, you can imagine what happens.

We drove around fallen trees and tree limbs, through sporadic smoke and dust and hot winds, for several hours until we passed out of Guanacaste and on toward the Central Plateau. We still appreciated the scenery during periods when conditions permitted. It seemed strange to us northerners to experience heat and high winds at the same time, but when we crossed the mountains surrounding the Central Plateau it became almost too cool. We even drove through a hard rain shower as we approached San José and were treated to the loveliest rainbow imaginable. What a contrast from the dry heat and smoke of Guanacaste. All this time Martha and I sat in the rear of the jeep with our luggage, a long, dirty, tiring ride.

The Hotel Bougainvillea being full, we found rooms at the Hotel Irazu, near the west end of town. They had some nightlife, a casino and salsa dance music, but we were too exhausted to participate. We were just glad to shower, eat and rest.

The Easteps were later disturbed by a phone call from Jack Hargleroad informing them that there was a jungle fire raging in the development at Nosara. Jack asked Chet, "Do you have any instructions in case the house is threatened?"

Chet replied, "There's a leather folder of papers in the footlocker by the bed. Grab that on your way out. Don't risk yourselves. Everything else can be replaced."

Martha became excited, declaring, "Oh, Chet, we should drive back!"

Chet vetoed that idea, responding, "Martha, there's nothing we can do! Let's just be glad we're here and finish our trip."

Skip and I agreed, but it was their decision, since they had the most to lose.

The next morning we headed for Golfito, a small seaport near the southernmost corner of Costa Rica.

61

Before we left San José we stopped for a brief visit with a young Tica named Bennie whom Martha and Chet had met earlier and hosted for a visit at Casa de las Flores. She was having marital problems and was trying to raise her young son under difficult circumstances. She was estranged from her husband because he was unable to leave his mother. Bennie volunteered to guide us through the city, since we had to go east and south to follow the Pan-American Highway toward Golfito.

The trip through town was pretty hairy, with Chet's rural style of driving at odds with the Ticos' Italian mode of driving. We dropped Bennie at the east end of town where she could catch a bus back to her apartment, and went on over the mountain pass toward Cartago, once the capital city of Central America. We bypassed it for now and proceeded up the next mountain.

Before long we could have sworn we were in Switzerland. We donned jackets and admired the chalets and wild hydrangeas. Chugging up the hills in the four-cylinder jeep, we were even passed by buses, but we were enjoying the fresh air and high-country scenery. Skip was reading the map and found we were climbing Cerro de la Muerte, the Peak of the Dead, highest point on the Pan-Am Highway. Much of the time we were in rain forest and cloud forest. Huge trees occasionally emerged from the mist, covered with bromeliads and orchids, whole gardens in their branches. They were wonderful to see but difficult to photograph, we learned, due to strong backlighting.

Emerging from the mountains, we followed a river valley that led us toward San Isidro, a nifty old-fashioned town near which we found a motel for the night. Now at a lower elevation, it was warm enough to enjoy the pool and relax with a rum and Coke. Most of the hotel guests were Ticos—unusual, in our experience. Apparently this was not a touristy area.

The next day we continued southeastward, reaching Golfito in midafternoon. We had reservations at Hotel la Paloma (The dove) but had great difficulty finding it. We drove back and forth along the strip of highway where it was supposed to be located, finally deciding to stop at Hotel las Gaviotas (The sea gulls) to inquire. It seemed to be the only decent place along the road, anyway. Guess what: this was it! They had changed the name since our reservation was made. Either that or the travel agent who had made the reservation for us had gotten his doves and sea gulls confused.

Everyone was tired again except Martha, so we wound up playing Pennies from Heaven before dinner. Later we strolled the grounds, enjoying the sight of sailboats coming in for the evening. One of the sailing couples chatted with us awhile, telling us of their adventures sailing from Seattle and stopping at ports in California, Mexico, and El Salvador. They said the entrance to Golfito, called Golfo Dulce (Sweet Gulf), was as pretty and secure as any harbor they had found. We sat and talked on the outdoor patio overlooking Golfo Dulce, surrounded by flowers, including orchids, as the sun set over the bay.

The next morning we began to hear of the fires in Guanacaste, including a large one at Nosara. It was reported on the morning news over the restaurant television, but as the story was in Spanish, we picked up only bits and pieces. Chet said, "What will be will be. Franco will see that our place is protected if at all possible. Let's not worry about it." What a philosophy that man had, and it was typical of him.

As we explored Golfito, we learned that the town had been abandoned in 1985 by United Fruit after some fifty years as its major employer, when the government began requiring more worker benefits, such as employer-paid health and Social Security coverage and paid vacations every year. Locals were angry, as graffiti on walls and fences expressed. It made us feel like ugly Americans, an unusual sensation in Costa Rica. The people felt abandoned in spite of the company's gesture of donating their buildings for a university. Unemployment was high and the lack of prosperity showed. Still, on a personal level, the people treated us graciously, as usual. There seemed to be a light tourism business, and we could see occasional sailboats anchoring to buy supplies and fuel. The big wharves, built in the early 1940s for the banana industry, were idle, their disrepair evidence of their disuse.

Chet approved of the rainfall here, obviously greater than in Guanacaste. He said it would save him an awful lot of watering. He practically drooled over the lush greenery and blossoms. Guanacaste has a wet season that corresponds in time with our summer and fall in Pennsylvania, seasons in which we like to be home. When we need to be in Costa Rica to avoid our nasty winters, Nosara experiences its dry season.

Chet said, "Maybe we should move here, to Golfito," sort of testing the waters.

Martha quickly responded, "No way! I need the beach, and Nosara's beaches are nicer. The skies are clear almost every day, and besides, I won't leave all our friends at this point." That settled that. End of discussion.

We have heard since that some corporation bought the United Fruit holdings and replanted them with African oil palms. We don't know if they are prospering or not at this point. Palm oil is used in soaps and cosmetics and such but is probably a less labor-intensive business than bananas. Oil palms grow wild in Costa Rica and provide the thatch for the traditional *ranchitos* used for housing, especially in the poorer areas. In later years, we learned to enjoy watching parrots tug the nuts loose from the palm next to our screen porch.

When we checked out of Las Gaviotas, Chet asked for a starting of an orchid he had been admiring that grew on the ground. (Most orchids grow in trees.) The manager called the gardener to help and gave Chet a very nice plant, no charge. We left with smiles on our faces, heading back north toward San Isidro.

Retracing our route, we were relaxed, enjoying more nice weather and scenery, when we were flagged down by a man in a military uniform. *What's this?* we wondered. The soldier said a few words in Spanish that we didn't comprehend. Finally we realized through gestures that he wanted to ride with us. He squeezed into the back of the jeep with Martha and me, and we headed on up the road.

After an hour or so we came to a junction with a sort of military checkpoint. We slowed and eased our way past them, but the man started talking and motioning for us to stop. We backed up to the military-looking men, and our passenger got out and just walked away. Another man in uniform came over to us and jabbered something we couldn't understand. Then another came to aid him, repeating the process. They checked our passports and looked in the jeep, still trying to communicate with us. Finally they waved us away, and off we went. We decided they were checking for traffic from Panama, looking for drugs. We hadn't crossed the border so didn't get a full search.

By late afternoon we reached the hotel at San Isidro where we had overnighted on our way down. At dinner we again saw pictures of the fire in Nosara, causing us to wonder further about Casa de las Flores and our friends there.

The next morning we drove downtown, parked the jeep, and began exploring the town on foot. San Isidro appeared to be a true "Tico town," not yet spoiled by tourism. We came upon a funeral procession with local folks dressed in their best, the men carrying the casket on their shoulders from the church to the cemetery. A large procession followed, also on foot, many of the women weeping. It made us remember our own mortality and appreciate their earthy simplicity. Somehow it was a good feeling. We tried not to be obtrusive while still observing closely, with honest fascination.

As we strolled up the main drag, looking into shop windows and watching people, we realized belatedly that we were still wearing shorts and that some people were taking notice. Many paid no attention and some merely glanced, while a few rendered hard stares. Skip, who was following behind, told us later that one matron who was sitting in a shop entrance doing some needlework gave Martha a wide-eyed look of indignation. Her look seemed to say, "What in heaven's name is an old woman like that doing in such obscene dress?!" She glanced away in time to catch Skip watching her and responded to his bemused look with a grin and confidential chuckle of her own. He winked at her and moved on, enjoying a silent belly laugh.

Our next stop was Orosi Valley, a green and beautiful place with flowers everywhere. Our reservations were for the Rio Motel. We thought we were lost as we followed our directions until the road became a two-track path between pasture fences. Finally we crossed a rickety wooden bridge over a small, fast-running river, turned downstream along its bank (nowhere else to go), and found our *cabinas*. They were cool and a bit damp and musty, but we were glad to have a roof and beds after our day's travel through the mountains. The dinner menu featured trout, not surprisingly, in a surprisingly nice restaurant.

The next day we visited the little old Orosi church, which seemed to suit this valley perfectly. It held icons and treasures, a history of its own, and was set in a beautiful garden of orchids and gaudy heliconia and bird-of-paradise plants. It seemed almost worth converting to Catholicism in order to partake of the peace and simplicity this tiny church conveyed.

We traveled back up the steep hill where we had entered the valley and parked at a lookout to view the Cachi hydroelectric dam. From there, we stopped at a house to ask directions and found an elderly American who invited us in for drinks and then escorted us to some people for whom Chet was searching. This garrulous old gentleman just happened to know them personally. The couple lived on a farm that produced macadamia nuts, coffee, and fruits. They plied us with drinks and samples of their produce as well. They had visited Nosara once and had briefly known Chet and Martha. Skip and I sipped rum and Coke and munched macadamia nuts as we listened to their conversation.

Heading back toward San José, we stopped near Paraiso (Paradise) to visit Lancaster Gardens, a property donated to the University of Costa Rica by a wealthy gringo. It is a large garden specializing in orchids, although it exhibits a sampling of other tropical plants. Chet, the garden lover, couldn't bypass that opportunity. The sign at the gate said they were open, but then a man emerged to tell us they were closed for some religious holiday. Oh, well, this was Costa Rica; businesses seemed to close for any reason. Disappointed, Chet drove us on to San José. This time, he let Skip do the city driving.

Back at the Bougainvillea Hotel, Martha called to learn about the fire in Nosara. Thankfully, the fire had bypassed Casa de las Flores, but not by much. Hundreds of acres of the development, a designated wildlife sanctuary, had burned, along with three gringo homes. We felt sad thinking about all the birds and monkeys and other wildlife that might have perished; some were like friends to us. We had spent hours each day watching their movements and daily habits. It goes without saying we also felt sorry for friends and acquaintances who had lost property.

We ran into George and Beverly Baumunk at the hotel and had dinner with them. They related their tale of escape from the fire. Initially deciding to stay with their house, they had second thoughts when the smoke began to make breathing difficult. Beverly had kept watch down the mountain slope at the back of their veranda, and when she began to see flames being driven toward them on the high winds she panicked, crying, "George, we've got to get out of here!"

They'd already had their bags packed, since they were about to leave the country anyway, so George threw the luggage into their Land Cruiser and they hurried down the mountain. At one point they had to drive through flames as well as smoke. George said he could hardly see the road, which was bad enough under good conditions, but he couldn't go too slowly because of the fire. He said, "That's an experience I don't want to repeat! Believe me, I was scared."

Beverly amplified, "Scared! I was petrified! I was never so glad to be off that mountain."

They went on to tell us that most of the gringos had prepared food for the fire fighters and had served it to them near the fire lines. That included our friends the Hargleroads, who had stayed at the house while we were traveling. What a first-time Costa Rica vacation for them!

They'd handled the experience with great equanimity, but they certainly had something to tell their neighbors when they returned home.

Martha and Chet left us in San José and returned to Nosara with a new batch of houseguests who met them at the hotel. Skip helped them load their gear in and on the jeep early the next day. What a sight! Baskets and suitcases piled on top of the aging Land Cruiser; every inch of interior space packed to the roof; six people squeezed in, elbows crammed against ribs. It looked top-heavy as they drove off toward the jungle.

At least Martha has company, we thought, and, *Poor Chet, a lone chauvinist with five elderly women.*

Skip and I had a couple of days remaining to tour the city and nearby areas before our flight home. We took the usual city tour, something we often do when we visit different locales, since they generally give a good orientation to the environs that you don't get bopping around on your own. This one had a good tour guide, so we learned a lot. The National Museum was informative, and the National Theater was old and lovely.

The next day we took a bus tour to Poas Volcano, seeing some countryside and eating some very good traditional Tico food, family style, at a local home along the way. We even visited a coffee plantation and picked a few beans. The volcano was clouded over, but the cloud forest was special to see. It was cool up there, in spite of our nearness to the equator. We were pleasantly surprised to find one of Skip's old Penn State professors on the tour with us, as well as the Baumunks. Small world; small country.

For our final free day we chose the famous Jungle Train trip to the banana country on the Caribbean slope. At one time it went all the way to the Caribbean port city of Limon (lee-MOAN), but due to lack of funds to keep the rail bed in repair and clear of landslides, it now stopped at the banana town of Siquirres. In fact, after boarding our bus in front of the hotel we learned that we would be bussed first to Turrialba for the ride to Siquirres. More landslides had closed the tracks from San José to Turrialba, so our ride on the Jungle Train was more bus ride than train ride.

"That's what makes Costa Rica so interesting," I told Skip, getting a knowing grin in response.

The rail system, small as it is, has been a symbol, of sorts, of the nation's economic and social development. It was begun in 1871 and completed in 1890, the first reasonable transportation link between the capital and the Caribbean. Later it was pushed on westward to the Pacific port of Puntarenas, finally linking both coasts with San José. This railroad made possible the banana and coffee plantations by connecting them to the seaports, as well as allowing a viable representational government. In short, an era of nationhood was ushered in, along with the beginnings of an international economy. The pattern of foreign investors and the use of foreign technology came with it and still exists today, although with increasing internal expertise. Costa Rica now has a strong focus on education, further encouraging foreign investment, but supplying more domestic expertise.

Apparently, participating in a global economy has its pitfalls, since the train we were bussed to was old, being replaced by trucks, buses, and a highway system. The bus deposited us at the station in Turrialba, a nifty old town named for a nearby volcano that towered well over ten thousand feet in altitude. We were ushered into a special touring car that had yellow granadilla fruits strung festively from the ceiling above each seat. The car itself was clearly an antique (Victorian?). Windows were open, since the weather was hot, and we watched local folks walk past toward other coaches.

Skip stuck his head out to look and said, ''Wow! Their cars are so crowded that they're hanging out the doors and windows.'' We were obviously getting preferential treatment, but we learned later that we had also paid well over double their fare, a common practice in the tourism business in this and other countries, we are told.

Our tour leader had given each of us a box lunch to enjoy during the wait for the train to move, so we checked it out. Not bad—a quiche, plus a coconut bar for dessert, a mango and a Coca Cola. We also sampled the granadillas, about the size of large lemons, having thin shell-like skins and a seedy pulp similar to grapes without skins. We enjoyed them, but then again, we take pleasure in eating almost anything, especially new and exotic foods. The mangoes were terribly juicy, difficult to eat without becoming a sticky mess, but wonderfully tasty.

Our lunches were more than sufficient, and apparently the local children anticipated this, since they were waiting just outside our windows with receptive looks on their dear faces. Other passengers were already handing food through the open windows, so we joined in. We were surprised to see two little blond sisters in the crowd, validating something we had read about the infusion of various European nationalities into the Tico gene pool, which otherwise tends strongly to dark hair and eyes.

One little guy with a very dirty face lingered outside our window with four lunch boxes stacked by his side on the concrete wall. He kept stuffing himself with leftover quiche and coconut bars, at a slower and slower pace, as if he intended to force it all down whether he liked it or not.

The train began moving, breaking the spell of those special moments. We waved to the children as well as to some older people who were watching our departure, maybe wishing they could go, too. They certainly are friendly people.

The train ride allowed us to enjoy a good slow look at the countryside. We saw toucans, tanagers, and parrots, along with other exotic birds. Passengers called out their excited sightings to one another. At one point, we saw a tree full of large, woven nests and were told the birds were *oropendolas*. They were large and apparently quite social in nature. It was a wonderful sight to see.

The train took us past a remote pueblo where we saw a man on horseback ride up to a small thatched bar to buy a drink without dismounting. I remarked to Skip, "Boy, that's convenient."

Skip replied, "Wouldn't it be a neat experience to be able to visit a place like that and talk with the people in their own language?" He has always wished he could speak other languages and has been working on his Spanish in an effort to make that wish come true.

At times the curves in the tracks were so tight we could see both the engine and the caboose out the same window. Often the ground seemed to disappear from under us as we were hauled along some steep hillside, where the outside track was held by posts or even cantilevered from the slope. Many such rugged places showed the remains of landslides that had been recently cleared away. Apparently nature has won the contest, as we later read with sadness in the *Tico Times* that the Jungle Train had been discontinued.

We left the Bougainvillea at 5:30 the next morning, in order to be checked in for our eight o'clock departure on LLACSA Airlines two hours early. LLACSA is the national airline of Costa Rica, and if you are slightly late, they will replace you with someone who *is* there. We don't take chances with them. The plane departed late, in spite of that practice, and was filled to the brim as usual.

Our late arrival in Miami International placed us in the midst of chaos. We had unknowingly scheduled ourselves into the middle of *Semana Santa,* Holy Week, the time between Palm Sunday and Easter. All of Latin America seems to travel somewhere during this week, and half of them funnel through Miami. Between this situation and the conversion to daylight savings time in the States, it is easy to miss a connection, as we have been known to do.

This time we had until 5:30 P.M. to get to our next boarding area and wound up with time to kill. We opted to take a taxi to the International Mall, near the airport. Since it was only a few miles away, we figured the taxi ride wouldn't cost much and we would get cheaper food there to offset the cost of the ride. Yeah, right! The round-trip fare plus tip cost us nearly thirty dollars, and our light lunch was no cheaper than airport food. Oh, well, as Skip says, you have to pay for your education. We're still learning, and we did have another great trip to the jungles of Costa Rica.

8

Maxine

The word came by the jungle grapevine: Maxine had been found lying by the side of the road. Poor Maxine, she was always getting into some kind of trouble. This time a young German woman named Monica was driving by, spotted Maxine there, and stopped, fearing a car had hit her. But it turned out that Maxine had lain down to rest and was not hurt but merely tired.

Earlier in the day, Maxine had gone to the market for groceries and had gotten confused on her way home. She had turned off the main road too soon and wound up looping down one of the river roads, emerging at a spot where some contractor's workmen had earlier dug some sand for their concreting needs. Not being a skilled driver, Maxine drove right into the soft area and mired her "Maroon Moose," the big old Dodge some slick car dealer had stuck her with.

She had begun walking back up the road, but being eighty years old and struggling along the sandy trail with her cane, she tired rapidly and decided to lie down and rest. Happily, Monica had happened along and driven Maxine to her condominium. Then she recalled that she had groceries in her car and had to beg a ride from one of her neighbors to retrieve them. Sometime later, she hired a trucker to extract the Maroon Moose, a rather commonplace endeavor for Maxine.

Maxine is a retired professor of English and still enjoys writing. She has produced, on her own, a very enjoyable unpublished work titled *Never in Nosara*, which describes some of the characters and events from earlier Nosara up through her own experiences of recent years. She writes well and with some wit, even poking fun at herself at times. She tells how she gradually hauled her possessions from Florida to Nosara, including her computer and word-processing gear. She is a pretty plucky person, by our estimation.

Maxine generally arrives in Nosara during the rainy season, spending most of the fall months in her apartment at the Condominio de las Flores.

One night after visiting a neighbor and watching one of those lovely Pacific sunsets, Maxine headed straight to bed, feeling very tired. However, she was unable to sleep, so she arose some time later and headed to the bathroom for water and a sleeping pill. As she passed the closet, a man emerged and grabbed her roughly. He held his hand over her face and a knife to her throat and demanded money. It turned out she couldn't give him much; her apartment had been burglarized earlier that same day. The man hit her and tried to leave, but the door was locked. He forced Maxine to find her keys to let him out! She then roused her neighbor, who administered first aid to Maxine's broken nose, and later drove her all the way to the hospital in Nicoya, the usual two-hour ordeal.

Maxine's life seems to go along like this in Costa Rica: periods of peace and productive writing, followed by trying incidents that would intimidate many a younger, stronger person. Yet she perseveres, apparently stout of heart, seeing life as that kind of adventure in which one must endure some adversity.

One of her trips to the grocery store included the purchase of some rather expensive bacon. She decided to stop at the beach on her way home to take a stroll and look for some shells, since, after all, she was on vacation. Those beaches do restore one's soul. Upon her return, she found that a dog had absconded with her bacon, the windows of the Maroon Moose having been left wide open. This disheartened Maxine for the moment, so, feeling suddenly tired, she drove straight home, grabbed a book and a pillow, and headed for her beloved hammock. As she swung into the hand-knotted off-white mesh with the confidence of familiarity, it betrayed her, throwing her onto the rock-hardness of the tiled balcony floor almost with a vengeance. Unable to rise, she had called for help and was rescued by a couple of Tico workers who fortunately happened to be within earshot. She had damaged her shoulder and ribs and hip but, with her usual pluck, commented dryly, "It would have been better had I landed on my head."

Driving is a constant problem for Maxine. It requires more strength and visual perception than most elderly women can muster to negotiate the rough, twisting graveled roads of the Nosara area. Just starting her car and going to town for gas could give Maxine fits. One day she got the right front tire off into the gravel that accumulates at the edge of the road and it drew her off, despite her most strenuous efforts. That steering had been giving her problems anyway, and as it was the rainy season, the roadside was soft. Soon she was mired to the hubcaps. A passing trucker stopped to pull her free, with the good-humored kindness found in many Ticos.

Next thing, after a couple of errands, Maxine's lights dimmed. Someone told her that her battery was failing to recharge. She drove home by the high road to avoid getting stuck again but could use only her parking lights because of the battery problem. She claimed she knew the road well enough to negotiate it in the dark but admitted it was a terrible strain. Steering was difficult because of the pain in her shoulder resulting from the hammock attack. She did arrive safely, however, but her shoulder pain kept worsening.

The bruised areas of her body deepened in color, as she put it, "from light blue to deep mustard to purple grape." Finally, Maria, her maid, insisted that she go at once to the local clinic. At that time the schedule was still the one-day-a-week visit by the itinerant Social Security physician, a couple of doors down from the post office. Maxine went at noon and was finally seen at five o'clock by the fatigued doctor, who took a quick look at her injuries and recommended that she go to the hospital in Nicoya for X rays. Oh, no! The dreaded two-hour trip again!

Meanwhile, Maxine had left the Maroon Moose with Aristedes, the local mechanic. He was to fix the steering and electrical problems, if possible. When she came away from the medical clinic it was raining, the usual afternoon downpour at this time of year, and she had to walk the muddy streets to get her car at Aristedes'. She accomplished this and even drove herself home.

A friend called Nicoya for a cab to take Maxine and her interpreter, Juanita Aviles, the condo manager, to the hospital. It cost about forty dollars to make this trip by taxi, fording the half-dozen streams, bouncing and weaving in order to get a little care for your body. It must have been painful for Maxine to endure this.

Nicoya is a very old town, with a touch of the old Spanish colonial flavor. It makes you feel like you are stepping back in time, especially around the square and the old church adjacent to it. The hospital, however, is rather modern, at least from external appearances, and is landscaped with—you guessed it—bougainvillea, hibiscus, and such. It is attractive, unless you have to wait in line for treatment.

Maxine's wait was between two and three hours. Juanita had to do a lot of interpreting to get Maxine into a waiting room, probably because of the Social Security red tape, as well as the usual multistage process that their nepotistic system breeds. Juanita had to chase back out to the cabdriver to ask him to wait longer. (They are used to that.) Maxine was then led to a room with numerous women in white, one of whom took her papers; then another wait. Hunger pangs began; it had been a long time since breakfast! The women working in the vicinity, however, seemed in a festive mood, as though focused on a forthcoming holiday. Finally, Maxine was taken into radiology, late in the afternoon. A young doctor, pointing to the X ray, showed Maxine a broken bone in her shoulder, laughing when Juanita told him how long ago it had happened and all that Maxine had been through since then. Maxine visualized a cast and restrictive bandaging and blurted out, "Oh, I won't be able to use my computer!"

Another doctor gave Maxine a quick bandaging. He taped across her back and up over her shoulder, then wrapped around her chest, under her right arm, and over her left. He had to puzzle a bit, working around her postmastectomy prosthesis and bra straps, but got the job done, finishing with a neck loop and sling for her arm. The whole contraption was bothersome and irritating. She was told to wear it for three weeks.

Juanita took Maxine to a restaurant for a much-needed dinner before the dreaded taxi ride back to Nosara, after which Maxine went to the rest room and removed half the rig that the doctor had installed less than an hour before. The ride home was rough. It took an experienced driver to manage the stream fordings and narrow bridge crossings. The next-to-last bridge was blocked by a pile of lumber, but the driver knew the ford well enough to negotiate a sand bar and avoid deep water.

Soon after this it was completely dark and still raining. Maxine offered to put them up overnight at the Hotel Villagio, a lovely but expensive resort not far from Nosara. This must have been misunderstood, not taken seriously, or just ignored due to the others' wanting to get home, for the driver just kept on going.

The little river just before Esperanza was raging over its banks. The tropical rains had elevated it, to a dangerous level. The big daily bus that hauls the mail, running late, also pulled up and stopped. The two drivers got out to inspect the water level in the glare of the headlights, concluding that they had to wait for the water level to recede before moving on. They discussed how the Guanacaste politicians had promised to have this bridge installed last year: "Mañana, mañana, mañana!"

The cabdriver, now in earnest discussion with the bus operator, disappeared into the bus, while Maxine and Juanita were left to their own devices in the taxi for an hour or more. Finally, Maxine had to get out and walk back down the road to relieve herself in the dark. Fortunately the rain had slackened. When she returned, Chaco, the driver, came from the bus, turned the cab around and drove to a lighted rancho-style building (a large thatched-roof structure), which Maxine wishfully supposed to be a small hotel. It was only a tavern, but it did have a telephone. Chaco called Nosara for assistance and was told that a truck would be dispatched.

After they returned to the river for another wait, the truck arrived on the other side, and they saw several sturdy young Ticos emerge and wade cautiously toward them. Although she was puzzled at first, it suddenly dawned upon Maxine that they were going to carry her across! They did just that, with one on each side of her, locking arms beneath and behind her. She was glad she had removed the sling, so she could put her arms around the young men's necks. What an ordeal with a broken shoulder! They proceeded to carry Juanita, then a mother with her small baby wrapped in a shawl. They did it safely, but it was a difficult crossing. One man lost his footing and was nearly swept away. They even carried Maxine's overnight bag across. Needless to say, she was delighted to reach home that night and tipped the driver very well. Just another day in Nosara.

Maxine had been around some and supposed herself to be reasonably worldly, but those Tico used car dealers in San José taught her a thing or two. Actually, used car dealers everywhere probably teach humility lessons pretty regularly to a lot of people.

It seems that Maxine turned out to be "the little old lady in tennis shoes" with $3,000 in traveler's checks. Her first purchase was a vintage Cadillac, for $1,500. But she learned as she drove toward Nosara that the roads required a vehicle with more clearance. The old Caddy brushed bottom too many times, and since the roads worsen toward Nosara, she decided such a low car would be a serious problem. About-face: back to San José. The next try was a 1971 blue Toyota Corolla, for $2,616. After driving out of the city, this one began to smoke. Besides, the steering was terrible, and when she turned it around to take it back, the left front tire became hung up on the fender. The dealer was nice enough to buy the junker back for $393!

Maxine forged ahead, undaunted in her efforts to acquire "wheels." She bought a 1973 Chevrolet Monte Carlo that she thought looked pretty good. They promised her a new battery, which somehow failed to materialize. This car made it to Nosara, but only barely. The radio quit and the

75

battery cable was knocked loose by the rough trip. That really didn't matter, though, since the battery had died. It was very hard on gas, smoked like a demon, and seemed to be misfiring a lot, too.

Chevies are not common in Nosara, so she had to order the parts from San José, along with a new battery, which alone cost $100. By this time she had $5,000 invested in trying to get a decent car, only to learn a few days later that the engine was shot. That was the day she broke down and cried. This plucky octogenarian had finally been beaten! She said later that she never even received title to the vehicle, that it must have been a Mafia or drug runner's car.

At the time of this writing, Maxine is still making her annual pilgrimage to Nosara. She sent us a note in 1997, scribbled on a copy of her 1996 Christmas letter. In it she told of her most recent visit to Nosara that September. It included her exodus during a heavy deluge that detained her and her driver in Garza, very near the same spot where she had been stopped by the flooded river described earlier in this chapter. She located lodging in Garza at what she later discovered was a brothel.

Maxine also described her graduation, at age eighty-five, from an advanced studies program in religious science. She went on to tell of an incident at a writers' conference at the University of South Florida where she lost her breast prosthesis, rendering a blush from a male conversant. Then she amplified the effect by later introducing him to a friend as her bosom buddy, causing him to flee her presence.

We haven't heard any more outrageous tales about Maxine since that letter, but we intend to keep our ears open. She is a wonderful character, and we have great admiration for her.

9

The Church

Chet's promise to God was on his mind. We noticed him sitting, staring, and apparently pondering. We could almost see his mind working as he watered his beloved tropical flowering plants. He verbalized, "Skip, I've got to get going on the church project. I made my promise to God that if I could be rescued from that little boat out on the Pacific I'd see that the church was finished. But how in the world can I do it? I don't know how."

The church foundations had been started some years ago. Monetary contributions from an earlier gringo visitor had supplied the impetus. The foundation had been laid and two long sidewalls started, but the gringo had left, and with him the wherewithal to continue. By now the two somber gray block walls amid weeds and vines had a bleak aspect, even under the hard tropical sunlight. Mass was held by a lay leader under a thatched *ranchito* shelter on the east side of the churchyard.

Several times a week Chet drove past the overgrown foundation and was forced to think of his promise to God. The magnitude of the task troubled him; this was no mean chore. The foundation was capacious, surprisingly so for a small village like Nosara. Skip estimated it as possibly fifty feet by seventy-five feet, with the existing weathered sidewalls perhaps sixteen feet high.

Chet talked to Cuyo, the farmer, lay leader of the congregation, through an interpreter. Cuyo hoped this church would be the religious center for quite a large rural area surrounding Nosara. With a gleam in his eye, he proclaimed, "Maybe someday we will even have our own *padre!*" Cuyo was delighted that Chet was interested in helping, in fact could hardly believe it, receiving it as great news inspired by God.

Chet became more and more excited about building the church, adding Cuyo's enthusiasm to his own more wistful hopes. But on a college professor's pension? How to begin? It was dismaying, he said, but he couldn't renege on his promise. *Maybe, a little at a time, just work along at it, just get started. . . ,* he continued to ponder, drifting off in thought. And it's a sure bet that we were aware of only a small portion of his musings and cogitations.

There was practically no money available from the Ticos. This was a poor community. If they had any money they would already have had a church. No, the money would have to come from gringos, either from the neighbors in the Playas de Nosara development or from back in the States. Chet hated to beg money from friends and neighbors. Thinking of getting money that way was dismaying. He stewed and stewed over his dilemma.

As Chet began sharing his problem with friends, people started saying, "Hey, Chet, I'd like to make a contribution to your church." One said, "I'll bet the Shippensburg Catholic church would be pleased to help you." This really started the ball rolling.

Chet was invited to make a presentation to the Council of Catholic Women. Skip was recruited to show slides of Nosara, and Chet told movingly of his promise to God on the Pacific Ocean and of the needs of a poor Costa Rican community. A fund was set up, and money slowly began to flow toward Nosara for the church.

There were never very large lump sums involved in this fund, but it commanded a loyal and rather constant flow, which served nicely to meet the needs of the building process. Visitors to Chet and Martha's residence would say upon leaving, "Thank you so much for a wonderful time. By the way, here's a check for the church fund." Once or twice a year a check for hundreds and, at special times, even thousands of dollars would arrive from the Council of Catholic Women. Our Lady of the Visitation Church of Shippensburg adopted the Nosara church as its sister and held occasional fund drives for its support. Chet was heard to say wryly, "Maybe when this church is finished I can finally get my foot out of that boat."

People asked Chet why he, a Presbyterian, would go to such lengths to build a Catholic church. He would say, "It's all the same God, and this church is for *them,* to meet *their* needs, not mine."

Skip and I have had to repeat this statement several times, too, in response to the same question regarding Chet's efforts. Apparently it is puzzling to some people that a person could be so broad-minded. I remarked to Skip, "It really is a good example, isn't it?"

As money started to flow, the need for a financial manager in Costa Rica emerged. Money had to be sent or carried from Shippensburg to

Nosara and then had to be converted to colones. A bank account was necessary. Finally suppliers, contractors, and workmen had to be paid after ascertaining that the work had been accomplished satisfactorily.

Chet asked Albert Muller to handle the primary financial end of things such as records, money accounts, conversion, and payments. Albert was ideal for this, being bilingual, a past resident of Nosara, and now living in Nicoya, where he had access to banks and better mail service.

Cuyo handled the on-site organization related to jobs and supplies. When Cuyo told Albert of supplies needed or contractors to be paid, Albert would make funds available. When the account was ebbing, Albert would call Chet in Shippensburg and Chet would inform Janice Illo of the Council of Catholic Women and casually mention it to friends. Soon money would trickle in to get things moving again. Martha did the telephoning, correspondence and local banking. She was Chet's aide-de-camp, a great front-line contact person, and an enthusiastic ambassador.

Work on the church moved along at a rather uneven pace, partly due to the nature of "the tropical personality" and partly due to the uneven flow of funds. Some of the local *campesinos* (country folks), fishermen, and others worked occasionally assisting the builders. Women of the congregation would provide food at special times. Mostly, however, the work was contracted and paid for with money raised by Chet and Martha and their network of friends and supporters.

Two large bells had been donated: a brass ship's bell by George and Beverly Baumunk of Pittsburgh and an antique cast-iron schoolhouse bell that I had bought at auction some years ago. We shipped these to Costa Rica by air freight. Skip had to build a wooden crate for our bell, and when we delivered it to the Harrisburg terminal the crate failed inspection. We had to return home with it, where he altered sharp corners on the crate to make it safer for the airplane's cargo bay, then haul it back to the Harrisburg air terminal, another three-hour round-trip. Shipping costs alone amounted to twice the original price of the bell. Then the bishop's staff in Costa Rica had the chore of retrieving the bells from the difficult Costa Rican customs offices, known as the dreaded *aduana*.

By 1990 the church was nearing completion. Then, on March 18, we experienced an earthquake. To be honest, our first thoughts were not of the church but of what to do to escape the terror of being helpless in the face of nature's power.

Martha and I had been serving lunch to Chet and Skip on the front porch at Casa de las Flores when the tremors began. We both ran off the porch after our first momentary reaction of paralyzed panic, leaving Chet and Skip sitting rather calmly at the table watching the hanging flowerpots swing back ånd forth and the tableware rattling. Skip later remarked, "I wish I had pictures of your faces when the porch began shaking."

After a while we began wondering, *What about the church?*

The next day we checked and were pleased and amazed to find little obvious damage. It set us to wondering, however, about the vulnerability of those high block walls.

The next year, when we hoped the church could be dedicated, a much stronger *temblor* occurred, and the structure was seriously damaged. The long-awaited dedication, which was to involve the bishop and many *padres* and other representatives from surrounding parishes, had to be postponed indefinitely.

It was back to raising more funds while the whole front of the church was reengineered to make it safer and more earthquake-proof. The answer was a steel framework strong enough to stabilize the whole building. This may have been a blessing in disguise, since the result was, in addition to being much stronger, much more attractive. Extra space was included in the form of an entrance foyer with small cubicles on each side, rising into a bell tower.

This pleased us very much, since now the bells were hung high in a real tower instead of being suspended on a crossbar between two rough poles in the churchyard, as had been the case before the earthquake.

Chet pondered over this as he did over the whole sequence of events from the fishing trip forward. *Why did we go fishing that day? I'm not a fisherman. Why did that banana freighter show up in the middle of the ocean when it did? Why did I even make the promise? And now the earthquake, and the church is being improved, . . . but it's still not finished. Will it ever be completed?* Chet was nothing if not a ponderer.

Unfortunately, Chet died before the church was completed. As with most World War II participants, he smoked cigarettes. At that time, everyone stateside was encouraged to cut back on smoking so our fighting men could have plenty of cigarettes. The USO distributed them, as did the Red Cross and the Salvation Army, even the U.S. Army itself. The result was that Chet craved his nicotine, and it killed him. He had several bouts with cancer: bladder, skin, and lungs.

I told Skip, "It's like the cancer is really trying to get him." The bladder cancer seemed in remission and the skin cancer was removed, but the lung spots grew too large. Chet had more and more difficulty

The Nosara Church, finally in use after many years of effort and delays due to earthquakes and lack of money.

breathing. He finally succumbed in May 1993, after a brief but difficult last visit to Nosara. Sadly, he had never seen the completed church.

Martha requested memorial contributions to the church instead of flowers. To our amazement, she carried nearly seven thousand dollars to Costa Rica in January 1994 for Albert Muller to deposit toward the completion of the church. She sat beside a stranger on the plane, and by the time we debarked in San José Martha had another twenty-five dollars for the building fund. Skip said, admiringly, ''Amazing. The unsinkable Martha Brown.''

At last the church was completed. It was dedicated on Wednesday, January 18, 1995, two years after Chet had last seen it. Martha attended, along with her friend Jane Bauer, Skip, and me. Many of the gringo supporters of the building fund came. Albert and Nora Muller, fund treasurers, were there, and Cuyo was beaming proudly. Flora Avila, Cuyo's *esposa*, was deeply immersed in preparing food for the great celebration to follow.

Bishop Hector led the mass, assisted by ten young priests, including handsome young Padre Victor, Nosara's very own priest! Busloads of

81

Plaque inside the church honoring Chet, reads: In Eternal Gratitude—to our dear friend—Chester Eastep—for his help with the construction of this temple—Bocas de Nosara 1994.

people from surrounding villages arrived, swelling the attendance to nearly seven hundred souls. They came from San Juanillo, Barco Quebrado, Garza, Delicious, Santa Marta, Silencio, Terciopelo, and Ostional, from pueblos up and down the coast, along with *campesinos* from the inland hills and valleys. It was a wonderful celebration, with choirs from various congregations singing and offering testimonies of support. Nosara finally had its church.

A fiesta followed, the women of the church feeding the majority of visitors under a *ranchito* in the front churchyard and the clergy on the veranda of the little priest's residence in the backyard. Special guests, which included our group, were to follow the clergy at the tables on the veranda. We were served rice with pork, palm hearts, *mondongo* (tripe), *chicharrones* (chitterlings, or deep-fried pork rind strips), beer, and Coca-Cola. We felt both proud and humble to be a part of such an event.

After eating, we went back inside the nearly empty church to survey the decorations and appointments. Now, for the first time, we saw a bronze plaque on the right-hand wall near the rear of the church. Skip choked up as he translated for us: "In eternal gratitude to our dear friend Chester Eastep for his help with the construction of this temple."

Tears flowed freely down many of our cheeks as we thought of Chet and the events and years of effort involved in producing this magnificent outcome. It was sad that Chet wasn't here to share this day, but the joyfulness of the people overcame our sadness. (Some say, "He was there . . . , he was there . . .")

10

1990, We Build a House

We had arrived at Casa de las Flores in early January 1990 to find the normally quiet, serene atmosphere disturbed by hammering, scraping, clanging, and the chatter of workers bantering in Spanish. Chet had hired Arepa, a hyperactive Tico of Italian descent, to build large gateposts at the two entrances along the road and to form the foundations and deck for a new house. It was to be our house.

Chet, nearing eighty, had decided that it would make sense for Martha and him to have younger people around as they aged, especially here in a foreign country. He was concerned about the transition period between the time he and Martha could no longer endure the trip to Nosara and the time his sons would retire and be able to care for Chet's beloved Casa de las Flores. He had probably also considered the likelihood that Martha would outlive him and that this arrangement would provide assistance for her, enabling her to continue wintering here. A final consideration was that another house would provide separate quarters for their second son. Chet envisioned both sons retiring to Casa de las Flores, happily puttering around the gardens and buildings as he did, while their wives enjoyed the beach. Chet tried to think of everything.

He pondered over this idea for a long time, then disclosed it to Martha and secured her agreement. Skip and I were chosen, probably for our compatibility, along with our availability. Skip had recently retired, and we had been looking for suitable wintering grounds. Skip was a capable handyman, and my homemaking skills complemented Martha's nicely. We had the bond of having shared the lost-at-sea episode, and of course Skip and Chet had worked closely together at Shippensburg University for ten years, continuing the friendship for over a dozen years after that. It seemed a pretty natural step, and certainly we felt honored to be invited to help build a house and be a regular part of their winter escape to the tropics.

Chet broached the idea to us during the summer of 1989. We were flabbergasted at first, then began to probe further. We had almost made up our minds to locate a winter home in Florida when Chet hit us with this, so we had to step back and do some serious comparing. Florida, of course, was less expensive to reach and would enable us to keep in better contact with our four children and their families as well as our parents. But Costa Rica was so exotic and beautiful, and the cost of living was less expensive once we arrived there.

Chet explained that he would fund the construction; we would only have to pitch in and help. We would be free to use the house or not, as we wished, no strings attached. They would like us to spend the winters with them as much as possible, but it would be our decision as to how much time we spent there and when. This began to sound like a great arrangement.

We talked it over, deciding that there were few negatives. It seemed almost too good to be true. We discussed it again with Chet and Martha as we hauled our bell to the air freight terminal to be shipped to Costa Rica for the church. That day we agreed to be part of their Nosara enterprise, no strings attached or, as Chet said, "No obligations either way." We had already visited three times, the last time for a month. With these visits viewed as test runs, the indications were positive so far.

Now, here we were, at Casa de las Flores, ready to begin what we hoped would be a long and pleasant involvement. All the activity was impressive. The Tico workmen had formed and poured the reinforced concrete pillars upon which they were now setting the floor joists to support the wooden deck that would become the floor of the new house. It seemed very spacious, thirty by forty feet, at the moment unbroken by any partitions. The men sheltered the new flooring with palm fronds to prevent rapid drying by the tropical sun, which would otherwise cause distortion and warping. I guess they never considered drying lumber before building, or maybe they knew something we didn't.

One of the men was hand-planing the floorboards, an unthinkably archaic task in the United States. The boards had been tongue-and-grooved by machine, but not surfaced. What a lot of muscle and sweat went into that task! Skip asked the muscular, good-looking workman using the plane what his name was, to which he responded shyly, almost haltingly, "Ferencio."

Arepa himself did the masonry for the bathroom. Masonry was his specialty. It had separate foundation pillars and a concrete floor and stood within the main framework at the upper side of the foundation. The bathtub/shower was formed out of concrete blocks and then tiled. The result was very attractive, featuring a lovely floral design.

Arepa, whose name means "pancake" or something of that nature, kept pressing Chet for a written contract. Chet was avoiding any legal involvement, since he didn't want Arepa to take over the whole process. Chet wanted Arepa only for the foundation work, but communication seemed always to be a problem.

Finally, when the gates, the main flooring, and the bath were completed, we heard Chet and Arepa talking pretty loudly. Soon Arepa stomped into the toolshed, grabbed his tools, and cleared out, taking his men with him. Chet had made it clear Arepa was no longer needed, seriously damaging his dreams of becoming a building contractor. After that, Arepa cheerfully supplied lumber on order from Chet, but merely on a cash-and-carry basis.

Looking back on that period, we think that some of the "contractors" and suppliers were probably overcharging some of the trusting older gringos, like Chet. Things happened slowly, supplies were difficult to obtain, and the language barrier was ever-present. Some folks were glad just to get something accomplished and therefore often overlooked puzzling discrepancies. After all, the exchange rate kept shifting, too, and it was hard to know just what a bill for 30,000 colones meant, especially when you weren't even sure what items were included in the bill. So Chet just paid the bills without much questioning.

When Arepa *was* on the job, it was fun just to see what would transpire each day. Upon his first look at Skip, Arepa exclaimed loudly, "Kennedy!" Ever after that, he would yell, *"Kennedy!"* every time he saw Skip, even when passing on the road. John F. Kennedy had visited Costa Rica in the sixties, and Arepa apparently saw a resemblance. JFK is remembered with high regard in Costa Rica.

Chet had hired a new caretaker since our last visit to Nosara. Franco, Chet's first caretaker, had quit, claiming that Chet and Martha had been trying to make his daughters into "little gringos." Whatever the truth, Franco was gone and Chet was very bitter about the separation.

A bright young charmer named Antonio had appeared to replace Franco, and Chet hired him immediately. Antonio had a woman called Chini who lived with him, and Martha hired her at times to clean house or wax floors. Chet and Martha enjoyed their new employees so much that they played cards together and socialized at times.

Arepa repeatedly called Antonio a lazy duck because he and Chini had no children, even after several years together. That probably hurt Antonio's feelings, since he had made it clear that they desired children but were having no luck. Not being able to have children seems to be a grave fault in rural Costa Rica.

Arepa then tried to weasel Skip into negotiating a contract between himself and Chet, but Chet rejected that out of hand. Still, Arepa remained irrepressible. Chet would put on a new audio tape so the workers could hear it, and Arepa would walk 100 yards from where he was working to tell Chet how good the music was. Then he would walk 50 yards in another direction to explain the great music to Skip. The day Chet put on a tape of Peruvian mountain music, Arepa literally trotted from one to another to praise the music. He knew its source, too.

Another day, driving toward Nosara, we came upon Arepa's car parked on the berm, Arepa himself flat on his back across the center of the road, his arms stretched full-length. Martha cried out in concern; Chet slammed on the brakes. Before we could get out to render assistance, Arepa jumped up, laughing with glee. He had just pulled a great joke on us and was delighted with himself.

Once, he walked onto the porch, limping. He proceeded to tell us an involved story of how he had seen a huge bull on the road and tried to herd the animal with his vehicle. The bull turned and charged his vehicle, denting it, and he somehow hurt his leg in the process. He seemed somewhat proud of that, too, as if it were a badge of courage. Then there was the time he came up on the porch at Casa de las Flores, walking very stiffly and carefully. Dr. Jack Hargleroad happened to be there and asked what was wrong. Arepa told him he had a sore place on his butt. Jack asked him if he wanted it examined. Arepa looked at Martha and asked, ''Is he really a doctor?''

Martha of course verified it, so Arepa gladly agreed to the examination. Jack had Arepa bend over the table and drop his trousers. Martha ran into the kitchen, out of sight. Sure enough, there was a nasty carbuncle. Jack asked, ''Do you want me to fix that for you?''

Arepa agreed, after another reassurance from Martha that Jack was a real doctor. Jack pulled his little Swiss Army knife from his pocket, got a cigarette lighter from Chet, sterilized the blade, and lanced Arepa's ugly, painful sore. Ever after that, Arepa happily called out ''*Doctor!*'' every time he spied Jack. Skip can't help but recall that scene whenever he and Jack are together and Jack uses the little Swiss Army knife to peel and slice a piece of fruit he is eating.

Arepa later abandoned the lumber and contracting business and now operates Nosara's taxi service. Actually, there's only one taxi, and he drives it himself. He will be glad to sell you a piece of real estate, though, if he can, since he does that on the side.

At any rate, once Chet dismissed Arepa, he and Skip, with assistance from Antonio, were left to complete the construction of the new house by themselves. They tore into it with a will, and soon partitions were rising from the decking that had been nearly completed by Arepa. Chet was the idea man, the designer, and Skip was the carpenter. With a mixture of old lumber from the former caretaker's house and new lumber purchased from Arepa, they built a spacious jungle home.

Building supplies were difficult to obtain. Most of the lumber was obtained locally, but nails, paint and roofing had to be ordered. One neighbor, a farmer named Justo (pronounced "HOOStoe"), had a truck and would obtain things in Nicoya for us. The problem with that, of course, was the language barrier. Justo spoke no more English than we did Spanish at the time. Some things came through nicely, while others drove us crazy. One of the latter was an order for nails. Skip needed some four-penny and eight-penny nails. They don't use that Old English description of nail sizes in Costa Rica. The order came through as several pounds of half-inch brads, literally thousands of them! We did get some correct items, though, so we kept everything.

As we talked it over at dinner, Chet lamented, "What will we ever do with all those little nails?" Martha decided that she and I would go to Nicoya on the bus to return the nails and get the correct size. Chet said he also wanted some paint, so that settled it.

The next morning, Martha and I were clad in clean dresses, waiting for the bus at 6:30, ready for a big day on the town. Actually, we were excited to get away from the confinement of our jungle routine for a day.

The bus ride was typical: bumpy, dirty, long, and tiring. We soon remembered how difficult it really was. Sometime after nine we arrived in Nicoya and walked through town to Ajoy's hardware store. Shopping was slow, not self-service. It required an interpreter plus some sign language, then selecting from the items they bring to the counter, having the bill written up, paying at the *caja* (the cash register cage), then taking the receipt to another counter to pick up your parcels.

87

By then we were carrying a heavy load of paint and nails, so we didn't want to do very much more shopping. We came by the grocery store for a couple of items unavailable in Nosara and then had a Chinese lunch at El Presidente. After that we headed for the bus station. Above all, we wanted to be certain to have seats for the return trip. We wanted no part of standing on a moving bus for two hours with the weight of all the items we were carrying. We wound up sitting in the bus for a half hour before it departed. The temperature was in the nineties, and the bus had no air-conditioning—just what we needed, some extra time sitting in that darned bus.

The bus dropped us in front of Casa de las Flores about 3:30 P.M., hot, tired, and dirty. We walked up the driveway to the house, dragging ourselves and our parcels up the stairs onto the porch. The guys came quickly to see how our trip had gone and burst out laughing when they saw us. I had just yanked off my sunglasses and had white circles around my eyes with curved black lines under them, where the glasses' frames had trapped dirt and sweat. Skip thought I might be related to a raccoon.

Still, we felt proud of our accomplishment, getting those important articles and returning all in the same day. We were conquering heroines, or something like that. The men hated to tell us that we still had bought the wrong kind of nails. They were very apologetic that they hadn't made it clear enough, that it was not our fault. But we did consent to repeat the trip again the next day, carrying samples of the correct size of nails. Somehow, the sense of adventure was gone.

Antonio, the caretaker, thought the world of Skip. As one of our guests said, "He just loves you, Skip!" Skip appreciated Antonio, too, and they delighted in teasing, joking, and occasional tomfoolery. Antonio regularly teased Skip by hugging me and standing with his arm possessively around my waist, acting the outrageous flirt. I had no problem with that, since I enjoyed the playfulness, too, except Antonio did this even when he had *el gripe,* as they call the flu. Of course, I'm the one who gets sick. It made me feel like a wimp and took some of the shine out of my vacation for the next week or so. I tried to avoid him when he had the flu, but it was difficult. I just couldn't be rude to him; he's such a sweet, playful guy.

Now and then a school of *sardinas* would come close to shore, which enticed the larger game fish to follow. Antonio, a born fisherman always with an ear to the maritime grapevine, was one of the first to know. If the timing was appropriate, he would invite Skip. Off they would go to fight the surf for several hours, sometimes risking their necks, in order to catch a few fish.

Antonio provided the bait by catching some minnows from the large schools that were being hunted by the game fish. This process amazed Skip. Antonio would wade into the school carrying his ball cap and ever-present machete. He would slash the machete horizontally through the minnow-laden water, flipping out several minnows, and then catch them in his hat! He would then stash them in his shirt pocket, or if he had a plastic bag, he would use that and tie it to his belt. He would give Skip some to put into his shirt pocket (phew), and they would begin casting.

Antonio had his line wrapped around a whittled piece of wood. He would cast by swinging his minnow in circles over his head like a lasso, then releasing it, holding the wooden "reel" so that the line could peel off freely, as from a spinning reel. He was very good at this. Antonio always caught fish, usually lots of them.

Skip occasionally caught a couple and was the brunt of much light-hearted derision by Antonio. Skip used a nice rod and spinning reel, while Antonio used only that hand line, yanking in three or four while Skip sportingly played one fish until it tired or broke free. We would generally have a dinner or two of fish after these forays. Usually Antonio had to supply the fish.

The *corvinas* (white sea bass) were the best to eat, then the *pargos rojos* (red sea bass) and *robalos* (snook). Less favored were the *jureles* (jacks) because they had the darker flesh; naturally, they were the most common. Chet and Martha didn't like to eat the jacks until one time Skip filleted them extra carefully, removing all bones as well as the liver-colored side stripes. Then we all found them more than tolerable, after I fried them in Italian-flavored bread crumbs. After that Martha asked, "Skip, why don't you go fishing more often?" She also said, when he came back empty-handed, "Well, why did you bother going?"

The reason he didn't go fishing more often was that he and Chet were building the house as fast as they could. They worked until noon every day, sweating profusely under the tropical sun. They lost weight and became trim, brown, and fit as the season progressed. The work moved along rapidly.

A visit by Eldon Neurenberger, a retired engineer from Chambersburg, Pennsylvania, gave them a boost. He helped Skip lay out the big rafters, which had to be nearly twenty feet long, a length unavailable in Nosara. Skip had seen how local craftsmen spliced planks with a Z-shaped joint and made a pattern. Eldon helped match pieces and calculate lengths and spacing so they would have enough lumber to complete the job. They did a fine job; Chet was greatly pleased. Additionally, Eldon was a large, strong man, a great asset in raising the heavy rafters into place.

Skip calculated overhangs of three feet to keep rain off the woodwork and avoid rotting as much as possible. The only wood left exposed was the front deck and stairs. They were concerned about that but, in the push to finish, left it as it was.

Most of the wood they used was *pochote,* from a common local tree that is covered with large thorns from the ground up, trunk, limbs, and all. The wood is very heavy because of the amount of sap it contains and bleeds profusely when it is punctured by a nail. (The lumbermen who cut and limb the trees bleed profusely, too, if they aren't careful, because of those thorns.) This characteristic protects the wood from rot and fire for a long time after cutting, making it a valued construction lumber. Additionally, it is very workable as well as beautiful.

Skip told Chet as he was painting some of the new woodwork, "You know, it's a shame to use this beautiful, furniture-quality wood for construction and then cover it with paint."

Chet nodded in agreement, replying, "Yes, but it's the only thing we can get, and we have to protect it."

Skip later lugged a couple of small pieces home with him, from which he created attractive fruit bowls. He said it was easier to form than any wood he could obtain at home, even white pine, and much more attractive.

Antonio's half brother, Gerardo, whom we called Gerry, worked with the guys for part of the season. I dearly loved Gerry. He was a sweet, pleasant, hardworking little guy who always tried to please. Antonio would give Gerry the hardest jobs and then dawdle at his own task as Gerry cheerfully tore into his assigned job. Gerry accomplished twice as much as Antonio and for less pay.

I told Martha they should have Gerry working for them on a regular basis instead of Antonio, to which she replied, "We can't let Antonio go. We just couldn't do that. I guess when we're done with the house I'll just have to find Gerry a job." She loved Antonio and Chini and wouldn't dismiss them, even in her own best interests. And when the time came, she did get Gerry a job.

The Carpenters: Skip, Antonio and Chet pause during a morning's work on the "new house" at Casa de las Flores.

By now the house was up, roofed, and screened, which are the essentials in the jungle. Chet, Antonio, and Gerry were painting and installing wooden louvers in the window openings. No glass was used in the house. Skip was hand-crafting doors and some of the furniture. He had a portable power saw and electric drill; otherwise he had only hand tools to fit together doors, cabinets, bed, and sofa beds. He did a lot with mallet and chisels. We used up some Band-Aids on the guys but had no major injuries, for which we were truly thankful.

We were able to sleep in our new house for most of March that year, which seemed very special to us. The house belonged to Chet and Martha, but they made us feel as if it were ours. The kitchen needed a lot of work, especially cabinets and doors, and the bedroom needed closet doors, but we could at least sleep in the house. Martha always wanted our company at meals, anyway.

Sometime in March the diesel fuel drum ran nearly dry. Chet told Antonio to order a refill by way of Justo and his truck. During a free moment, Skip checked the fuel drum and found a layer of dirt and rust in the bottom. He said, "Holy smoke! I've got to clean this out or the old jeep will start coughing and let us down." So he used the remaining

91

fuel to rinse the drum. He strained the ugly mixture through cheesecloth, then dumped it back into the barrel, swished it around, and dumped and strained again. Finally, he deemed it clean enough to satisfy the jeep.

He told me, "It's a good thing that Chet always strains the fuel as he fills the jeep." Actually, Skip usually did the refueling during this period, but thankfully he'd followed Chet's practice of double straining; straining once as he filled the jerry can from the barrel, then again as he poured from the can into the gas tank. Maybe Chet learned this system in WW II, in the South Seas.

The propane ran out, too, near the end of the season. Martha commented, "Isn't that the way it goes? Right at mealtime, and just a few weeks before we leave."

Skip and Antonio lugged the heavy tank from under the porch and fifty yards to the jeep. They hauled it to Nosara and swapped it for a full one at the SuperNosara, picking up some groceries, the mail, and some hog concentrate for Simona's pigs at the same time. The full tank, much heavier than the empty one, had to be lugged back under the porch and attached. Skip stepped on a bougainvillea thorn, which pierced his flip-flop and his foot. Shades of Jimmy Buffet's *Margaritaville*! "Stepped on a pop-top, blew out a flip-flop . . ." Such is life in the jungle.

Martha and I spent a good bit of time in her tiny kitchen, preparing food and serving it, then cleaning up and doing dishes. Proximity was so close we joked about "dancing cheek to cheek," especially if there were guests helping. If we were hosting a party, things got pretty hectic. At such times, Skip would be mixing drinks in the kitchen, too, crowding it further.

One of our specialties for entertaining was "heavy *bocas*," meaning enough appetizers, or hors d'oeurves, to serve as a meal. Folks tend to enjoy trying different taste treats while chatting and sipping various rum drinks. We specialized in smoked oysters (from a can) on crackers, French fried yucca, chayote and carrot strips and dip, cream cheese wrapped in smoked chipped beef, plus the usual cucumber and tuna salad sandwiches. Some type dessert, often a cake, was usually included. People looked forward to such diversions here in the jungle, so attendance was generally good. The house guests of our friends were always included, swelling attendance beyond expectations at times. Then it was back to dancing cheek to cheek as we performed cleanup duty.

By early April, Skip and I were ready to head for home and see our children and grandchildren. Chet and Martha stayed on for another month or so, to avoid the cool weather back home, but we had to get back and do our income tax. Besides, our tourist visas allowed us only ninety days without an exit fine, so all things combined to motivate us on our way.

Chet said with his usual great sincerity as we were leaving, "Skip, I don't know how to thank you."

Skip replied, "Chet, we feel the same toward you. As Chipper says, it's truly a privilege to be here with you." We wished one another safe travels and were on our way, ending another season in Nosara.

11

1991, Becoming Nosaraños

January 8, 1991, we had Howard Teyssier, operator of the Mature Gentle-men's Limo Service, pick us up at our door and drive us to Hagerstown Airport to start us on our way. I told Skip, "That way, if it snows, we don't have to ask friends or family to risk their necks to drive us to the airport." That's exactly what happened. It was snowing hard and six inches had already accumulated by 5:00 A.M. when Howard arrived. It was so early the snowplows weren't on the road yet, but Howard, a retired driver education instructor at Chambersburg High School, had no trouble getting us to the airport on time. That was only step one, however. The airport was nearly abandoned, and the few staff on hand were no surer of flight schedules than we were.

After some anxious waiting, more passengers showed up, and a small commuter plane appeared in the snow. We flew through heavily falling snow all the way to Baltimore only to learn that air traffic was so delayed that we couldn't land. The pilot circled the airfield in the blinding snow while everyone hoped we wouldn't have to go somewhere else to land. Finally, after an announcement that fuel was getting low and an alternate landing site was under consideration, they did get clearance to land. We had at least reached Baltimore but were facing more delays before takeoff.

They did board us, but we sat on the approach strip for two hours as they repeatedly de-iced our plane. We were awfully relieved to get into the skies and climb above the weather. Soon we were looking down on the tops of the quiet, soft-looking clouds that had caused us so much nervous tension that morning.

As we approached Miami, the pilot smugly announced the sunny, eighty-three degree weather awaiting us on the ground. We smiled at each other, wondering jokingly, *Why in the world do people put up with Pennsylvania weather this time of year when there are places like Florida and Costa Rica?*

Then, just as we were approaching touchdown, the engines revved and the plane nosed back up into the sky. Skip said, "What's happening now?"—the same thought you could see on other concerned faces around us.

Immediately the pilot announced, "Sorry for the unexpected move there, folks, but we spotted a small craft where he shouldn't have been. We'll make a new approach and have you safely on the ground in a few minutes." We liked the "safe" part, but we were getting pretty late for our connecting flight to San José.

The weather certainly was lovely compared with the snowstorm we'd left in Pennsylvania, but we had missed our ticketed LLACSA flight. Fortunately, there was an underbooked Pan Am flight in about an hour, which we gladly accepted.

We had an uneventful flight to San José, and were glad to see the beautiful mountains as we made our approach at Aeropuerto Juan Santamaria. We perspired as we passed through Immigration and waited at the baggage conveyers. Skip grabbed our two regular suitcases but couldn't spot the footlocker that we had loaded with supplies for the new house. We waited and searched until the area was nearly cleared of people, then found the Pan Am baggage agent, who had us fill out a form. The agent, Carlos, told us that it would probably turn up tomorrow, but the term *footlocker* puzzled him. Skip described it as best he could, even drawing a picture, and then we proceeded to get a taxi and go on to our hotel, the Bougainvillea.

We met the Easteps for dinner that evening and reviewed our plans together. Skip and I were staying in San José for a little over a week while he took some intensive tutoring in Spanish. Chet and Martha were driving to Nosara the next morning. They were in town because they had left Nosara to go to Florida to be with family over Christmas and had timed their return to meet with us. They asked us to get some serious money changed for Chet and bring it with us when we left San José. The hotel owner usually provided this service for Chet, but he was out of town at the moment. I was concerned about carrying so much cash, but we felt obligated.

After getting business out of the way during dinner, Martha told us of an incident that had happened to her on her way into the country in October. The customs folks at the airport were inquisitive about a cardboard box she had with her, so they opened it as it sat on the conveyor. It required a knife, but the man sliced a little too deep, causing oatmeal to spill out of the box and onto the conveyor. Martha was embarrassed as people in line shuffled impatiently, waiting for the oatmeal to be swept up and removed so the conveyor belt could be restarted.

The next morning we helped load the Land Cruiser after a six-thirty breakfast. Skip carefully stowed bags, boxes and parcels in the back of the jeep and then climbed up on top with more baggage, chairs and foam rubber mattresses, plus ropes, bungee cords, and plastic sheeting to secure it all. There were so many things we needed in Nosara, so much to buy for the months ahead. Chet said, "Why do I always feel like a pack mule?," his blue eyes twinkling.

The jeep looked severely top-heavy, almost bulging at the seams. We shook our heads and laughed as the Easteps pulled away, wishing them a safe and untroubled trip while knowing that the odds were unfavorable.

We returned to our room and I began packing while Skip called the language school. The driver was prompt, delivering us to the school in jig time. I waited in the lobby while Skip completed registration with Wilma Castro, the director. Then the driver, who turned out to be her husband, drove us to the house of our home-stay hosts. Our host was José Maria Jimenez, a professor of languages at the nearby University of Costa Rica. Teaching is not highly rewarded in Costa Rica, so Professor Jimenez supplemented his income by hosting foreign language students.

Our arrangement included a nice room for two, a bathroom shared with other students, plus breakfast and dinner daily. We were expected to speak Spanish at meals but cheated a good bit, since I knew so little. Besides, our host's children liked to practice their English with North Americans. (People "south of the border" are a bit touchy about we folk from the United States calling ourselves Americans, as if no one else was. To them, we are either gringos or *Norteamericanos*.) Still, we heard a good bit of Spanish and became able to decipher some of it. However, we learned to be careful with our low-literacy interpretations, because, while some of our misunderstandings were hilarious, others were potentially disruptive or misleading.

The Jimenez children served as guides on occasion, since they were teenagers and quite competent at getting around the city. It was pleasant to observe their natural warmth with their friends as they encountered them on our jaunts about town. Often they would hug and sometimes kiss, especially the women or people of opposite sexes. We occasionally saw young men holding hands or with arms draped about shoulders as they sauntered along the streets. And don't jump to the conclusion that they were gay, either, since Costa Rica is still largely behind closet doors in that regard. Our impression is that they are nearly fifty years behind in tolerance of "alternate life-styles." Overall, we were impressed with the gentle warmth and good humor of our hosts, as well as that of Costa Ricans in general.

The meals were traditional, typically beans, rice, a modest piece of meat, and a cabbage salad. A small dessert, often fruit or Jell-O, and coffee would top it off. Senora Jimenez would vary the menu slightly each day, but there was little culinary excitement after the first few days.

Still, mealtime was always a pleasure, due to the mix of individuals. There was a counseling psychologist from Texas, a sociology professor from Maryland, and a retired horticulturist from British Columbia. In addition to the three Jimenez children, two of whom were university students and the other in high school, there was a university student from the United States. Everyone participated in discussions and shared daily experiences to the degree they wished.

One event dominated our conversation early in the week: the advent of Desert Storm. Professor Jimenez had panicked and begun to buy supplies wholesale, hoarding coffee, rice, beans, sugar, canned goods, toilet paper, toothpaste—anything he saw in the store that he could imagine running out of. We guests helped him unload his car and carry bags and bags of his purchases into the house. Then off he would go for another load. We were reminded of how some of our neighbors had reacted during the Cuban crisis back in 1963. He was one busy little man.

Meanwhile, I made almost daily trips to the airport, trying to obtain our piece of lost luggage. It was quite an ordeal for me, since I spoke so little Spanish, and Skip couldn't go because of his all-day language classes. He would call about the luggage at times, to place a little extra pressure on Carlos, the agent, but it seemed we were getting nowhere.

Thursday before noon I took the bus into the city to meet Skip over lunch hour, and we walked to the Bougainvillea Hotel to pick up the money to carry to Chet in Nosara. Hans, the owner, was occupied, but he had authorized his secretary to handle our request. A couple thousand dollars translate into a large bundle of colones, and I carried them in my purse as we walked the streets back to the city center. Skip had class yet that afternoon, so he saw me to the bus. From there I was on my own. Believe me, I hugged that purse pretty tightly as I rode the bus and then made my way on foot down the hill to the Jimenez home. I was greatly relieved to arrive safely.

Finally, on Friday, we decided to make as thorough a list as we could of the contents of the footlocker, believing we would have to resort to making a monetary claim. Of course that was when we made a last desperate call, only to have Carlos casually respond, "Oh, didn't anyone inform you? We have your luggage. You can get it anytime." We were too grateful to be angry. That piece represented many items meant to stock our new house.

Skip's cousin, Don Carey, had recently taken a new job in Costa Rica. He was working as a horticulturist for Linda Vista, S.A., a corporate producer of flowering plants that was developing a system to air-freight cut flowers to other countries. Don was involved in solving problems related to that endeavor. He looked us up at the Jimenez home and made plans to show us some points of interest we had yet to see. Don promised to help us get our footlocker and haul it out in his car.

Sunday morning he picked us up and introduced us to his date, a Canadian embassy employee, and off we went to the airport. By now, I knew my way around pretty well. We went to the upstairs administrative office of Pan Am, only to be shuttled around to two other offices, with everyone disclaiming any knowledge of our situation. Finally, Don took over, being much more competent in Spanish than we were, and made one of the officials understand.

We were sent downstairs, where they admitted only Skip and led him into the deep, dark bowels of the building. There Carlos awaited. He unlocked a screened luggage lockup and waved Skip inside. After a short search, Skip located our footlocker. Carlos asked him to open it but didn't do any sort of inspection. Skip emerged into the sunlight lugging that heavy, homely, but valued container. What a relief!

We spent the rest of the day visiting a butterfly farm and an aviary, both of which were fascinating and educational. At one point, as we were cruising down a highway, Don yelled, "*Pipas!*" Some young Ticos were selling green coconuts at the roadside. They hack off a shoulder of the hull with a machete, making a small opening, into which they insert a straw. This creates a simple, tasty, portable drink, which costs the boys nothing and they can sell for fifty colones, all profit. Don was delighted to treat us to our first *pipas*, and we were just as pleased to share them. The green coconut milk was watery and mildly sweet, with just a touch of coconut flavor.

That night we prepared to leave our Tico family. At dinner, we discussed our early flight to Nosara on SANSA, the domestic airline of Costa Rica. One of the young people brought up the problem of a trial daylight saving time that the government was attempting to implement that very night. Everyone was confused. The teenagers contested their father's position on whether to move the clock ahead or back, and he became angry. After some time of wrangling and near shouting, they agreed on which was correct and settled down to their usual congenial mode of behavior. This was one of the rare times we ever observed irate behavior exhibited by Ticos.

The professor called the taxi service, ordering our pickup an hour early, just to be sure. We heard him say, forcefully, *"En punto!,"* meaning, "on the dot." We were still worried whether the appointed time, 3:00 A.M., was understood by the taxi company as standard or daylight saving time. It was to change at midnight, and we wanted to be at the SANSA bus office by 5:00 A.M. to be shuttled to the airport. Oh well, we agreed, by leaving at 3:00 A.M. we should be covered either way.

We said our good-byes to the family and other guests, double-checked our packing, and retired early. The street noise seemed unusually loud that night. Dogs barked. Garbage cans rattled. We tossed and turned, gradually dozing fitfully. After we finally fell into a deep sleep, the alarm went off at 2:30. We splashed water on our faces, brushed our teeth, dressed, set the bags out, double-checked the room, and then carried our bags to the street. We moved on down to the corner to wait for the taxi.

Skip checked his watch. It was a quarter of three. We waited and watched, a little bleary-eyed from the early hour.

"What time is it now?"

"Eight 'til."

"I hope the taxi is on time."

Slowly time trudged on. Three A.M.; five after; ten after.

I said, "Skip, we better do something. After all, Mr. Jimenez said, 'En punto.' "

Skip agreed and went up the hill a couple of blocks to try to hail a cab on the main drag. I wondered if there would be much action even there between 3:00 and 4:00 A.M. on a Monday, but about fifteen minutes later a taxi came zipping down the hill. Skip and the driver hopped out and loaded the luggage, and off we went.

Skip said there were lots of cabs moving, but he had to wait for an empty one.

We reached the SANSA office about 3:50 A.M., and waited in the cab a few minutes, but no one was stirring. We discussed what to do and were about to get out and wait on the curb, though that didn't appeal to us, when the driver offered to take us on out to the airport for a few dollars more. Problem solved.

Things were just as lonely at the airport; it was closed for the night. Skip said, "What do you expect at four-fifteen A.M.?"

I replied, "Yeah, if it is four-fifteen." We were so confused by now that we had no idea what time it was or if anyone else did.

After paying and thanking the driver, we sat with our bags in the dim glow of a lonely bare lightbulb at the decrepit entrance to the SANSA terminal. Before long, a night watchman came by and eyed us carefully, apparently deciding we were harmless or, at most, crazy, to be sitting in the near-darkness at this hour. He disappeared into the night, leaving us alone to wait.

It seemed a long time, but all things pass. Another couple appeared in the twilight, and we quietly shared our conjectures about what was going on. Then more people appeared, and finally some official came with a key to open the door and let us inside to sit in chairs.

About five-thirty the officials began weighing us and our luggage on old medical scales. Someone spoke earnestly to Skip about the weight of our luggage. Skip didn't comprehend it all but handed the man a couple hundred colones, which he pocketed. Then he pushed our bags on down the line to be loaded. Apparently everything was now acceptable.

Bob and Kathy Benish, whom we had met in Nosara the prior year, appeared among our fellow passengers. After the usual hugs and greetings, Bob said, "Have you heard? There is a *temporal* stuck over Nosara."

I asked in ignorance, "What is a *temporal*?"

Bob explained that it was a cloudy weather front that carries rain, and in Guanacaste, rain is rare January through March. It would be our first experience with wet weather in the jungle.

Sure enough, we flew in over clouds above the ocean and landed, for once, without the usual cloud of dust.

Chet and Martha were there to pick us up, but instead of a hot, dusty trip to Casa de las Flores it was pleasant, clean, and green. We had never seen it like this.

We soon learned, however, that this nice, cleansing rain had a drawback; everything felt damp. Clothing never fully dried. Tools rusted. Things mildewed.

The *temporal* left after only a day or two more, and then we were back to our usual bright, sunny weather. It is always a pleasure to see the beach for the first time after being away. It simply brings joy to the heart to walk out of the jungle onto such a wide, pristine strip of sand with the great Pacific Ocean as a backdrop.

The guys were so busy again working on the new house that we didn't get to the beach as often as usual. Sometimes Martha and I went without them. It was one of those times when we saw a panther and her two cubs cross the road. I had never seen the variety of small panther which inhabits the jungle here. Antonio called it *el gato del montaña*, the mountain cat. They are so fleet that the sighting leaves you wondering if you really did see them. Martha and I excitedly verified what we had seen and tried to get the details clear in our minds. What a wonderful experience! Skip was envious when I told him all about it. He said, "Now I really wish I had gone to the beach with you! How lucky you were! I've never seen a panther here. A mother and two babies!" He was so excited.

The following week, on our way to the post office, we saw a couple of coatimundis cross the road. They were moving rapidly, but each had its tail straight up in the air as usual. From time to time we'd seen them in parade formation, traveling through the jungle behind our house, all with their tails straight up, occasionally a dozen or more in the troop. Their tails are ringed, like that of a raccoon, but are twice as long. Sometimes as they traveled through low underbrush nothing but the tails could be seen, floating above the bushes, all in a row. Skip said, "I wish Gary Larson, the cartoonist, could see this. He'd make something hilarious out of it."

We went on to the post office, only to find that it was closed all week due to a fiesta in Nicoya. The Nicoya post office was where the Nosara mail was sorted and placed on the bus. This second-class treatment aggravated Martha, who relished getting her mail. A letter was read aloud in the jeep on the way home and then studied carefully once or twice more while having a cold drink on the porch. It may be further reviewed while writing a response. Martha is such a social communicator that she even writes to strangers and people she doesn't truly care for. She certainly makes life interesting for us, though.

Jan MacLean, a regular beach buddy of Martha's, appeared one day looking somewhat sheepish. Jan said, "Oh, Martha, I completely forgot about dinner last week. You'll have to forgive me. I can't even remember

101

my name anymore. Between getting old and staying out in the sun too much, I'm losing my memory."

Martha responded, "Did I invite you to dinner? When was that?"

They both laughed, and Jan said, "Last Thursday evening. Don't tell me you forgot, too!" Then they laughed some more. Martha loves to laugh, a very endearing quality.

Martha said, "Yes! I don't even remember inviting you, but while you're here, let's set a date." They proceeded to set up a dinner, and both remembered that one.

We made the acquaintance of an undertaker from New Jersey who had been visiting the area, a happy sort of guy in spite of his line of work. He liked to joke and relate humorous incidents. One day Martha had driven two of her friends and me to the store for groceries, one in front with her and me and another in the back. We had completed shopping and were loading the jeep when the undertaker walked up to kid us about all our bags and parcels. We were all laughing as we completed loading and began to climb into the back of the jeep. Martha began climbing into the rear of the jeep, saying loudly, "You girls get in front! I'll ride in back this time."

I said, "But, Martha, you're driving!" We all cracked up, the poor undertaker laughing so hard he nearly rolled on the ground.

We enjoyed following the progress of the daylight saving time experiment. The bus driver compromised by going halfway between standard and daylight saving time. The schools tried to follow government advisement and use daylight saving time, but the bus schedule fouled that up. Workers ignored the "new" time as much as possible. Chet said, "I knew it couldn't work. I bet they'll never try it again."

On March 16 at 1:05 A.M. we were shaken awake by an earthquake that registered 5.7 on the Richter scale. It lasted for several seconds, long enough for us to awaken and "still have time to enjoy it," as Skip later quipped. I sat up and tried to jump out of bed, but Skip grabbed me and held me in bed until it stopped, ordering, "Stay where you are! This is a good, soft, safe place to be." This quake was strong enough to open our locked doors. It certainly scared me!

We learned the next day that Beverly Baumunk had done exactly what I tried to do. She had gotten out of bed and lost her balance due to the shaking. Then she fell on the tiled floor and hurt her elbow and shoulder. I guess it's human nature to take flight during such frightening moments, even when it is potentially harmful.

We also learned that Bob and Shirley Leonard's house was seriously damaged by the quake. John Frazier, who had originally built the house, offered to fix it for them, but they decided to sell out and leave. Shirley couldn't stand the sun, anyway; their house had been broken into and robbed earlier this year, and now the earthquake damage was just too much. In answer to protestations by nearly everyone to losing these good citizens, they promised to return and either rent or stay at the hotel. But they could not be dissuaded from selling out and leaving at the end of this season. Skip and I later visited them at their home in Colorado Springs and had a nice long reminiscence about the folks of Nosara and whether Pacific sunsets really do have green flashes.

Soon it was time to pack things away again. In the tropical jungle there is more to leaving than merely closing up. Each item's safety is considered in the face of the decaying dampness of the rainy season. Nearly every item not too large is packed into a footlocker with mothballs. The mothballs are intended to stave off the intrusions of insects and mildew. Furniture is stacked and covered with plastic. Refrigerators are cleaned and propped open. Sometimes a lightbulb is left on in a confined area to help stave off the penetrating dampness. Even so, finding mildewed clothing upon return is not uncommon. Then the smell of mothballs lingers for a week or two after reopening the following year. That's life in the jungle, and we were beginning to feel truly at home with it. We were becoming "Nosaraños."

Our departure this year was complicated by the closing of the airport—too many pigs, dogs, and chickens, bicycles, and pedestrians. As a result we had to get up extra early and drive to Samara, then a little farther to Carillo, where there was an unpaved strip still in operation.

Chet and Martha both accompanied us in the jeep. Antonio and Chini had asked the evening before if they could ride along. When we stopped for them at 5:30 A.M., no one was up. They didn't have an alarm clock. We fidgeted as we waited, not wanting to miss our flight. The tickets said to be on hand at 6:00 A.M.

Antonio and Chini soon appeared, plus Gerry, a surprise, which overloaded us somewhat. Now we felt we were late, so Skip drove faster than usual. It seemed dangerous and after we forded the river the brakes were wet, but we kept pressing onward. Skip wasn't familiar with the route, so Chet and Martha had to direct him as needed.

The final leg was along a pretty stretch of ocean, very inviting in the dawn mists, with a lovely row of palm trees paralleling the road. The airstrip was only a short distance from the beach, and there we were . . . all alone. Not another soul was in sight.

Skip said, "Gee, there's no one here. It's only six-ten. Surely the plane hasn't come and gone yet."

Chet reassured him, "No, I wouldn't think that. All we can do is wait. Someone will show up."

Someone did. First it was a couple of kids driving a herd of cattle down the runway. I said, "Look at that. And the Nosara strip was closed because of the same thing. We drove all the way here for this."

Then someone came and opened the decrepit little outhouse-sized shed that must have been the business office. We waited some more. A little after seven a car pulled in not far away.

About seven-thirty an airplane circled the strip and landed. Ah, finally! We got our luggage out of the jeep and prepared to board. Skip walked on over to check things out. It was a pretty small plane. The people from the other car drove up to the plane, handed over their luggage, and crawled in. They waved Skip away, indicating that it was a charter plane. Then they all flew away, leaving us still sitting there.

After another hour and much discussion, we decided to drive to what Martha called Del Pacifico's. She said, "They'll know what's going on." I wondered who Del was.

We drove to a nice neat tropical hotel bearing a sign, LAS BREEZES DEL PACIFICO. So . . . Del Pacifico was a hotel, not a person. Should have known.

Antonio and Skip went to the reception desk to inquire about the muddled airplane situation. The lady at the desk said something in Spanish, then asked a man in the back office a question. She said something more to Antonio and Skip; then the two of them had a discussion. Antonio asked the lady something else, then repeated a response to Skip. Finally, Skip came back to the jeep and told us that our plane was expected to arrive at the Carillo airstrip at eleven o'clock. Transportation to the airport would be available from here at the hotel at that time. He explained that he hadn't understood all that was being said, but he was familiar enough with Antonio's translations to add it all together and was pretty sure that the information was correct.

So . . . our tickets that read, "Be at the airport before 6:00 A.M." were a bit inaccurate. Surprise, surprise. We suggested that Chet and Martha go ahead and drive back to Nosara. Chet said, "I hate to go off and leave you here in a strange place like this." Bless his heart.

104

Chet and Martha squint into the morning sun at the dirt airstrip at Carillo, near Samara. The plane was over four hours late. The Pacific Ocean is in the background.

Skip replied, "Oh, no, Chet. We'll be fine. Thanks so much for all your trouble. We'll just wait here at the hotel and ride out with their guests."

Chet shrugged, "Well, if you're sure you'll be OK . . . "

I gave Chet a big hug. "You've spent enough of your day hanging around, waiting. You all have plenty to do back at Casa de las Flores. We'll be fine now."

Saying good-bye was sad as always, leaving good friends, including Antonio, Chini, and Gerry. But we smiled and hugged everyone in true Costa Rican style, waving as they drove off in the old jeep.

Now we were alone with our bags, hoping the information we had obtained was correct. Carrying our luggage with us, we entered the restaurant area, parked our bags against a wall, and ordered some *gallo pinto* (rice and beans) with eggs for breakfast. We hadn't had time for breakfast before we left Nosara, and the morning had been stressful. It was very relaxing to sit, sip our coffee, and chat about our morning as we awaited breakfast. We noticed that many of the guests spoke German and were amused by one German gentleman who wore shiny black wing-tip shoes and black silk hose that covered his calves, along with bikini-type swim trunks and a Hawaiian shirt.

After eating, we moved to a bench near the bus stop where we couldn't fail to see the airport shuttle when (if?) it arrived. It seemed like a long wait, but we were reassured when other travelers began showing up about ten-thirty.

Sure enough, just about eleven o'clock a van and a small pickup truck pulled up and began taking on passengers. The hotel guests seemed to have priority, so we wound up on the back of the little truck with the luggage and one other couple, traveling alfresco.

The other couple were German, younger than we, and spoke some English, so we chatted about our travels in Costa Rica and our impressions of the country. Skip mentioned the destruction of the Berlin Wall and how he had never expected to see it come down in his lifetime. That struck a chord with the German couple, and they shared their delight at its demise. They conveyed a very personal view of the event and had taken the time to go see it. It seemed to have been the greatest event of their lifetime, and we could sense how emotional they were about it.

We reached the airstrip before the plane but waited only a short while before it thundered down the runway. Not one of their usual boxy Brazilian-built workhorses, this was a real antique, a WW II vintage DC-3. It held twice the number of people but had little swivel-mounted fans with rubber blades instead of air-conditioning. Skip's father had a 1938 Ford pickup in which a fan like that served as a defroster. Skip adjusted it to get the maximum wind flow on our faces and quipped to the German couple about the quality of the air conditioning. They laughed and lamented the lack of the real thing as we awaited takeoff in the ninety-degree weather.

Soon we were lumbering down the gravel runway and into the air, on our way to San José and home. We had planned to do some shopping in the city, but most of the day had been wasted—well, let's just say we had used it up—on another surprise adventure in Costa Rica.

106

12

1992, a Really Good Year in Nosara

This was an exciting year for us. Our daughter and her two children were coming along to Nosara with us. They were our first guests in the new house, and they were as excited as we were. Our tales of Costa Rica had intrigued them, since as Laurel said, "You guys make it sound like an adventure in paradise."

Laurel closed her ballet school for two weeks after the New Year's holiday in order to make the trip. She had secured a passport for herself and the necessary papers for the children. The latter included, to our surprise, an affidavit attesting that the father approved of the children leaving the country with their mother. We had never heard of that. Perhaps there had been problems with one parent stealing children from the other.

Of course the airplane flight and connecting travel were a great adventure for them. Laurel hadn't traveled much, and the children were still in the wide-eyed stage of the very young. Carey was nearly five and Luke was closing in on three. They asked questions and commented on nearly everything. Even as we stayed overnight at the Hotel Bougainvillea in San José, they asked, "When will we be in Costa Rica?"

We explained that we were in Costa Rica, but Carey responded, "Well, there's no beach here. I mean the *real* Costa Rica." There was no escaping it: they wouldn't accept that they were in Costa Rica until they saw the Pacific Ocean and some monkeys. We flew to Nosara the next day.

When we arrived, Martha and Chet picked us up, but Martha didn't seem to be moving at her usual speed. I mentioned this, and Martha grinned sheepishly, saying, "I hate to tell you what happened to me. I fell through the deck." She went on to explain how she had walked out onto the deck that reached from the front porch to the back deck and had fallen through. The slats had become rotten from the rainy season and just plain given way under her weight. She had fallen straight down and would have gone clear to the ground below, except her ample breasts and arms stopped her passage.

I exclaimed, "My goodness, Martha! Did you hurt yourself?"

She replied, "I'm still sore around my ribs and back, but I'll be OK. I wouldn't want to do it again, though. Chet tried to pull me out and couldn't do it. He ran down under and stood with my feet on his shoulders for a while, but I was still stuck. Then we heard a couple of Ticos talking on their way home from work, down on the road, so we yelled, but they didn't understand English. Finally Chet ran down the driveway and called to them. They ran the whole way up to the house. They were so nice; one got on each side of me while Chet pushed from below, and they tried to pull me out, but I was stuck too tight. Then one of them got a saw from the bodega and cut off a couple of the boards around me. That made me loose enough that they could get me free. I'll tell you, I was glad to be out of there."

Chet added, "Yes, and I was glad to be out from under her," drawing a laugh from everyone. They went on to inform us that the offending wooden deck had been replaced by a new one made of concrete; no more rotten decks.

Martha and Chet enjoyed the children, as did their other houseguests, Harry and Ginny Sweely, who were also old friends of ours.

We all hit the beach the next day and enjoyed watching the children experience the surf for the first time. They loved it. Luke said the water chased him in and then he chased it out. Best of all, it was so warm that the kids didn't shiver or have their lips turn blue, as so often happens up north. They were so tired afterward that they slept all afternoon. The sun and water had worn them out.

Laurel, who has a moderate fear of spiders, had a very large one above her bed on the wall that night. She kept a wary eye on it but had heard Skip quote Chet's philosophy of coexistence with the jungle creatures and accepted the spider as a neighbor. It worked fine; they didn't bother each other except to maintain a respectful distance of a couple feet.

After dinner the next day, Martha gave Luke some Hershey Kisses to distribute to all who desired them, limited to two or three per person. Harry Sweely, who taught developmental psychology and enjoyed relating to youngsters, grabbed a handful of Kisses from the dish, just to see what the reaction would be. Luke never moved or said a word; he just fixed Harry with a cold, baleful blue-eyed stare until Harry replaced the proper amount of candies to the bowl. Harry nearly burst trying to hold in his mirth and has since retold the story many times.

Two days later, after Harry and Luke had gotten to be pals, they were strolling along one of Chet's landscaped paths. Luke said, "Look at this stone I found."

Harry responded with great seriousness, "That's a real fine rock you have there."

Luke, with equal sincerity, asked, "What's the difference between a stone and a rock?"

Harry was momentarily dumbfounded, but he related the conversation to the rest of us after Luke went to bed. Harry laughed until his eyes teared. The rest of us laughed, too, as much at Harry's reaction as at the story.

Meanwhile, Laurel became fascinated with an armadillo that habitually wandered around the grounds, dubbed "Tank" by Skip. She quietly followed it from our house down past Meditation Circle and back up toward the main house. Once in a while it would sense her presence and stop, prepared to leap, but she, too, would stop until it would feel safe again. Then it would wander on, snooping under leaves or branches for morsels.

The armadillo's pointy snout and hard shell allowed it to wedge through plants and jungle debris like a tank, hence its name. Laurel continued to follow it with the patience of a true nature lover until she was called to dinner. By that time the creature had meandered clear through under Martha's house and on up the hill into the dense jungle. Laurel had watched it eat insects and nibble at fallen fruit, although she couldn't see everything it ate.

When Laurel returned to the house she found everyone on the back deck listening to Carey reading from her little storybook. Still in kindergarten, Carey could read quite competently and had a very appreciative audience in the group of educators seated around her. Martha had been a second-grade teacher, Ginny was an elementary school counselor, Harry was a developmental psychologist, and Chet had been a school psychologist before becoming a college dean. What a lot of high-powered evaluation was taking place there in the jungle! But Carey was just enjoying having an appreciative audience.

A troop of howler monkeys was considerate enough to rouse us from our beds the next morning. Our guests wanted to see those guys as much as anything and watched and chattered and pointed until their necks ached. Our guests delighted in mimicking the sounds of the howlers, getting them to answer. Skip cautioned them not to disturb the monkeys too much. Later he said he was afraid he had been a wet blanket on their fun. Still, it had been a great experience for all, watching how the monkeys had clung to the branches with hind paws and tails while reaching out and pulling blossoms and new shoots to their mouths with their hands.

Laurel commented, ''Don't they eat your bananas?,'' to which I replied, ''No. That's a myth, at least where howlers are concerned. We only see them eat blossoms and young shoots, and they seem to have favorite trees even for that. They'll nearly strip a tree, then leave and return a few days later for the new growth. Sometimes we wonder if the tree will survive. They almost love a tree to death.'' We never cease to be fascinated by nature, and our children and grandchildren seem to have inherited our interest.

That evening after dinner, Martha and Ginny turned out the lights and brought a brightly lit birthday cake out onto the porch to the strains of ''Happy Birthday.'' It held six candles plus one to grow on and made Carey's eyes shine with delight. The two ladies had also created a few small animals from shells they had brought from the beach and presented them as gifts—very thoughtful indeed.

Too soon their time with us was at an end, and we helped them pack their shell treasures for the trip home. Skip and I accompanied them on the SANSA flight to San José, since Laurel was new at international travel. Besides, it gave us another day with them, and we could show Laurel around town a bit. Carey got airsick in the little plane, and I helped distract her by playing games but still kept the ''barf bag'' at hand, just in case.

Our room at the Cacts Hotel wasn't ready, which wasted some of our time. When it was ready, the kids were tired, so I stayed with them to allow them to rest, while Skip took Laurel on a hurried tour up Avenida Central to show her some of the shops.

Laurel enjoyed the Guatemala Shop, with all its colorful fabrics and unique handmade clothing, but she was delighted by the Mercado Central. This was the first time she had ever seen such an old-fashioned, exotic marketplace, complete with wonderful smells, sights and sounds. It has an atmosphere all its own yet is reminiscent of such bazaarlike markets worldwide. You walk among crowded stalls smelling richly of spices in this area, then of fish, then of cut flowers in another section. You pass hardware shops with dozens of machetes right next to leather shops redolent of beautiful saddles, bridles and braided whips, adjacent lariats, and colorful saddle blankets. Then come fruit and vegetable stands with produce, some of which you've never before seen, followed by festive clothing. (Ticos love colorful garb.) There are handmade shoes and leather watchbands, jewelry, guitars, wooden ox carts, and a large array of carved wooden souvenirs.

The market includes food and drink, mostly true Costa Rican cuisine, and the aromas here were nearly always too much for Skip. He had to take time from the fast-paced tour he was giving Laurel to treat her to a *guanabana refresca*. They both marveled at the tasty blend of fruit, milk, sugar, and water. They were tempted by the savory smells of the beans, rice, chicken, and seafood but had to hurry back to the hotel to take the rest of us to dinner.

The next morning we accompanied Laurel, Carey, and Luke to Aeropuerto Juan Santamaria and helped them negotiate the unfamiliar procedures of departure. We hugged and kissed, shedding a few tears in the process. We last saw them rounding a corner into a secure area, where we could go no farther. There was nothing for it but to leave and head back to town, feeling a bit empty for the moment.

Our agenda included a few errands, one of which was a stop at a drugstore. While waiting for service, we spotted some birthday candles in a showcase. This struck us, because Antonio's birthday was coming up later in the week. Better yet, we realized that these were the type of candles that defy being extinguished! Picturing Antonio's reaction made us laugh right on the spot and lightened our mood considerably, after the separation from our dear ones. Now we were anticipating a cheerful trip back to Nosara the next morning.

Antonio's twenty-second birthday arrived without his knowledge. I keep track of such things and had mentioned it to Martha, who, as usual, took over the planning. She had alerted him the day before so he could tell Chini and be prepared to come for cake and ice cream that evening.

Once Antonio remembered his birthday, he teased Martha by asking about the cake every time he saw her. "*Queque grande para mi?*" (Big cake for me?), he would ask with a devilish twinkle in his eye. "*Muchas regalas para mi?*" (Many gifts for me?) "*Fiesta para mi?*"

It was his nature to constantly tease and banter with good humor. He even sneaked under the porch while Martha was sitting on it and gave it a hearty shake, which he did occasionally to cause Martha to think she was experiencing an earthquake. Martha never failed to provide the desired response: a horrified look on her face and a cry of, "Holy Heaven!"

Meanwhile, Skip and I were alerting everyone to be watching when Antonio tried to extinguish the candles.

After happy hour and dinner, Martha told Chet to turn the garden lights on, which was the signal for Antonio and Chini to make their way up the hill from the pueblo for the fiesta. We sat on the porch and chatted as we watched for their arrival. They came, padding quietly up the slope in their flip-flops, only vaguely visible in the dim garden lights. As they emerged onto the lighted porch, they had the usual big smiles on their faces. Antonio patted his chest, saying, *"Queque and regalas para mi,"* sounding sure of himself.

Martha and I served them soft drinks with ice, which they consider a great treat in itself, here in the tropics. Then Skip produced gifts that he had carried from the States for his friend. He had monofilament fishing line, hooks and sinkers, some feathered jigs, and other lures. I gave him an inexpensive watch and a couple of T-shirts with NFL team logos on them. I also had a bright T-shirt and denim skirt for Chini, so she wouldn't feel left out. Everyone chattered and joked happily.

Then we sat up to the table for our cake and ice cream. Martha seated Antonio in the place of honor at the head of the table. The porch lights were turned off, and the brightly lit cake emerged from the kitchen to the enthusiastic strains of, "Happy birthday to you."

Everyone applauded and encouraged Antonio to blow out the candles. Antonio, grinning from ear to ear, blew heartily. The candles flickered, most going out—but then they flickered back to full brightness. We all cheered for Antonio to try harder, which he did—and did—and did some more. He got the most puzzled look on his face, along with a silly grin, but redoubled his efforts. Finally he sat back, out of breath, but giggling happily.

We were all laughing hard by now, Skip and Harry nearly rolling on the floor, some of us with tears streaming down our faces. Antonio was clearly having the time of his life. Ticos pay little attention to birthdays; some of the older ones aren't even sure how old they are. But Antonio certainly enjoyed his birthday fiesta.

Martha, who felt obligated to be a social leader in the community, had scheduled a beach party for January 19 at 4:30 P.M. Murphy's Law kicked in and the Guanacaste winds came on full-force. Martha got on the CB and and changed the venue from the beach to Casa de las Flores, saving the great event from defeat. *Then* she told Chet.

112

This was one of the infrequent times when Chet reacted strongly. If looks could have killed, Martha would have been pushing up daisies. He didn't relish having three score people, more or less, crowding his house. A number of them would be strangers, and his peaceful afternoon would be down the drain. He salved his temper by watering his plants some more, staying out of sight until the last minute.

We never learned exactly how many people came, but three score was an underestimate. With the high winds keeping people off the beach, this was a great diversion. We were afraid the porch would collapse, so we tried to steer people out back or down to the shuffleboard court, the horseshoe court, or the game room.

Thankfully, the porch held, and everyone had a good time. Martha was the heroine of Playas de Nosara, much to her satisfaction, though she didn't dare rub it in to Chet. The only casualties were a few paring knives and spoons, though we did gain a few other items of different patterns. Martha was so high, we had to play cards extra late that night to wear her edge off. Later folks said that was the biggest gathering ever for a beach party.

One February morning Martha and I were picked up at six-thirty by Kathy Benish and her mother for a shopping/sight-seeing trip. Kathy drove an Isuzu pickup with a club cab, so there was a backseat of sorts for us and plenty of room for purchases. It is a serious shopper's vehicle.

We began with a stop in Nicoya, since that is practically the only way out of our Nosara hinterlands. We turned northward from there toward Santa Cruz, then east on a side road just before reaching that town. This led us to Guaitil, a quaint little village that holds minor fame for the quality of its traditional pottery. They maintain the old Chorotega Indian style of crafting, and it seems that every other household has a large beehive oven in its backyard. The people were very friendly, allowing us to look around, handle their wares, and even peep into the ovens.

Needless to say, we each bought a few items of deeply colored pottery, mainly jars and vases. Their predominant color was a dark blood-red, usually combined with a lighter beige with a pinkish cast. A few artists included some black or very dark brown items, occasionally combined with a light tan. The decorative patterns had a primitive Indian appearance and would not look out of place for sale on a Navajo reservation. Prices were reasonable, with our small pieces (bought with an eye to packing them in a suitcase) costing only a few dollars each.

113

Driving on through Santa Cruz, we decided to head west and return by the more adventurous coast road. It was rough but very scenic, impossible in the rainy season, but February is the middle of the dry season.

We stopped at Junquillal (pronounced "hoon-kee-YAL") for a late lunch and a much-needed drink, all within view of the long, rolling surf of the Pacific. We hadn't paid much attention to our thirst, and that's not a good idea in the tropics. We had another drink, and feeling somewhat refreshed after our hot, dry travels, crawled back into the little pickup and took off again.

The road passed through some forested areas, then a little pueblo and on past some pasture land with a few large trees blossoming pink or yellow. Then we would break out on a hillside with a wonderful view of the Pacific, no civilization in sight, just us and the scenery. Then we would bounce along some more over the dusty dirt road, and the whole process would repeat itself. It stayed the same yet varied constantly.

We saw a grand ox cart, pulled by two large, strong, well-groomed beasts with placid eyes under long, dark lashes. The people we saw generally waved and smiled, reminding us how much we enjoyed the Costa Rican temperament.

After San Juanillo came Ostional, where the landscape became familiar again. Ostional is the location of a wildlife refuge where the Olive Ridley sea turtles are being studied. The local citizens are allowed to take a portion of the eggs to use or sell, and in return they help police the refuge in order to guarantee a perpetual supply. The eggs are sold throughout the country for use as *bocas,* gulped raw, or added to drinks in bars. We were told there was a smidgen of hope in the back of the user's mind that the myth of aphrodisiac properties is true.

After a quick stop at the *supermercado* in Nosara for a few items we were soon home. Martha and I felt greatly indebted to Kathy for the lovely day out. We babbled happily to Skip and Chet about our adventures as we ate dinner that evening. They were quite patient listeners, but of course they had already enjoyed their happy hour before we had arrived and were feeling mellow. To top it off, Martha and I beat the guys at bridge that evening. What a day!

Skip was still crafting doors for cupboards and closets but took increasingly more time off to accompany us to the beach. The house was becoming more comfortable all the time.

Chet divided his time between gardening and creating more projects. He began to work at the basement of our house, developing it into a sort of apartment, although we could see it had shortcomings for that purpose. Still, Chet seemed driven to keep working at something, whether or not it was necessary or even useful. I commented to Skip, "Have you noticed Chet puffing as he comes up the grade to the house? Sometimes he stops to rest. He acts like he's looking at his plants, but I think he's really out of breath."

Skip replied, "Yeah, I *have* seen that. The other day when we were working under the house, he said, 'Skip, I'm glad you and Antonio can handle this job. I'm not worth anything anymore.' I felt bad for him and told him he was our idea man and that he kept us on the right track. I know what you mean. Of course he is closing in on eighty."

The next day we went to the beach at low tide and headed for the tide pools. Mary Yost, a longtime winter resident of Nosara, now living in one of the condominiums, came toward us, almost at a dog trot. She is about Martha's age and is a retired physical education professor from Ohio State University. Mary is also a retired army officer and exudes a confident, tough demeanor.

She intercepted us, telling us that she had backed her old Land Rover into the barbecue pit next to the parking area, due to people parking so haphazardly. She would need our help getting the Rover unstuck, so we'd better not leave without doing so. We dutifully promised to pick her up on our way back to the jeep.

Off she went, back to the first tide pool, her favorite for snorkeling. Mary is an avid snorkeler and shell collector. She has a museum-class shell collection, both in Nosara and at home in Columbus, with specimens from all over the world in the home collection. Her favorite shelling spots are Belize, some remote islands in the South Seas, and Costa Rica, although she fears the quality of shelling in Costa Rica is diminishing. Many of the old timers agree; good finds here are becoming rare.

Although she couldn't gather shells at the Great Barrier Reef off northeastern Australia, she considered it to be the most spectacular of all snorkeling locations. For a woman nearing eighty Mary surely gets around. She was back in the water before we reached the second tide pool, Martha's pet hangout.

We enjoyed some time in the pool; then Skip and I walked our usual route to Guiones and back while Martha sunbathed and entertained anyone who happened by. She was educating some strangers about the glories of Nosara when we returned, telling them where to eat and trying to sell them on buying property and becoming regulars. She introduced

115

them to us and wound up inviting them to stop by Casa de las Flores before they left. Standard procedure.

We took another dip in the tide pool before heading back toward the parking lot. Before we reached the first tide pool, we spied Mary Yost hurrying out of the water to gather up her belongings. She merged with our parade like a loaded pickup truck entering from a freeway ramp. There was no way we could have missed her, as alert as she was.

We chatted about shells and such on the way back to Baker's Landing, the location of our parking area, which is also used for beach parties and barbecues. She was obviously agitated about her situation, but it didn't look that bad.

Skip said, "Give me your keys. I'll try to just drive it out."

Mary replied dryly, "It wouldn't come out for me."

Skip experimented with the shifters, trying to find four-wheel low range. Soon he drove it right out of the pit, making it look easy. Then he got out and walked around the Rover, spotting a very low tire, saying, "I thought it was sagging a bit on that corner, Mary. You better get going and drive it straight home and get it fixed."

Mary barely said good-bye, hopped in the old car, and hurried on her way, crouching over the wheel as if to force it to do her will. Skip stood there, grinning after her, saying, "There's only one Mary."

This was our best year for tarantulas. A medium-sized one was spotted amid all the kitchen action right near where Martha's belly rubs the edge of the countertop when she cuts up the fruit and vegetables. It was just under the overhang, black and furry, between three and four inches in diameter.

The same week another one the same size appeared in the guest bedroom, but at a time that caused no great disturbance.

A third tarantula, this one quite large, showed up in Martha's kitchen a few weeks later, only to be chased out with a broom. The final one, between five and six inches in diameter, was nearly stepped on as we started up our stairs after returning from a party one night in the dark. Skip was leading the way with a small flashlight and glimpsed a patch of black on the concrete step that shouldn't have been there.

I held the light on it while he ran for the camera. We prize that photograph of that beautifully ugly, much-maligned creature of the jungle. As with snakes, we humans are too likely to strike first and ponder later. We agreed with Chet: the jungle is a good place to learn to live and let live, to coexist and appreciate.

116

Each year the old jeep, the 1976 Toyota Land Cruiser, gives us problems of one sort or another. This year was the battery phase. We had parked at Baker's Landing as usual to go to the tide pools, and the jeep failed to start when we returned. Fortunately, there was someone else there with a vehicle to give us a jump start. When we stopped at the Gilded Iguana to make a telephone call home and the same thing happened again, Richard Buferd, co-owner of the Iguana, cheerfully provided the jump start. Then Martha was chattering and looking around on the way home and hit a bad hole in the road that jolted a shower of rust down on us. We had to shower the rust out of our hair and rinse it out of our suits when we got there.

Fortunately, George Miller and his right-hand man, Bolivar, were making a trip to Nicoya shortly thereafter and brought us a new battery. The jeep started fine after that, but we still occasionally received more rust showers.

March 6 brought us another earthquake. The clock stopped at 7:55 P.M. as recorded by Martha's kitchen clock when the electric supply was cut off. We couldn't play games that evening, so we retired early. We learned the next day that the tremor had reached 6.0 on the Richter scale.

March 7 was the day of the big wedding to be held at the Hotel Playas de Nosara. Gifts are difficult to come by due to limited shopping facilities in the area, but Skip came up with an idea. We had an unopened bottle of insect repellent, a Central American brand with COFAL on the label. He sat down at the table and worked out a poem that he deemed suitable to the occasion:

Aid for Newlyweds

Newlyweds must take care how they roam
   Round the *casa* they call home.
*Sin ropa** is the best, to really get it off your chest.
But *enemigos* may *visito* in the form of the mosquito.
   So instead of putting on your pants,
     Use this stuff for mosquitoes and ants.
       (Hope this poem's not a bore,
       We wish you oceans of amor.)

---

* Without clothes

We dressed in our finest that evening: guys in their best shorts and guayabera shirts and gals in colorful tropical dresses. We had to be at the hotel beach an hour before sunset. There was to be dining, drinking, and dancing, a 3–D affair!

Mickey and Don were middle-aged, and this was not the first marriage for either. Mickey had grown children who were on hand to participate in the wedding. Roger Harrison, one of our residents who was a retired Episcopalian priest, was engaged to perform the ceremony just before sunset. Then, as the sun sank into the Pacific, Mickey and Don were to ride off into the sunset on horses. What symbolism!

They failed to take into account the tide. High tide had narrowed the beach below the hotel to such a degree that most of the guests stood on the stairs and paths that led down to the beach. The wedding party kicked off their shoes and sandals and hiked their skirts in order to position themselves properly for the ceremony. Roger kept his sandals on but was still standing knee-deep each time the surf rolled in, since he was positioned with his back to the ocean, facing the wedding party.

The roar of the surf made it difficult to hear the service, but they proceeded as best they could. At one point the audience gasped as a wave nearly buckled Roger's knees. The maid of honor displayed a beautiful pair of legs as she pulled her lovely lace-trimmed skirts up around her waist to avoid soaking them in seawater.

Except for the tide, their timing was perfect. The ceremony was completed just as the sun, a great red ball, was sitting on the rim of the ocean. To our right we caught a movement and looked over to see a couple of Ticos leading a pair of horses followed by a young foal toward the wedding group. Mickey and Don were helped into the saddles and rode off down the beach at the moment the sun disappeared in a blaze of glory. It was one of those scenes never to be forgotten.

We all applauded and then made our way back up the paths and stairs to the hotel dining room for drinks and a lovely buffet as Antonio's Nosara Marimba Band began some lively salsa music. Skip and I danced every chance we could, between eating, drinking, and chatting with friends. It was a great evening, but it was cut short for us when Chet said he was ready to head home. Apparently he was tired, just another little sign that all was not well with him.

Nonetheless, we chattered gaily and even sang some old songs as we drove homeward in the moonlight. Once again Martha said, "I still don't understand how the moon can be behind us when we start out and

118

in front of us when we get home.'' Chet and Skip had tried time and time again to explain this phenomenon to her, but somehow she couldn't retain it. We all laughed one more time.

The following week, Skip nearly stepped on a slender green snake with a diamond-shaped head about thirty feet from our back door. Wearing nothing on his feet but sandals, he felt pretty vulnerable. He looked it up, finding it to be a type of vine snake, probably nonpoisonous.

We also caught glimpses of a deer, a rabbit, an anteater and another panther at one time or another during the season. The deer in the tropics tend to be much smaller than those in Pennsylvania, more like the Key deer in Florida. Skip read that there is some kind of principle involved that dictates that within a family the species get larger as one progresses from the equator toward the poles. It seems to be valid within the deer family, from the tropical deer and Key deer in the south to the white-tail, the elk, and then the moose in the northlands. Maybe.

The Guanacaste winds were strong this year, keeping us inside the houses parts of several days. A huge amount of debris was blown about. Limbs and leaves and dust were everywhere. Cleanup took a couple of days of hard work, with the women mopping and wiping and dusting and the men raking and dragging and burning and repairing. Then, next time at the beach or store, everyone discussed who had the worst damage, where the road was closed, and what accidents may have occurred.

The storm happened to tear a big limb from one of our largest mango trees, and it was carrying a bumper crop of unripe fruit. Antonio and Skip picked up sacks and boxes of the green mangoes, loaded them into the jeep, and hauled them down to the village. The neighbors were delighted to receive the fruit, since they have developed ways of using mangoes either green or ripe. Youngsters gathered around the jeep, toting off the bags and boxes in all directions, wide smiles on their faces.

The next thing to catch our interest was a swarm of bees that had settled high in the mango tree above the parking area between the two houses. We'd heard the swarm humming as they moved in a cloud above the house and watched them edge slowly toward the mango tree, where they finally chose an upper limb to call home. No one seems to know why they choose a particular spot to settle, although the queen is supposed to be at the center and where she alights the others follow and surround her.

We had read about the African strain of honeybees, both at home and in the *Tico Times*. These ''killer'' bees were supposed to be advancing northward through Central America this year. Reports were coming in of occasional attacks on people and animals. The United States was already preparing for the border crossing, probably within two more years.

We had no trouble with the bees for several weeks. We even knocked mangoes out of the tree, being careful not to disturb the bees too much. We kept a cautious eye on them, watching the nest grow larger each day until it was somewhat larger than a half-bushel basket.

Then one night a coatimundi apparently got a hankering for some honey and tried to raid the nest. That's when we found out they were killer bees. Chet and Martha heard the screams of that poor coatimundi in the night. Normally coatis can get away with stealing honey, but not with killer bees. Each bee's sting is roughly equivalent to that of a typical honeybee, but the African strain, when aroused, goes crazy and attacks kamikaze style. They don't know when to quit.

The next morning when Chet and Martha came out on the porch to prepare for breakfast, it was only a matter of minutes before the bees noticed their presence, though nearly one hundred feet from the nest. Martha dived through the door, but Chet was slower and was stung three times before he could get the door shut. Then they were trapped, prisoners of the bees bouncing off the screens, reminding them who was in charge. They had to keep out of sight for an hour before the bees retreated and allowed them to cautiously ease their way outside. Martha said, "Believe me, we kept our eyes and ears open for a while."

They reported the incident to the project manager, Michael Sandweg, who relayed the information to the government agency designated to deal with the bee problem. Within a few days, a "bee man" showed up to exterminate the nest. That problem was now off the list; on to the next.

Chet had ordered a table and chairs for the new house from Alfredo, the village carpenter, a year ago. Alfredo was skilled at many things but specialized in woodwork. Chet had advanced Alfredo $100, but his weaknesses overpowered his good intentions, and he spent the money on women and *guaro* (Costa Rican sugarcane moonshine). Chet had complained to us about the situation, so back in January Skip had taken him down to the village to have a talk with Alfredo. The language barrier still loomed large, but Skip's Spanish was improving, so they returned with new promises. Chet said, "It's been almost a year. I'll never see a thing for my hundred dollars."

Skip replied, "Well, we can at least keep after him about it. I know he can't have it ready by next week like he guaranteed, but we can keep the pressure on."

Chet grunted. "Yeah, he said he'd have something for me next week. That's a laugh."

Finally, one day in March, long after the promise of "next week," Alfredo and a husky neighbor boy came up our driveway balancing a pair of coffee tables on their heads with their hands! They happily brought the tables up the stairs and into the living room, proud of their work. Indeed, the tables were rather nicely crafted, with carved borders and feet and gracefully curved legs, made from some extremely dense, heavy wood. But they in no way filled the bill as a dining table and chairs. So much for communication once again.

Skip discussed it with Chet, who replied wryly, "Let it go, Skip. At least I got something for my money, and that's more than I expected after waiting over a year."

Mary Yost, our Ohio State friend, had us for dinner at her condominium one evening, starting with a nip of Abuelo rum and some tasty *bocas*. The latter included macadamia nuts (now a Costa Rican product) and smoked oysters on crackers. Skip and I studied her extensive and carefully displayed shell collection as the others reviewed the latest gossip. Then, after watching the sunset over a small patch of the Pacific from her balcony, we pitched in to help her serve a lovely dinner as the night chorus of insects tuned up. The tranquillity was regularly disturbed, however, by the yapping of Mr. Yost, her Shetland sheepdog, every time a motorcycle or horse passed by on the nearby road.

Mary likes beets, and she asked me to peel them each time we had dinner there. Another ritual that delights her guests is the gruff order, "And don't stack the dishes. That way I only have to wash the tops," delivered in her deep, tobacco-roughened voice. She is one of those endearing characters who lend color to our lives.

On March 17, Roger Harrison, the retired priest, drove down the mountain in his battered 1973 Mercedes to get Skip to help him install the main door on his new house. Roger had helped on the construction of our house in order to learn something of building techniques here, and Skip felt he owed him some help in return.

Roger had told Skip the door was salvaged from a church near San José, but he was still amazed at the dimensions of it. The door was of wood panels set in a heavy framework, nine feet high by four feet wide—a passageway for giants! Skip returned by dinnertime, the job complete. He grinned as he described the door and the process of hanging it but obviously felt satisfaction from it. He enjoys working with his hands and helping other people. He said that Roger was pleased, too. I got to see it later, and it truly is a beautiful old door.

The army ants came again as we approached the game room for our regular session at Martha's favorite haunt. Some guests were leading the way and inadvertently stepped on them. They were pretty good dancers, too. The bites are sharp, like hot needles, and although they don't last very long, they are difficult to ignore. Most visitors to this part of Costa Rica learn a dance step or two from the ants. It's a small price to pay for the privilege of visiting. The rule is simple: move aside; let them go on their way.

Toward the end our stay this year we had a little surprise. On our way back to the new house after playing games with Martha, we took the high path. Skip led the way as usual, with a flashlight, always watching for snakes as per Chet's rule. As we climbed the steps to our front porch, the light fell on a sleek object along the wall to the right of the door. We spotted it before we reached the top of the stairs, so we were looking at it nearly at eye level: a lovely boa constrictor. Part of it, perhaps five or six feet, stretched along the wall. Another two or three feet of snake was aimed straight up the wall beside the door, in an attempt to reach a young squirrel that was attached to the screen above the door. I say attached because he was obviously frozen with fear, trembling with dread.

We called to Martha and her guests, who came quickly to observe our new visitor. After a few minutes of hearing our excited chatter, the snake apparently began to feel crowded, so it doubled back on its length, rounded the corner, and slithered under the back stoop. The squirrel still wasn't about to move, so we all proceeded to go our own ways. Soon we all were in bed and everything was dark.

I felt the bed jiggle. Skip whispered, "I'm going to see if he's trying to sneak back up to get that squirrel."

I smiled to myself in the dark. *How predictable,* I thought. *If that snake is out there, he'll stay out all night to watch it.* To be honest, if anything interesting were to happen, I would have joined him.

He eased the back door open and stuck his head and the flashlight around the corner. There was the big, flat head of the boa, lying on the edge of the stoop, ready to approach the squirrel again.

Skip quietly shut the door and sneaked back to bed, "Shoot," he whispered, "I'm afraid I disturbed him. Now he may not come back up onto the porch."

We listened from the bed, and after a while Skip checked again, but the boa had disappeared. Finally, we drifted off to sleep.

First thing in the morning we checked again. Still no snake, but the squirrel hadn't moved. He wasn't about to come down from the screen with that big snake down there somewhere. We discussed what to do about the squirrel. I said, "He'll soon become dehydrated if he stays there. We'd better get him down."

Skip solved the problem with a broom. He brushed the terrified squirrel off the screen. The animal hit the ground running for dear life. We laughed as he disappeared into the jungle in high gear.

As Skip swept the porch he spotted a cluster of stems and leaves that started him thinking. He walked away from the house to higher ground to get a better view. Sure enough, there was more debris on the roof just above the pile on the porch and above that the remains of a squirrel nest high in the Guanacaste tree.

Then Skip remembered a thump he had heard before dinner the prior day. He had even walked across the compound to see if anything was amiss and also recalled a squirrel chattering in the Norfolk pine in front of the house. He had assumed that the squirrels had knocked a dead limb onto the sheet metal roof and dismissed it from his thoughts.

Now it all fit together, he explained. The boa had climbed the giant Guanacaste tree and tried to get into the squirrel nest. It had "gone out on a limb" too far, and the nest had given way, with the snake and young squirrels, falling onto the edge of the roof, then bouncing on down to the porch. Skip asserted, "That's how it had to happen to explain all those little details. Too many coincidences otherwise."

I replied thoughtfully, "Yeah, it does all fit; the debris on the roof and the porch, the squirrel on the screen, the boa on the porch. Why else would they be there, and all at the same time? Makes sense to me." We felt like a team of jungle detectives, pretty satisfied with ourselves.

This year we left Nosara a week early in order to see some more of the country. We packed our clothes and stored everything away for the season. Martha prepared an early breakfast for us, and we said our good-byes to her and to Chet. George Baumunk, who was making a run to Nicoya that day for some purchases he couldn't obtain in Nosara, gave

The "new house" at Casa de las Flores. It was the fulfillment of one of Chet's dreams, but we got to live it.

us a ride to the bus station. After another round of good-byes with George at the bus station we were on our own.

Skip used his so-so Spanish to buy tickets to some spot along the Pan-Am Highway that had no name but was a dirt road junction leading to Monte Verde Cloud Forest. We were uneasy about the vagueness of our arrangements, or rather lack thereof, since this was really our first time just "bopping around the country" on our own.

Our bus route was north through Santa Cruz to Liberia, then east on the Pan-Am to the dirt road junction. The driver's assistant was prepared for our departure and gave us a nod before the bus stopped at what appeared to be close to nowhere. We hurried forward with our overnight bag and out the door. The assistant yanked our luggage from the compartment under the bus, motioned toward a building a little way down the road, and was gone.

We looked at each other and laughed. Where were we? What happens next? I stayed with the bags as Skip walked back down the highway to the building to see what he could learn.

After ten minutes or so, he returned to tell me that the dirt road to Monte Verde did indeed depart from near the building and a bus was supposed to stop there later in the afternoon. He had even located a little restaurant down the lane. That cheered us considerably, and we lugged our suitcases down the highway and on down the lane.

We were hungry enough to enjoy the usual rice and chicken, but still had to wait nearly three hours for the Monte Verde bus. Time crept on while Skip tried to talk to a few young people who happened by. A couple of road-worn kids were camping around the country on a shoe-string budget. They had just come from Tabacon, the hot springs near Arenal Volcano, and said they had enjoyed the hot baths there. They were on their way to Monte Verde, too.

It passed the time when we had been told the bus would arrive, so we became concerned and tried to learn if anything was amiss. Nothing came clear to us until one young man explained in good English that the bus from Puntarenas had broken down along the way and it was the one that continued to Monte Verde.

We waited some more and a couple of school buses arrived. The drivers and another man discussed things thoroughly, and finally they indicated that we should all board the school buses. We all lined up, then realized there were many more people waiting around than we'd suspected. The lines were so long that we wondered if we would get seats.

One old man was in charge of luggage and seemed to be giving some of the travelers a hard time about the size or amount of their luggage. He asked us if our bags were large. Skip shrugged and got out a couple 100-colon notes, worth a little less than two dollars each at the time, and handed them to the man as he began sizing up our two large suitcases. He took the bills, said something like, "Not so big," and stowed the bags away very handily. Money greases the wheels.

Next they indicated that the bus with our luggage was full and directed the rest of us to the other bus. We weren't pleased to be parted with our luggage, but somebody said both buses were headed to the same place. We were packed in like sardines, holding our carry-ons on our laps, since the school buses had no overhead storage. We surely hoped that our other luggage would arrive where we did.

The space problem eased, however, as schoolchildren were dropped off along the way. The bus driver, on the other hand, frightened us with his crazy driving. He drove at high speed on the terrible roads, beating the poor bus to death on the rocks and ruts, rounding hairpin turns on the inside lane, ignoring steep drop-offs. We wanted to get to Monte Verde before dark, but not at the risk of our lives. He seemed to be angry at all the delays. This ride set an enduring record in our experience for rough, dirty, dangerous bus rides.

An occasional stop allowed us to catch a breath of relief as he dropped off a school student or picked up another passenger. One man he picked up loaded a large chain saw into the front of the school bus. The man was dirty and sweaty, as if he had just emerged from woodcutting in the forest.

Night deepened as the bus pounded ever upward. Finally we entered a large village high on the mountainside. This was Santa Elena, and everyone began debarking. Skip hurried to find the other bus and locate our luggage as I stood by a wall and held onto our carry-on bags. No problem, the bags were there as expected, so he came back with them and we started to walk toward an inexpensive hostel he had tentatively picked from the list in our guidebook.

As we lugged our baggage down a steep hill, a nice-looking young man strode up beside us and asked if we had reservations for the night. We said we didn't but were heading toward a place we had heard about. He introduced himself as Marco and then said he would take us to a nicer one, up the hill. "It has a good cook, and we'll even drive you to the park entrance or anywhere else you want to go," he promised. "We can provide a bag lunch and come get you, whatever you want. It's a new lodge called Arco Iris. That means 'Rainbow' in English. We'll take better care of you than anybody."

We looked at each other, trying to decide if this was a hustle of some kind. Skip asked, "How much per night?"

"Thirty-five dollars a night. No charge to drive you up to the park entrance."

"Any meals included?"

"Breakfast. And I'll carry your bags up the hill for you."

That did it. We were seriously tired, and we had no idea what the other accommodations were like. We said, "OK," shoved our two large bags at him, and trudged up the steep hill after him. We were truly glad to get settled in and sit down to a good meal that evening. That shower, followed by a lovely steak dinner, did wonders for us. Not wanting to waste any time, we made arrangements after dinner for a packed lunch and a ride to Monte Verde Cloud Forest following an early breakfast the next morning.

We arose at 5:30, breakfasted at 6:00, and were ready to travel by 6:30. Marco helped us into a beat-up car, but it wouldn't start. He tried another. It wouldn't start, either. Another man came to help. They tried drifting it downhill but then realized the other car was in the way. Everyone laughed about that. Finally they got one car going and Marco drove us up the rocky, rutted road in a terribly beat-up VW Beetle. He even took our admission fees to the head of the line, returned with our tickets, and sent us toward a park guide, around whom a group was forming. Nice treatment, as promised.

Monte Verde limits the number of tourists admitted to the park to 100 at any given time. After that number is reached, no one else is permitted to enter until someone leaves. They call this environmental impact control. It seemed a good idea to us.

Our leader was Alex, one of the indigenous people who had been trained as a naturalist-guide. Alex seemed finely attuned to the forest around him, being alert to any sound or birdsong we inquired about, able to spot creatures beyond our ken. We heard the call of the quetzal, the national bird of Costa Rica, as well as the *glung* of the bellbird, but failed to see either. Actually, it was a poor time to visit the cloud forest, since we were at the peak of the dry season. We didn't even need the rubber boots they typically lend to visitors to allow them to slog through the muddy trails. As a result, wildlife activity was at a low ebb. Still, we enjoyed the unique environment and walked other trails, even after Alex dismissed us. From one lookout we saw a volcano in the distance, wearing a halo of steam and smoke that the breeze stretched off to one side, ruining its symmetry. At another spot, Skip took my picture amid a mass of pink wildflowers.

Shortly after noon we returned to the park entrance to eat our lunch at a picnic table and check out the gift shop. Then we walked down the road a short distance to the Hummingbird Gallery. A couple of photographers had set up shop here and became interested in the variety of hummingbirds that came to their feeder, so they added more feeders, creating what we decided was the best attraction on the mountain. Their photographs were very nice, too, but the hummingbirds stole the limelight.

Several feeders were practically assaulted by the most amazingly colorful bird life imaginable. Little iridescent rockets shot out of the forest to hover and drink and challenge other feisty little blurs of color. In the Eastern United States we enjoy our single species, the rubythroat, which is admittedly beautiful. But here one species supped beside another and another and another . . . each one fascinating, lovely, and different. Some would drink from a perch, others would hover—some hovered with tails up, others with tails down. Some were solid colors, iridescent green or blue; others were multicolored, perhaps green and black with a dash of red or perhaps a white or buff breast to counterpoint a bright back. A few were less colorful, tending to olive or dark green. All were fascinating, holding us spellbound.

One man beside us commented knowingly, "There's a magenta-throated woodstar. And that large purple one over there, he's the largest species of hummingbird in the world." We were duly impressed, although Skip did check the man's information for accuracy as soon as he could, finding it correct. We watched, enthralled, until it was time for our ride back to Arco Iris.

A different driver arrived in the VW junker. His name was Marvel, he told us, "You know, like in Captain Marvel." Marvel was talkative and fun, babbling all sorts of information and teaching us some Spanish in the process.

We mentioned that we would like to see the creamery and cheese factory that produced that great Monte Verde cheese of which we were so fond. Marvel was only too happy to comply with our wishes, telling us that a group of Quakers had been so taken with President Figueres's 1949 disbanding of the Costa Rican army that they had formed a settlement on Monte Verde in the 1950s. They were also responsible for the development of the cloud forest reserve that had lured us here. We had read this information in guidebooks, but being here brought it home to us. Skip commented, "Good citizens."

We returned to Arco Iris with some cheese direct from the processing plant and then spent the afternoon walking trails, enjoying scenery, and bird-watching. We saw nearly as many birds here as in the reserve, including a pair of pretty toucanettes. We were so high that we could make out a vague patch of the Pacific Ocean. It was almost like being in the Alps.

At dinner that evening, we met a couple from Colorado who were also touring Costa Rica. The man was grumpy about his experiences: it was too hot in Puntarenas; the accommodations were not as good as in the States; the animals in the reserve were not to be compared with those in Colorado; the food was not to his liking. When the waiter brought his meal, he said, "Take this back and get that rice off the plate! I told you no rice." Then to us he continued, "They serve you rice with every meal! I never want to see rice again." We eased our attention away from him, embarrassed for the waiter and ashamed of the man's "ugly American" behavior.

The next day we pretty much repeated our first day, but with more independent hiking and more time videotaping the hummingbirds. That evening we packed and made arrangements for the next leg of our expedition.

Marvel met us early and carried our luggage back down the hill to the Santa Elena bus stop. He helped us make the proper arrangements to get to Tilaran, where we would change buses for the trip around Lake Arenal and past Arenal Volcano to La Fortuna, the access point for viewing that volcano.

It was another rough ride, but not so difficult as the prior ride up the mountain to Monte Verde. The driver stopped to receive and discharge passengers and a few parcels, to pick up his lunch, and once to help chase some cattle into a corral. One of the cows challenged him, but he stood his ground and the cow gave up, retreating through the gate. We all clapped as he returned to his seat behind the wheel. We passed on through high hills with long vistas of farm and pasture land, greener than the dry Guanacaste scenery, reaching the small city of Tilaran before noon.

Tilaran was a picturesque town with lots of flowers and palm trees, orange-tiled roofs, and a park with benches in the center of town, in front of the Catholic church. We walked around the town center as we waited for our bus, enjoying the color and peacefulness, smiling to passersby and saying, "Buenos dias." For lunch we tried black bean soup, which is truly black, contrasting with an egg broken into the center of the bowl. It was quite good except for an overdose of cilantro. Ticos seem to develop a high tolerance for cilantro, adding more and more to their dishes until the untrained palate cries, "Whoa!" At that point Skip says it tastes like it was cooked in a rusty pot.

Back on the bus for another extremely rough ride around the north side of Lake Arenal. The road was pure potholes, the lake scenery pure heaven. Then we rounded a bend and there it was . . . the most perfect volcano we'd ever seen! Mount Arenal was the volcano of artists' dreams, reminding us of pictures we had seen of Mount Fuji. It rises out of low rolling hills, forming a near-perfect cone encircled with a vague wreath of smoke. We craned our necks to catch every glimpse we could as the bus traversed the uncoiling road around bends, through patches of forest, and up and down hills.

The road passed right over the mountain's apron, leading us into La Fortuna. We could see the volcano's effect on the town; it had created a resort out of a farming center. In truth, the volcano had destroyed the town many years ago, but now it was reimbursing the people for the damage it had wrought. Tourism was growing. It didn't have the affluent look of North American tourist centers, but we could see some rather nice homes, restaurants, and a few hotels. There was more activity, more people and buses than in a typical town of several thousand people.

We carried our luggage down a side street, following a number of people toward a decent-seeming hotel we had located in our guidebook. We waited our turn as people were checked in, only to learn that they were filled before they reached us. Not to worry. A young man said he would take care of us; just kindly wait until he settled the others in their rooms.

In half an hour or so, the man appeared around a corner on his bicycle. He had accommodations for us. Just follow him this way. Abandoning his bike against a tree in the hotel garden, he grabbed our bags and led us around the corner and down a back street. It was quite a walk, the heavy bags bringing beads of sweat out on his forehead.

We entered a gate into a pleasant single-story house, where he introduced us to an attractive Tica. She and her husband rented rooms to tourists when the hotel overflowed. I'm sure the hotel received a kickback for delivering the customers, since that's the way things operate here, and she at the same time earned a nice income without having to solicit guests. We were simply glad to have a pleasant, quiet place to stay.

The man from the hotel invited us to join an excursion to the volcano that evening, for a price, of course. We signed up, and he suggested that we wear bathing suits under our clothes. Hmm, bathing suits for a trip to a volcano? Then we walked around town, had something to eat, and watched the ever-changing volcano.

Our group met at the hotel about dark. We hopped into a couple of pickup trucks carrying coolers for sodas. Being the elders of the group, we were offered the front seat, which we gladly accepted, thinking, *This isn't the way tours are operated in the States or even in San José, although it* is *more adventurous. I hope they know what they're doing.*

It seemed like just a bunch of young guys who said, "Hey, we have wheels. Let's start a tourist business!" We wished ourselves luck and a safe return.

Our first stop was on the far side of the mountain, the west apron, where we climbed out of the pickup trucks and followed our guide up a rough trail to a viewing area. There we could see glowing lava oozing from fissures in the side of the volcano at several places. We'd sort of expected the lava to overflow the rim at the summit rather than squeeze out the sides as this was doing. The shades of red and yellow and orange alternately glowed and dimmed, an eerie scene in the darkness, while the strong odor of sulfur made us wrinkle our noses. Sudden squirts of lava would occasionally pop out of the darkness and run down the slope, creating short, glowing yellow snakes in the night. The snakes graduated to orange and then red as they solidified and darkened in the cooling air.

The scene before us had a smoky, slow-motion quality, like trying to run in a nightmare. Moments or minutes passed between episodes as we waited and watched. We were torn between wishing for a large burst and fearing that one might occur. After an hour or so it seemed apparent that nothing was changing, so our guides led us back to the pickup trucks. Off we went to our next destination.

It seemed just a wide place in the road when our drivers pulled over next to some trees. We piled out again, realizing that this was a "hot creek" and we were allowed to hop in and enjoy a soak. That's why we'd been told to wear bathing suits! Another surprise due to the communication barrier.

The area was entirely undeveloped. We climbed down the creek bank in the dark, our guides offering helping hands as we felt our way around brush and over slippery stones, unable to see what we were getting into. Frankly, it was a little scary; maybe there were snakes or broken soda bottles lying in wait. It was a relief to find a likely spot in the stream and sit down in the hot water. We began to enjoy the experience. One of the guides handed us cans of chilled soda, and we listened to the quiet chatter around us as we sipped and soaked. I thought, *Gee, here we are enjoying water that has been heated by the very volcano we were watching only half an hour ago.*

After clambering out of the stream and up the bank, we struggled to pull our clothing on over the wet suits, then endured an uncomfortable ride back to the hotel and finally our residence. We went straight to the shower and then to bed. We were even too tired to enjoy the books that are our constant companions when we travel.

Skip took more pictures the next morning as we walked around La Fortuna after purchasing our bus tickets at the station. He said the mountain called to him, saying, "Take more . . . more. . . ." Skip obliged. The

Arenal Volcano, from the *fútbol* field in front of the church at la Fortuna in northwestern Costa Rica.

volcano was "wearing its sombrero," as the local saying goes. That means there is not enough wind to blow the smoke away and it hangs around the summit. It made a wonderful photo composition from the soccer field, with the mountain as a backdrop for the church and the playing field in the foreground, an unforgettable scene.

The bus for San José departed in midafternoon, taking us through some lush countryside, small towns, and a couple of small cities. One town, Zarcero, had nicely sculpted topiary, animals and such, in front of its church, as its focal point.

We changed buses in Alajuela, a sprawling city near the national airport, which still retains a small-town flavor. We were told the characteristic pastime of Alajuelans is to sit in the park and christen passersby with nicknames, generally of an uncomplimentary nature. When General Noriega was in the limelight in Panama he was known as the Pineapple here, due to his pockmarked face. I guess it takes some courage to walk

132

past a group of park loungers in Alajuela. One would be inclined to think, *I wonder what they are saying about me?* Our observation was that probably half the population in Costa Rica has derogatory appellations, such as Fat, Skinny, Bowlegs, Chinese Eyes, Limpy, Shorty, Paleface, Polecat . . . on and on. Alajuela is considered the culmination of this national pastime.

For our last free day in "Ticoland" we took a day trip to Guayabo National Monument, a pre-Columbian archaeological site near Volcano Turrialba. There we enjoyed the bird life and scenery as we explored the excavations of an Indian city that had been in use for over a thousand years before and after Christ, according to interpreters. We were the only ones on the tour with a driver, a guide, and her apprentice. Getting to know them was just as pleasurable as the tour itself, not an uncommon conclusion in Costa Rica, we have found.

Our trip concluded with a tour of CATIE, the Center for Tropical Agronomy Investigation and Education, roughly translated, which seemed to be the equivalent of one of our agricultural experiment stations, except this focuses on tropical crops. It receives some of its support from the United States, and in addition to research it supports a gene pool for some major crops, such as cacao, the source of chocolate. We saw numerous varieties of cacao as well as other tropical crops, some of which we had never heard of before.

Back in San José that evening, tired but happy, we prepared for our trip home. It had been our year for growing to feel at home here in our adopted tropical world.

13

1993, Hard Times a-Comin'

Chet and Martha had stayed several weeks after we left last year, as they normally did. As they were preparing to depart in early May, Chet was feeling weak and listless but hid it from Martha. By the time they had completed the rugged drive to San José and then the flight to Miami, followed by a commuter flight and the drive to their son's home, Chet needed to be hospitalized. He was diagnosed with pneumonia, but further tests confirmed that he had lung cancer. This began a sad decline for Chet, although we look back and see that his decline had been in progress for several years.

The prior year, Martha and Skip had had to administer chemotherapy treatments by catheter to his bladder during a bout with bladder cancer. His doctor hadn't been very pleased that laypeople were the only ones available to complete this treatment out in the jungle, but Chet got through that. Then the lung cancer was diagnosed, followed by an ugly, knobby, cancerous lump on his head. I told Skip, "It seems like the cancer is out to get him and won't let up until it does."

Our first visit to see Chet after they'd arrived back in Shippensburg was a shock. Chet looked terrible, weak, thin, wobbly, and with that awful knob on his head. We were shaken by his appearance. Still, he was dressed, reclining on the couch in the front room, and had struggled to stand and put up a brave front. When we protested, he said weakly, "No, I have to keep moving. I want to be ready to go with you to Costa Rica in January." We held back the tears, trying to agree cheerfully, reassuringly.

As the summer progressed, Chet made modest gains. He stabilized enough to have the lump removed from his head, which was at least a great cosmetic improvement. But he was still breathing with great difficulty and was obviously quite weak and unsteady on his feet.

Martha later took Chet to Florida when the weather became cool in the fall, so we hadn't seen him again until they came aboard our plane on January 4, 1993. Martha had been so upbeat in her communications that we were unprepared for our meeting as we watched their son Tom guide Chet down the aisle to their seats in front of ours. He was a wasted old man, wobbly and pale. His eyes and nose were dripping, and he was wracked by coughing as Tom steadied him and guided him into his seat. We said our hellos, totally inadequate expressions of all that we were feeling at the moment, as we choked back our sadness and tears. We also knew he shouldn't be here.

Chet gasped out an apology for his emotional state, a heartbreaking display of his usual graciousness. Skip reached around the airplane seat and tried to pat Chet and reassure him. Everyone knew this was a last-ditch effort, a final trip to his beloved Costa Rica. He still hoped the tropical climate, the flowers and peace at Casa de las Flores, would work a miracle on him, and everyone else wanted to give him the chance. But we all knew deep down that this was it; this was Chet's last look at Costa Rica.

The trip was stressful. We wondered about airline policy related to having someone so obviously ill on board. It was a relief to have Tom along to help with Chet as we negotiated the airport, baggage handling, and taxi ride, finally getting Chet to bed in the Hotel Villa Tournon. Tom is a big, placid man, and handled his dad gently and compassionately. He helped relieve some of our stress.

It was like a pilgrimage for Chet, seeing everything as if with new eyes, knowing it was for the last time. He made an effort to comment on many little things that stimulated memories, but we tried to discourage that, since speaking caused him to gasp and cough, and the coughing spells scared us. Sometimes Martha would administer some codeine-based cough syrup to stem his coughing.

We helped Martha do the shopping while Chet rested. We had to stock up on necessary supplies for our stay in the jungle, regardless of other circumstances. Francisco Vives, caretaker of the jeep, brought it to the hotel and did the driving. He also took Martha to visit the lawyer who keeps the legal papers for their "corporation," the recommended way to hold property in Costa Rica.

The next morning Skip and I packed the jeep. We were to drive it to Nosara, get the opening-up process started, and then meet the plane in two days to pick up Chet, Martha, and Tom. The jeep was loaded with groceries, cooking and cleaning necessities, and five people's luggage, plus a foam mattress and four chairs tied to the top. We left at eight-thirty, feeling as if we might do a "wheely" at any moment since the jeep looked so top-heavy. We made a wrong turn before we got very far but got that straightened out and finally began to relax, getting that free feeling as the road unfolds ahead and the wind blows through your hair.

Uh-oh. The jeep began to feel wobbly. Skip checked for a flat, and sure enough, there it was. The tire had enough air to allow us to make it to the next exit, where we found a small shack of a garage within the first half-mile. The jeep was piled so high that we could pull only partway inside the low building. They weren't equipped to mend the tire but did remove the wheel and install the spare. They sent us on into the town of Naranjo (Orange), where we found a better-equipped service station and there had a new inner tube installed for a very moderate price. The valve stem had broken on the old one, so a patch was impossible.

Relieved, we happily went on our way, but the delay had caused us to just miss the Tempisque River ferry at the upper reaches of the Gulf of Nicoya. The midday heat was heavy on us, having just come from the northlands, but the river crossing, as always, was picturesque.

Soon we reached Nicoya, where we filled the jeep with diesel fuel and enjoyed a Chinese dinner before tackling the final leg of our journey. Oh, that rough, dirty final leg! It is always a challenge!

Still we reached Casa de las Flores by four-thirty, hot, tired, dirty, and thirsty. We were more than glad to see Antonio and Chini, receiving hugs and smiles, and willing help with the unloading. We continued to work nonstop until after nine-thirty, well past dark. Everything had been stored away, so we had to air out mattresses and bedding and then make our own bed, as well as hang out clothing that had been stored in moth-balls. Some of the clothing would need washing in order to be wearable, especially if mildew had crept into the storage boxes.

The work continued all the next day. Antonio and Skip lugged the washing machine out to its place under the overhang at the back side of the house, allowing me to begin washing the most malodorous and soiled items of clothing and bedding. We hung numerous bedding items over the deck railing to air and dry and had the clotheslines loaded when I noticed some dark clouds moving toward us from the direction of the ocean. I mentioned this to Antonio.

He said not to worry: "It won't rain. It doesn't rain here in January, February, or March."

Well, it rained. We all scrambled madly to get things under shelter, not quite making it. Then it teased us by raining off and on throughout the day and most of the night. I chided Antonio about his weather prognosticating. He just grinned and shrugged.

The rain had surely frustrated our efforts to get everything in order for the arrival of Chet, Martha, and Tom. In addition, Jack and Helen Hargleroad were supposed to arrive at the same time. Jack had offered his medical services in Chet's time of need. Martha had told us not to feel we had to get everything ready, but we really wanted to, for their comfort. It would be impossible, now.

I began breakfast at six-thirty as Skip made the run to Nosara to pick them up. The morning was bright and sunny. The rain had washed all the dust from the vegetation and temporarily cut the road dust. It was good to be alive, but the thought of Chet's condition hung over us, just as the dampness remained in the clothing and bedding.

It was sad to see Chet being led up the path from the jeep, knowing it would be his last time at Casa de las Flores. After breakfast and a short reacquainting, everyone helped to conquer the chaos. I had made sure Chet's bed was ready, knowing he would soon need to rest, but he wanted to walk some of his precious landscaped paths before lying down. Tom and Jack helped him around while the rest of us labored on.

Chet made it around Meditation Circle and was too fatigued to go farther. He seemed to expect to become well and spry just by being there. The spirit was willing ... but he was perspiring and puffing as they helped him back up the path and porch stairs to his bedroom. He still said, between puffs, "This is the best I've done in a long while."

The next day, January 9, he turned eighty years old. Tom and Jack helped him out on another short walk, which he survived a little better, still seeming to cherish his hope of a miraculous Costa Rican cure. He returned to the porch, where he puffed out a request for Skip to get the little tape recorder and play a new tape Helen had brought for him. Soon we were listening to a reproduction of an old Nelson Eddy–Jeanette McDonald recording that included "Indian Love Call" and other musical hits from before my time.

Apparently Chet was feeling in a nostalgic mood, for soon he was in tears. His sobs brought on a coughing spell. Martha had to give him another dose of the codeine cough syrup. He gasped out his regrets for making a scene, trying to tell Skip that his emotional control had never

137

recovered since that close call in the boat. Tom and Martha helped Chet back into bed.

We made Chet's birthday cake and decorated it with eight candles. Luckily, Martha's little kitchen range was gas-operated, since the electricity shut off as a result of a mild earthquake about ten-fifty that morning.

We made a run to Nosara for fruits, vegetables, and other staples we hadn't obtained in San José. The electricity remained off until nearly six, and the lights came on just as the sun went down, allowing us to gather at the table to sing "Happy Birthday" to Chet for the last time. It was a bittersweet party, but all in all as pleasant a day for Chet as it could have been under the circumstances.

Our work in getting the place in shape was constantly interrupted by visitors as word got around that Chet was back in Nosara, probably for the last time. Chet received everyone graciously but invariably wound up becoming emotional, triggering a coughing fit, which required his being helped to bed until he settled down and rested.

Chet's former caretaker, Franco, came to pay his respects one day. Franco had been Chet's first caretaker. Chet had taught Franco English and treated him like a son. He'd provided Franco with a house and a regular paycheck, brought him and his family gifts, including the first television set in Esperanza, took his family to the doctor—in short, treated him as family. Martha had treated Franco's daughters like grandchildren, teaching them some English, buying them dresses and shoes, allowing them to hang around as she worked, giving them M&Ms on a daily basis, and loving them.

After ten years or so, Franco had come to Chet and complained bitterly about Chet and Martha separating his family from their Tico heritage. Chet was very hurt, became incensed by this harsh reaction, and dismissed Franco on the spot. As a result Franco brought suit against Chet for severance pay, which Chet contested but paid. Feelings between them had been bitter.

Now Franco had come to say good-bye to his one-time loving employer. We all felt tense about it. Chet had only occasionally mentioned Franco over the years but recently had expressed regrets and the wish to set things aright. This was an emotional moment, probably for both of them.

After twenty minutes or so Franco emerged, followed by Martha, both in tears. Franco hurried away down the path, keeping his eyes averted. Martha took a couple of minutes to collect herself and then related to us that Chet had forgiven Franco and how relieved they were. Helen, with tears streaming down her face, stammered, "Wow . . . that's heavy!"

Everyone was swallowing back emotion, but Skip later told me, "I wonder if Franco felt he needed forgiveness. I know they needed a reconciliation, but I bet they saw it different ways. There were big cultural differences operating here." We'll never know the inside truth, but we were certainly glad they were able to finally find some kind of resolution.

At another time, a whole cattle truck load of people from the church in Nosara dropped in one afternoon to pay their last respects to Chet. They filed around his bed with woeful faces and sad demeanors, unable to otherwise communicate their sorrow to him. It was extremely touching to witness, leaving Martha, Helen, and me in tears. Jack and Skip were swallowing hard. It was an emotionally tiring day.

John Frazier rode in on his motorcycle on another afternoon to spend a little time with Chet. They had served some years together trying to make the hotel a success and had some feelings of comrades-in-arms. Chet had been a friend-in-need to John and was therefore held in high regard.

We were headed across the driveway a little later when we spied John sitting on his motorcycle with his head drooping. We sidled over to say a few words to him and found him in tears. He apologized, sobbing out, "I just can't talk now. I'm just too sad . . . that poor man . . ." Skip patted John's shoulder and we helplessly left him to his grief.

Many others came to visit Chet during his final few weeks in Nosara. Most were shocked to see how he had deteriorated since they had seen him the prior year and were saddened by the suddenness of it. No one could doubt the imminence of his demise. All visitors left with grief written on their faces, knowing Chet would never return to Casa de las Flores.

On January 14, Tom Eastep had to leave for his home in Maryland. He is a professor, as was his father, and the term was about to begin. Meeting classes is an extremely high priority to a teacher, but Tom was leaving with reluctance. His dad was now in worse condition than when he came here.

Skip and I gently suggested to Martha that this would be a good time to get Chet back to the States, where she could be close to good medical care and have Tom's assistance getting there. She talked with

139

Chet, returning to say that he wanted to stay; he still had hopes of Costa Rica making him well. They had decided to try to stay the full three months and return with us.

Their decision seemed unrealistic to us, but Martha is an eternal optimist. We tossed a lot in bed that night, listening to another surprise rainstorm drum loudly on our sheet metal roof. Skip rose early to drive Tom to the airport before breakfast. Poor Tom, he had to be wondering if he would ever see his dad alive again.

The rain poured again that evening as we entertained George and Beverly Baumunk with a fish dinner. They had just arrived, and Martha made a yearly practice of providing them with dinner on their way from San José. Chet forced himself to eat his meals at the table, pretending everything was OK, so we were all gathered together making the best of it.

I happened to notice that George's shirt was soaked, suddenly realizing that the porch roof was leaking a steady stream down his back. George, consummate gentleman that he is, never said a word and wouldn't have if I hadn't spoken. He said, "Oh, that's all right. It's no trouble at all." At least Martha was finally convinced that she needed a new roof.

Chet stabilized again, so Jack and Helen asked Martha to borrow the jeep for a trip to Guaitil, the village where the Indian pottery is crafted. The roads were dampened and the temperature was moderate, making it an ideal time for a jaunt.

Skip drove us away at six-fifty the next morning, our mood lighter than it had been for a while, feeling the freedom of rolling along the dirt road with the cool morning air blowing through the jeep. After a stop in Nicoya to buy eggs and frozen chicken for Martha, we drove the highway north toward Santa Cruz, enjoying the change of scenery. One large tree in a meadow along the way was so full of pink blossoms that Skip stopped for a photo session. He and Jack "oohed" and "aahed" until Helen and I chuckled at them.

We strolled the village of Guaitil unhurriedly, just inspecting the wares the first time around, making our purchases on the second pass. Helen and I bought a nice pot for Martha, a low, wide one with a narrow mouth, deep red, encircled by a narrow black zigzag stripe.

On our way out of town, we stopped at another shop where a man had his oven fired. He showed us around, although we couldn't comprehend much of his explanation in Spanish. Since the work area was an extension of his home, we could observe their living conditions, which seemed quite poor to us. Living quarters were a pole *ranchito*, boarded around the sides, with a steep palm-thatched roof. The kitchen was under a sort of porch overhang. His wife cooked in the pottery oven when it was fired or on a small, elevated wood fire when the oven wasn't in operation. They had a single outside water tap with a hose attached where they apparently bathed and obtained water for cooking. It seemed a poor, dusty place to live, but some beautifully crafted pottery emerged from that *ranchito*, more art than comes from our big, solid, clean houses.

The ride home was uneventful, except for passing a picturesque yoke of oxen dragging their cart, flanked by the *boyero* with his whip. Again we pulled over for some photographs, wishing we could be more unobtrusive. Such scenes are wonderful and fast disappearing, but I still hate to treat people as scenic objects.

As the days flowed by, Chet gradually worsened. We still went to the beach pretty regularly, but now one of us would find an excuse to stay behind and keep Chet company. The beach pulled so hard at Martha that she would convince herself that Chet would be OK alone "for a little while." So the rest of us took turns making excuses to stay with Chet while Martha pretended not to know what was going on. Jack had a speech he was working on for the historical society; Skip had some repairs to do on the water line; Helen had too much sun, or her foot hurt—anything to rationalize Martha's going to the beach while one of us kept watch.

The following week Chet went into a tailspin. Martha called from the bathroom, where Chet was on the commode, his bodily systems shutting down. His breathing was shallow and he was pale and cold, covered with perspiration. Jack yelled for Skip, who ran to assist, and they carried Chet in his sitting position to the bed, where they stretched him out and covered him. Jack administered some medication and sat with him until his breathing smoothed out.

Skip took Jack aside later to explain that Chet wanted to return to Florida to see Randy, his younger son, once more, and then be buried in Shippensburg. Jack looked astonished, saying, "Is that true? I was under the impression he wanted to die here in Costa Rica."

Skip explained that Chet had been vacillating about that decision, but now he seemed set on returning home to die.

Jack said, "Well I'm going to talk with them about that. If he wants to return home, he'd better soon do it. I think this was a heart seizure he just had, and it was a close call."

141

After Jack cleared the air with Martha and Chet, Martha came to us in a very agitated state. She now knew she and Chet should leave immediately if they didn't want Chet to die here; Jack had made that clear. But Martha couldn't envision how she could get Chet to San José, into a hotel, and back to the airport with all their luggage, and so forth. She was stewing and vacillating, even still wanting to remain in Nosara, hoping for a recovery, then rejecting that idea, knowing it was time to leave. She talked about having difficulty getting a room at the Bougainvillea, nearly in tears thinking of what to do if they were full.

Skip took hold at this point, saying, ''Here's how we'll do it.'' We were rarely able to wrest the reins of control from Martha, but this was a desperate time. Skip told her we should arrange the earliest flight possible to Miami with first-class seats and then charter a plane for an early flight out of Nosara to meet it. There would be no need for the trip into San José, nor for a hotel room. She could have Chet at Randy's by the middle of the afternoon.

It took some more persuasion, but she began to see the light. Then she remembered that their passports were in the safe at their travel agent's office in San José. She felt she would still have to go into San José. Skip suggested that she have the necessary exit papers delivered to them at the airport at departure time by messenger. Martha contemplated this and decided she would do it, except she would have Francisco Vives pick the documents up and bring them to the airport.

Now Martha was ready for action. She and Skip drove straight to Nosara to make the phone calls. They arranged first-class passage for the morning after next, which allowed Chet an extra day to rest after the near-miss episode he had just experienced. Then they chartered a small plane to get them from Nosara to the airport just in time to make the connection. They called the travel agent, then Francisco Vives. It all came together, partly because of the emergency quality of the situation, partly due to the respect people had for the Easteps, and partly due to luck. We all felt no better arrangements could have been devised under the circumstances. If only everyone did their part, it should work . . . if the Guanacaste winds didn't blow. If . . .

Word got out, and more people arrived to say their farewells to Chet. Another group came from the church to pray with Chet and thank him for his help. They wanted their pictures taken with him and of Martha sitting with him. One boy sat on the bed and leaned back, nearly on the pillow in order to have his face next to Chet's in a photograph. It was so sad and emotional that Chet experienced another bad spell, and we had to try to limit visits to a brief peep into his room. Everyone was tearful.

Finally the last night came. Our distress was now mixed with a touch of relief that Chet would be heading home in the morning. We went to bed hoping for some much-needed rest.

The winds blew. Each of us lay awake that night, January 27, listening, fretting, dozing fitfully, wondering if the little plane would be able to make it into the Nosara airport. What could we do if we couldn't get Chet out? What of all those arrangements we had struggled to make?

We were a haggard lot the next morning as we appeared on Martha's porch for coffee and cereal. No one really had an appetite, but we ate a little out of habit and the knowledge that we would need our strength that day. And the winds were still blowing.

We had contacted Bob and Carol Ormsby, nearby neighbors and friends who had a larger, smoother-riding vehicle than ours, to drive Chet, Martha, Jack, and Skip to the airport. They arrived on schedule. Chet tried to walk with our assistance, but Skip stepped in front of him on the next-lower step and lifted him piggyback. He carried Chet to the car very quickly and helped him in, and they were on their way with time to spare. The car was too full to accommodate Helen and me, so we stayed at the house. Our final good-byes to Chet were all too brief due to the hurry and stress of the moment.

Jack and Skip filled us in on the details when they returned. They told us how Chet had panted out his pet peeve of how the road should have been located differently over the ridge to Nosara and that Skip gently suggested he should rest, fearing he might aggravate another coughing spell.

There were more people at the airport than usual, and others trickled in as they waited to see if the plane would arrive. It became obvious that folks were coming to see Chet off. There was no fuss or commotion, no speeches or planned events, just a large number of local folks who had quietly appeared to honor the final departure of one who had served them well. Chet peered out the car window through watery eyes as we discussed the wonderment of it in low voices. But the wind was still blowing.

Word came that the regular SANSA flight would not make it this morning. As we quietly worried and debated, the winds slackened somewhat, and soon someone said, "I hear a motor." All ears were strained skyward, all faces intense. Then it appeared, that little plane, wobbling on the errant wind currents as it made its approach.

Everyone bailed out of the car, and Skip again piggybacked Chet to get him to the plane without loss of time. Skip stood Chet on the ground and, as Jack held him, climbed upon the wing and bodily lifted him up, then dragged him into the passenger compartment. The pilots stowed the luggage as Jack helped Martha aboard, and in moments they were off.

It was a rough ride. The winds buffeted the plane, bouncing the passengers constantly until they passed over the high hills toward the interior. Skip had to hold Chet down to keep his head from hitting the ceiling, since he was too weak to brace himself. But finally the ride smoothed out and they began thinking ahead. Skip called to the pilots over the engine noise to ask if they could radio ahead for a taxi to meet them at the terminal. That would speed their transition to the main airport.

It was all coming together. The taxi pulled in just as they touched down. Skip helped Chet into the taxi, Jack grabbed the bags, and Martha paid the charter agent. In minutes they were at the main terminal.

Martha paid the cabdriver, Skip ran to American Airlines' first-class check-in to see if Francisco was there with the necessary papers. If he wasn't there, the whole plan could go down the drain. He was there. Not only waiting with the papers, Francisco had gone to the counter and had the papers in the works, needing only Chet and Martha to complete the process.

Skip greeted Francisco warmly and gratefully, then returned to see if Chet was making it to check-in OK. He found Jack and the taxi driver helping Chet through the doors with Martha leading the way.

Soon all was in order and Skip turned to face Chet for a final good-bye. Chet was panting, his eyes wet and his nose dripping. Still he had that dignity about him that elicited admiration from others. He tried to thank Skip again in his usual gracious manner, and Skip muttered, "Good-bye, old friend," with a quick embrace and wishes for a good flight to Florida.

Skip told me later it was a totally inadequate farewell, but then most good-byes are inadequate. He kissed Martha, who was in a pretty agitated state, and tried to reassure her. Then he watched them disappear into the bowels of the air terminal.

Skip and Jack were suddenly relieved of a great weight as they went with Francisco and climbed into his red Bronco for the ride to the bus station in San José. The transition seemed strange, leaving them unburdened of the swirling concerns and emotions they had been dealing with for several weeks, and especially for the last day or two. They chatted

144

with Francisco about Chet's situation and the events leading up to his departure, gradually tapering into inconsequentials such as the weather and Francisco's new car as the stress began to drain away.

Francisco dropped them at the Alfaro Terminal where they bought bus tickets for Nicoya. They also purchased a few tangerines from a vendor to assuage their thirst during the long ride.

They arrived in Nicoya by midafternoon with sticky fingers from the tangerines and large appetites, so they went straight to the Restaurante Nicoya for a large lunch of what Skip calls "Tico Chinese"—Chinese food done with a Costa Rican flair. Jack evaluated it handily: "Boy, this is good!"

Then they went to the taxi lineup at the park and dickered for the hard ride to Esperanza. They accepted a bid of forty dollars and were soon on their way home, arriving before dark. They said they got to practice their Spanish with the driver and taught him a little English in return.

Helen and I were as relieved to see them as they were to see us. Shadows were growing long as they came tiredly up the walk between the crotons and hibiscus plants to hug us and plop into the old leather-seated rocking chairs on the porch.

We listened to their story of how the day went and questioned them on the details. We were all very sad but undeniably relieved as we sat in the darkening evening and sipped cold drinks, listening to the music of insects and night birds. We went to bed early, mentally and physically drained.

The next morning after breakfast, Will Scarlet drove up the driveway in his usual busy manner to invite us up for sunset drinks and dinner. He and Ann had figured that we were in dire need of "R and R," so he made a special trip down the mountain to deliver the invitation. No debate over that!

Ann prepares wonderful *bocas*, Will mixes memorable drinks, and the view of those stupendous Pacific sunsets from their veranda is unparalleled. We recuperated about 90 percent in the first hour there. They had also prepared a tasty fish chowder, followed by fresh Key lime pie, made with limes from their own tree. Great food and great friends; we were thankful for both.

We began to heal; still we had Chet's plight in the backs of our minds. And poor Martha still had to deal with weeks of watching him approach death. Skip commented, "In spite of her gift for denial, Martha is a very strong woman. She'll handle it." I had to agree, but I was glad I wasn't in her shoes.

On the way to the beach the next day Helen hesitantly broached a topic that she had kept from Martha, due to the situation with Chet. Helen had set her purse on a living room chair when she had arrived and then had gone back out onto the porch. Later she happened to glance through the door and had seen Chini, who was dusting in the area, with her hands on the purse. To avoid a scene Helen had waited and checked later, finding sixty dollars or so missing. She wasn't absolutely sure of the amount, but she was pretty certain that money had been stolen. Helen had decided not to say anything about it but then decided we should know. Jack had wanted her to forget it.

Chini, Antonio's wife, had become a trusted friend of Martha and Chet and was an occasional employee in the household. We absolutely hated the thought that she couldn't be trusted, although I had had earlier suspicions.

Helen and I concocted a scheme to trap Chini. Martha had arranged for Chini to clean the master bedroom after they departed, so Helen and I planted a ten-dollar bill under a vase on Martha's dresser. After Chini cleaned the room and left, the money was gone. I got Skip to talk to Antonio about the money disappearing. Antonio replied, "Posiblemente Chini," with a shrug.

He disappeared down the path, and soon Chini arrived in an agitated state to hand over the ten-dollar bill, offering lame excuses. Skip tried to talk with her about how important honesty is to us gringos, which elicited a few tears, but his basic vocabulary probably didn't deal well with such heavy issues. We continued to have difficulty trusting Chini, which is sad. I guess that she saw our wealth, moderate though it may seem to us, as something endless that she ought to be able to take as she could; why would we even miss such small bits?

Soon Jack and Helen had to depart. We drove them to the airport, glad for the nice day after a few days of wind. We all thought of that morning when we had helped Chet and Martha get to San José and were thankful for the calm weather. We would miss the company of Jack and Helen; this was our first time living alone in Nosara.

We were busy cleaning and putting things away in the main house when Roger Harrison showed up for a visit. We chatted about our ordeal with Chet, and he told us of his ninety-two-year-old Aunt Mary. He had brought her here from New York State. She was declining mentally but was still alert most of the time.

We had seen Aunt Mary at beach parties as well as at Roger's house, and he seemed to take good care of her. He had assistance from Alfred, a younger black man who also lived with Roger and did the cooking as well as designing fashion wear on the side. Together they would doll Mary up in colorful clothes, lipstick, nail polish, and hair ribbons when they took her out. Her white hair would be brushed, and her blue eyes would sparkle like the necklaces, bracelets, and rings with which they adorned her. Folks always paid their respects to her and asked if she was well. She typically responded, "I'm happy to be here."

Chet had enjoyed quoting her when people inquired about his health, saying, "I'm like Mary; I'm happy to be here," eliciting chuckles from his listeners.

We soon began to enjoy our solitude, spending more and more time watching the birds and other wildlife. Our front porch was so high that we were on eye level with the monkeys at those times when they dined on the trees directly in front of our dining table. We never tired of watching them. A dynamic society, they were always changing. There would be howling battles between neighboring groups, times when the females were noticeably pregnant, then babies in various stages of development, sometimes twins. We saw "teens" competing in jumping and chasing contests, watched by babies and tolerated by their elders. We saw older males evicted from the tribe and loners hanging around, watching pathetically from a distance.

When they camped for the night above or behind our house we knew we would be awakened by their roaring before daybreak. And roar they do. We guessed that all the roaring had something to do with establishing territorial boundaries, the equivalent of, "You guys stay on your side of the road! These trees in blossom over here have belonged to our tribe since before my grandfather's time."

This week we watched a little fellow leap a very long distance from high on one tree to low on another, catching only small branches. Skip laughed as I stifled a scream. Then we marveled as a mother leaped the same gap with a tiny baby on her back, gripping tightly to her fur.

While eating lunch one day we saw the lead male of a troop chase a smaller male and knock him from the tree. The small one climbed back up only to be chased back to the ground again. He then hurried along the ground until he disappeared into the jungle. It is dangerous for monkeys to

147

be on the ground, since that is where most of their predators are, so we felt sorry for his having to undergo both the trauma of separation and the fear of being on the ground. He must have felt terribly lonely and vulnerable. We guessed he must have been becoming a threat to the alpha male. This was the only time we had ever seen such a spectacle.

We also got to see the *chachalakas*, the wild jungle fowl that resemble pheasants or small turkeys. We have already mentioned their calls, which are so loud and raucous we almost needed ear plugs. They would peck gravel from the driveway and check the faucets for drops of water, always with a wary eye out for danger.

With the area being quieter due to the absence of Martha and all her guests, we were able to spot birds we hadn't seen before. Two of the most exciting were a pair of elegant trogans. We had seen another species of trogan, also beautiful, but these were special, with bright rose pink breasts along with the usual black backs and wings with white trimmings. The black-headed trogan has a yellow-orange breast and a big pale blue ring around its eye. We had been awed by them at first, but now we were accustomed to them, so we were highly impressed by these different new visitors. Human nature, I suppose. We also enjoyed a colorful pair of toucans, brown robins without red breasts, necklaced magpie jays (ornery as our jays and twice as large), and a blue crowned motmot that caught large insects and bashed them against the tree limb before eating them.

Another day while eating lunch we noticed two iguanas posturing in the driveway. They moved toward each other, stopped and bobbed their heads up and down, then moved closer and repeated the bobbing. Then all was still for a long moment. Suddenly one dashed at the other and grabbed it by the mouth with its needle-toothed jaws. They writhed and rolled with their jaws locked together. Then one tried to shake the other. After another burst of rapid rolling and twisting, they let go, and the larger one chased the other up a tree, quick as a flash. We had noticed the posturing behavior before but had never seen it evolve into physical combat. Probably neither was hurt very badly; just another territorial dispute.

One day we watched a small gecko molting. Like snakes, they shed their skins as they grow. This one stayed put for an hour as he slowly shed and ate his skin. It seemed hard work, too, as he strained to split it and then tug it off with his mouth. He was very vulnerable during the process, an easy catch for a predator.

Once again we watched the neighbor boys cut palm thatch for a roof this week. It's always interesting to see them shinny up those tall oil palms and hang on while they hack off the fifteen-foot fronds. They say it takes 250 to 300 for a typical *ranchito* roof. They drag them a few at a time down the main road to the village. Even those owning a concrete block house with a tin roof often have a thatch-roofed area alongside to use as a porch or outdoor kitchen.

We went for the mail, but the post office was closed. We saw where Maxine had broken the barbwire fence, though. She had gotten her mail, then stalled her car. When she restarted it she raced the engine and pulled it into reverse at the same time. It spurted backward through the fence before she got it under control. It's interesting having Maxine around.

It's interesting having Roger around, too. He had us up for dinner again, serving ''sundowner'' drinks as we watched for the green flash of sunset on the Pacific. No green flash this night. No dinner for a while, either; the chicken was still frozen when we arrived. Still he and Alfred put on a very nice dinner, always with some special touches. One time when Martha was with us they served *mondongo*, fried tripe mixed with rice, as a side dish. Martha would have none of that!

We were told that another time Roger had a big frozen fish in his bathtub, still trying to thaw it when his guests arrived. It was ten o'clock before dinner was served that evening.

The prior year Roger had brought a Weimaraner puppy, which he called Champ. It was a beautiful dog, but very rambunctious. Roger and his two cousins were serving dinner with linen, flowers, and long-stemmed wineglasses when Champ leaped right up on the table, making things fly. They regained control, but Champ was still on the loose, jumping up on guests and sniffing everything. He took a liking to me, as most pets seem to do, and grabbed me playfully by the arm. His sharp puppy tooth slashed a vein, and I began bleeding profusely. Roger had no medical supplies on hand, not one Band-Aid, but he did find a cotton ball, which I had to press to my arm as I tried to eat. I was not happy with Roger that evening, despite the lovely table setting and interesting food. I still bear the scar.

Within two weeks Roger brought Champ to the tide pools and he jumped playfully on the backs of my legs, breaking a vein beneath the skin. It swelled and continued to be painful for several weeks. We tried to avoid Champ after that, though we hated to hurt Roger's feelings.

Champ has since gone to obedience school, perhaps due to some suggestions made to Roger, and has become a very nice dog, looking

149

and acting every bit a champion. He often accompanied Roger and his friends to the tide pools, but no one had to avoid him after that.

Roger had made arrangements with Jan Buferd at the Gilded Iguana to hold a birthday party for his Aunt Mary, but she died before her birthday, so he retained the reservation and held a memorial party instead. Meanwhile he lost track of her body. It was sent to Nicoya, but he couldn't locate it there. He tried at Liberia, with no luck. Finally her remains were located in San José, where she had been sent for cremation. Roger said with relief, "At least I found her!"

The memorial party was interesting to us; we had never been to such a thing. There were drinks and *bocas* provided, and the mood was somewhat festive, although mildly subdued. Roger called for attention after half an hour of socializing, then related some fond memories of Mary as tears streamed down his face. Alfred, Roger's companion and housekeeper, did the same. Then Roger invited others to contribute their recollections of Mary. Several did so; Ann Scarlet spoke very movingly. We agreed afterward that the memorial get-together was a very nice thing to do.

Antonio still enjoys taking Skip fishing. He likes Skip and appreciates having Skip drive him to the beach where the fish are feeding. Additionally, he enjoys the entertainment that Skip provides at times. Skip caught a small *corvina*, a white sea bass, and was trying to wade to Antonio to put it on his stringer. Antonio waved at him to loop around a certain spot, but Skip didn't get the message or perhaps was in too much of a hurry to pay attention. He dropped into a hole clear over his head and had to let go of the fish in order to swim out. After a moment of concern, Antonio grinned and then laughed his usual falsetto giggle. Skip grinned sheepishly and went back again to his casting.

During the first week of March we received word that Bolivar was about to begin replacing the roof on Martha's house. Bolivar Bermudez is a local contractor financed by George Miller, a friend of Martha's from near Harrisburg. Bolivar is George's right-hand-man and a good guy to know, since he provides trustworthy service in a land where we gringos are never quite sure of ourselves.

That week we packed things away for the year since we expected no more visitors. This required all the usual cleaning, wrapping, bagging, and mothballing to ensure the survival of Martha's possessions. We stored them carefully in the first guest room.

Just as we finished we got word from Martha that a couple of her acquaintances from Chambersburg had wanted to use her house and they were already on their way. They were expected to arrive about the time Bolivar's men should have the roof completed. We hoped we would have time to clean Martha's bedroom for them.

The morning they were to arrive, Bolivar's men finished the roof. It had been completely removed, exposed to the sky. Dirt, sawdust, and leaves from nearby trees littered the room, not to mention roof nails, screws, and pieces of boards.

We dug in and cleaned the room from top to bottom. Then we moved the bed and other furnishings back into place and replaced the bedding. We were pretty pleased with ourselves, having everything ready before the Neurenbergers arrived.

Since Martha's kitchen items had been stored, we had Eldon and Louise for dinner at our house. They arrived right at mealtime, and Louise was embarrassed that we had to feed them, under the circumstances. After all, as she said, *we* hadn't invited them. But Big Eldon didn't mind; he confessed that he had gotten a speeding ticket in his rush to get here, but he had flashed the patrolman a twenty-dollar bill and continued on his way. We assured them that we were prepared and the food was ready.

At dinner I commented that Louise looked very tired. She explained that she was trying to recover from the flu, but traveling so continuously kept her tired. They were just coming from an Elderhostel program that had kept them busy for the prior week, and Eldon was keeping her on the move.

Knowing that she would want to retire early, I explained that the guest room wasn't available; that we had already stored Martha's gear there, but her bedroom was available; and that we had just cleaned and prepared it today. Eldon said he preferred the guest room he had used during a prior visit and suggested that we move a few things around.

Skip and I explained the situation again with a few more specifics, not relishing the idea of undoing so much careful work. But Eldon stuck to his request and wanted to see for himself what the rooms were like. So we all walked across the compound to the main house, only to be greeted by a long line of army ants. The column of ants marched from the garden area in front of the house, up a porch post, across the porch, through the bedroom and bathroom, then out the back toward the jungle. It truly was an army of ants, marching in formation.

151

We looped around the ants, stepping over them at one point, and showed Eldon how the guest room was piled full of stored items. He grudgingly gave in to our wishes, and after waiting for the ants to conclude their passage, we settled Eldon and Louise in Martha's bedroom. But before we returned to our house, Eldon insisted that we dig out a toaster and some utensils to allow them to have breakfast on their own on the porch. I must admit that I grumbled a bit to Skip before drifting off to sleep that night.

The next morning as we prepared to eat breakfast, Eldon strode purposefully across the path to our house, his huge frame shaking the floor as he crossed the porch. He informed us that the gas stove wasn't working and they couldn't make coffee.

Skip returned with Eldon to check out the problem, finding, naturally, that the tank was empty. We invited them to breakfast, promising to go to town for a new tank of gas before noon. Finally we had them settled in for the week.

A couple of days later, as they were exploring the area in their little rental car, Eldon was eyeing a senorita and drove off the road into a ditch. One drive wheel was hanging with no traction, so he needed help to get out. Luckily, a contractor's truck loaded with workmen came by and stopped to help. The whole bunch simply bailed out of the truck and lifted the little rental car back onto the roadway one end at a time with Louise still aboard. They accepted no recompense, only grinned and waved, hopped back aboard the truck, and went on their way. Typically Tico.

The night before the Neurenbergers departed, the winds arose, reaching near-hurricane levels before the night was over and causing an electrical outage. Undauntable Eldon still had Louise up early enough to drive through countless fallen tree limbs and reach San José in time to return the rental car and make their flight out.

Many homes were damaged by the winds that time. We surveyed the damage around the compound, finding Chet's little Meditation Circle pavilion blown to the ground and limbs and shredded foliage virtually everywhere. Antonio was in for days of raking, carrying, and burning.

Some folks had it much worse. Some *ranchitos* were destroyed, and our nearest neighbor's beautiful new home, known as the Palace, lost large sections of roof and was inundated with dirt inside. We walked across the road and up the steep hill to offer them what comfort we could. Carol was in tears. Her lovely Persian carpets were nearly hidden by dirt and leaves that had blown in. All we could say was, "This is rare, Carol. We've never seen it this bad. Hang in there. Remember how beautiful it can be." She and Bob agreed but were still awfully blue.

With Chet and Martha gone, we were able to move the CB radio to our house, which enabled us to keep up with the local news a bit. It was not a high-grade installation, so we missed a lot, but still we could at least call out or receive a call now and then. Skip usually turned it off before going to bed so we wouldn't be disturbed.

One night during the windy spell we awoke to loud sputtering and static coming from the CB in the kitchen area. Skip said, "Darn, I forgot to turn that crazy thing off!" and hopped out of bed to do so.

By now we were puzzled by a flickering glow reflecting off the ceiling above the partitions. As he went through the door, he cried, "Holy smoke, there's a fire starting out here!" Sure enough, the refrigerator plug had caught fire, apparently from all the surges caused by the power going on and off. The flame was slowly climbing the wall.

Skip yanked the plug and beat the infant flames to death with a wet dishcloth. We were kind of worked up over the thought of what could have happened had the CB not alerted us. Skip commented wryly, "Well, I guess that proves the wiring isn't really adequate. It always looked suspiciously deficient. Besides, it's stapled directly onto the wood, and Alfredo even drove some of the staples clear through the insulation. We'll have to keep a sharp eye on it from now on. I'm going to bring a U.S.-quality outlet for that refrigerator next season and run number-twelve wire direct from the entry box."

I was worried. I hated the idea of awakening to a fire in the house, especially since this house was all wood and screen. But here we were, and it's our nature to hang in there and make the best of it. I vowed to sleep more lightly, especially on windy nights.

Our stay for this season was coming to a close. We met with Paulina Anderson, who oversees the caretaking of properties and the paying of gardeners, taxes, water rents, and such. Skip wrote checks to cover such expenses and discussed Antonio's wages, hours, and duties with her.

Antonio seemed depressed as the season wore on. He dawdled at his work and wasn't as jovial and teasing as usual. Skip commented, "There's something wrong with Antonio. I'll try to have a talk with him."

I replied, "He surely isn't getting much work done. He's been dabbing at that gate with whitewash all morning and is barely started. He isn't earning his pay."

Skip talked with Antonio, reporting that he had responded blandly, "I'm a serious kind of guy," when Skip asked why he seemed so down.

Skip queried, "Is there something wrong at home?" to which Antonio shrugged and said, *"Posiblemente."*

That was that; nothing changed before we left. We suspected that he and Chini were having some difficult times.

We were in the middle of packing things away when the winds rose again. I was tired of cleaning up the windblown dirt that had accumulated during the storms via the screened ventilation areas all around the top of the house. In addition, the electricity went off for fifteen and one-half hours.

Still we got everything ready, gave our remaining food to friends, said our good-byes, and were on our way on schedule. We left Casa de las Flores at 6:30 A.M. and were waiting at the Tempisque Ferry at 9:30, snacking on sweet little "lady finger" bananas from Martha's stalks, munching some homemade cookies, and drinking ice water from an old plastic Coke bottle we had saved for that purpose. It's always pleasant to "people-watch" here, and the scenes are exotic and colorful.

We made good time in the old jeep, arriving at the Cacts Hotel in San José during the noon hour. We felt lucky to have had no problems and were looking forward to the change of scenery and another little jaunt around Costa Rica. We enjoyed sampling the food at different restaurants and bopping around the shops and markets, too.

Skip called Francisco Vives right away to make arrangements for him to pick up the jeep. He's Martha's regular car caretaker and gets it ready for the next season, in addition to storing it for her. He picked it up the next day, and we were relieved to hand the keys over to him. Now we were on our own, with no more responsibilities to anyone except ourselves. We relished that free feeling.

The folks at the Cacts, always friendly and helpful, recommended some tours they thought we'd like. We already had our hearts set on seeing the Tortuguero Canal area on the northeast coast, so we signed up for a tour that included that plus a tour of a banana plantation. We also made arrangements to be dropped off on the way back at Siquirres, where we could take a bus to Limon. From there we could catch another bus farther south to Cahuita to see a small national park on the Caribbean. (Somewhere we had read about this park having Jesus Christ lizards, which can run across the surface of the water!) We would be on our own for this segment of our travels, but the desk clerk did make a reservation for us at a little hotel in Cahuita. We were excited to get going!

The little tour bus that picked us up the next morning held only about twenty passengers, which seemed to encourage our getting acquainted quickly. We were soon chatting with other tourists and acting like authorities on Costa Rica, having a great time. One vivacious lady who was leading a small group from Milwaukee pumped us for information about living in Costa Rica and had us all in stitches with her quips and commentary. They were a fun group to travel with.

Our first stop was a large banana plantation near Siquirres on the road to Limon on the Caribbean slope. They showed us how the banana bunches were enclosed in chemically treated bags while still on the stalk in order to prevent insect and disease damage. An extensive system of cables strung on pulleys mounted on poles allowed the harvesters to cut the large, heavy bunches and attach them to hooks on the cables. The cables carried the heavy bunches back to the processing center from anywhere on the plantation. Ingenious, but still very heavy, hard work.

At the processing center the bunches were washed and inspected, then packed and shipped, by both rail and truck. Each tourist came away with a Chiquita Banana sticker on the back of one hand.

As we waited for the last stragglers to reach the bus, we noticed a couple of young boys playing with something that seemed to move on its own, so we walked over to watch. They had a pair of the largest beetles we had ever seen, both approaching three inches in length and half that in diameter. The boys would hold these giants apart briefly and then bump them against each other. This aggravated the beetles into wrestling. They would latch onto each other with legs and mandibles and roll all over the little patch of barren earth between the boys in a fierce "hand-to-hand" struggle. Finally the beetles would separate, each lumbering off in a different direction. The boys then grabbed them and held onto them while the beetles rested for the next match. One boy tethered his beetle with a string tied to its leg. We were amazed, having never seen or heard of such huge beetles before. The boys smiled at us, apparently pleased to have an audience.

We hopped on the bus, not wanting to be last on, and observed the dusty but lively scene out the window. One scruffy-looking Tico caught my eye. I pointed him out to Skip since he was so unusual. Even laborers are usually relatively neat about their appearance, but this tall, slim guy was ragged and dirty, with long hair and a beard, a real standout character.

155

Skip tried to sneak a candid picture of him, but he disappeared behind some other workmen. Soon they moved out of the way, allowing Skip to attempt another shot. Again the man moved out of sight. The sharp-eyed rascal had caught Skip's effort to photograph him and was playing hide-and-seek! Perhaps he had been through this before with other nosey tourists, for he was quite adept at the game. As our bus pulled away, the "character" stood away from the crowd and grinned at us.

We drove north from Siquirres to a landing on a river that connected up with the Tortuguero Canal system. We had been traversing dirt roads for the last hour and now felt we were really out in the jungle. There were few amenities at the landing, but it presented a colorful scene. There were native peddlers trying to sell carvings and trinkets and fruits. Drums of diesel fuel were stacked near the river. One boy had a green parrot on his shoulder; another was trying to sell some fish on a stringer he had just toted up the riverbank from a long dugout canoe.

There was no pavement in the area, only bare ground surrounded by jungle and some grassy places where the traffic was less wearing. We tourists wandered around the dirt paths looking at everything and smiling at the natives until the ferry pulled into the landing to discharge a returning group of tourists and locals. We began to realize that it wasn't just an excursion boat; it was also the main transportation for the Ticos who lived along the river and canal. This was the way they came to town; first by boat, then bus—a long, slow trip.

After the passengers disembarked, a few "longshoremen" dressed in shorts and T-shirts loaded some sheet metal, fuel, and other supplies before we were told to go aboard. Some natives joined us, returning from their visit to the outside world, perhaps to visit relatives and friends and do some shopping, perhaps to go to the doctor or take care of some business.

It made us think of how different their lives were from ours, how much slower and perhaps harder. Yet maybe they feel they have something we don't. Some of them wonder why we northerners come all the way down to Costa Rica. Some think they have something better than we have, such as climate, beaches, scenery, food, pretty girls, maybe even better fishing. Antonio has mentioned such thoughts to us, seeming pretty certain that Costa Rica must have something special to lure so many *Norteamericanos* so far from home at such great expense.

Soon we were clambering down the slippery dirt bank to the rough, narrow gangplank that led onto the ferry, ending our philosophical interlude. There were two levels to the boat, a fact that always requires a decision. We opted for a lower-level seat, but it wasn't long before we realized it didn't matter. Shortly the boat was poled out into the current and we could move about to explore the boat as we wished, though some of the passageways were crowded. Even that hindrance ended after fifteen or twenty minutes, as people settled down.

The jungle shoreline was pretty constant except for occasional clearings where native families had *ranchitos* and small farms, which they call *fincas*. Cattle might be standing belly-deep in the river getting a drink, or children would be swimming and splashing, appearing very much at home in the water that doubled as their front yard. They looked very happy, more so than our modern-world youngsters who walk the mall for recreation looking bored.

Suddenly the ferry slowed its downstream pace and made a long U-turn back upstream, causing us to wonder what was going on. We gradually interpreted that there had been a small emergency boat tied to our stern when we started that was now missing. We continued back upstream until they located the rowboat and recovered it. Perhaps that is a legal requirement, to have a lifeboat available. At any rate, I'm sure they didn't want to lose it.

After proceeding downriver for a while, we put in at another small landing where they loaded some more cargo, including large sheets of corrugated roofing. One of the crew cut his hand badly on the sheet metal. Another worker helped him wrap it in a bandanna, and he continued to finish the loading. After we were under way again, Skip went over to ask the man if he was OK, and received a very nonchalant, macho response: "*No problema*," and a cavalier wave of the wrapped hand. Very Tico.

Along the way we watched for birds and mammals, wanting to see a sloth, which we were told were commonly seen on this trip. Sure enough, a sloth was spotted high in a tree at the water's edge. An elderly Tico gentleman with whom Skip had exchanged a few words reached over and tapped Skip on the shoulder, pointed, and said, "Slot." The problem was that even with our binoculars we could only make out a small, dark blotch against the green leaves and blue sky; not a very satisfying encounter. Still, we could at least add it to our list; we had seen it.

157

We saw some interesting birds and a large area covered by water lily blooms, but not very much to excite us for a five-hour trip. Yet it was a pleasant trip. They served us sandwiches and soft drinks, and we did enjoy the peacefulness of the trip through the lush jungle. The main break in the monotony was observing the occasional homesite and waving to the people. I suspect that observing us might have been an important break in their monotony, too.

Tortuguero, accessible only by boat, is an unusual village that lies on a narrow, overgrown strip of sand between the canal and the Caribbean. There are no streets, only footpaths that wind between houses of wood or thatch and sooner or later lead to the beach or a landing on the canal. Some of the houses include small shops that sell crafts, trinkets, and sodas. At the southern end of the main path is a visitor center for the Tortuguero National Park, which is renowned as a major nesting site for the large leatherbacks and the smaller green sea turtles.

At one time Tortuguero served a thriving turtle industry, providing turtle shell, eggs, and turtle meat for soup to exporters. Now the turtles are a protected species and many local folk find work in the tourist industry and with the National Park, protecting the very turtles they used to prey on. I wouldn't be surprised, though, if many of the locals still quietly consume their share of turtle eggs.

On we went after our stop at the village to a little resort complex about a mile farther north on the other side of the canal. This place felt really isolated, surrounded by heavy jungle, with no access other than by boat. There were boarded pathways, and we were told it was a good idea to stay on them to avoid wet feet as well as poisonous snakes and frogs. This was wet jungle, unlike the dry jungle where we normally stay on the Pacific side of the country. Our cabinas were large, but there was a damp feel to everything. Still, we were glad to get settled in after a long day's travel.

The evening meal was very nicely done, typical Tico food, and we all relaxed and got better acquainted. After dinner there was a lively singalong on a patio overlooking the canal and landing. Some rum and beer loosened our inhibitions and helped make the evening very enjoyable. Our tour guide, Jaime, turned out to be a fine guitarist and vocalist, a really vivacious personality.

Some of our group left after dark for an optional tour, a boat ride up some side streams to spotlight crocodiles. Skip and I went to bed early, since a nature hike was to start before breakfast the next morning.

We learned from the group that the night tour had seen only one crocodile, spotting its red eyes in the flashlight beam, but had seen a few other creatures to make the trip worthwhile.

We were issued black rubber knee-high boots for the morning hike. Our goal was to see some tiny red poison dart frogs. The pace was slow to accommodate the less fit, and our guide pointed out many tropical wonders along the way. The plant and insect life was marvelous, but the poison frogs and a small but deadly fer-de-lance snake were the highlights of the morning.

The tiny frog, which could sit on your thumbnail without much overhang, was a shiny orange-red. The guide placed it on the back of his hand, saying that it wouldn't have much effect unless he rubbed it on the underside of his arm, but he definitely didn't recommend eating it.

The little fer-de-lance seemed to have a touch of red and yellow low on its sides but was mainly rather dark, as far as I could see. Small as it was, the guide said it would still be quite poisonous, so we all kept our distance. Snakes do have a way of fascinating us.

After a big Tico breakfast of rice and beans, fruit, and coffee, our main hike began. It would be moderately strenuous, we were told, not too difficult for anyone, although those who didn't want to exert themselves could go to the beach with a different guide. The hike was to ascend Mount Tortuguero, a little knob that rose above the jungled tidal plain that surrounding the area, so we were told.

Jaime led us on a winding trail around the base, zigzagging back and forth in our ill-fitting black rubber boots as the hill became steeper and steeper. The trail was wet and slick in places. Soon Skip was helping the older and heavier of our group, and at times I had to help and be helped. A few spots required an all-out hands and knees effort almost straight up, around rocks or over logs. I was amazed that they had told us we would all be able to make this climb; it was clearly too much for some of our group.

The view from the summit was grand, however, encompassing miles of jungle, the canal, and the Caribbean Sea. Jaime said we were seeing into Nicaragua as we looked northwest. We could also see the remainder of our tour group lolling on the sandy beach beside the mouth of the canal, those lazy, lucky lowlanders! We still had to descend this nasty little knob, and some of us were praying we could get back down without any breaks or sprains. We were already dirty and sweaty, some with blisters or scratches.

By helping one another we made it back to the bottom without incident, though some were complaining and threatening to write letters of protest to the tour company. But we were provided with soft drinks as they boated us back to the lodge, where a shower, a change of clothing, and a nice lunch began to elevate our collective mood. Then a call to look at a large colony of *oropendola* birds nesting in a nearby tree distracted and delighted us to the degree that we were happily ready for an afternoon trip back to Tortuguero Village to explore some more at our leisure.

Another nice dinner followed by more music and some dancing completed our stay. Doing the limbo stretched our tired muscles, and we were certainly ready for bed this night.

We arose before six for breakfast and were packed and on the boat by seven for the five-hour ferry ride back to the landing where we left the bus. The canal scenes were unchanged; some bird life, water lilies, and friendly natives who smiled and waved were all that there was to break the monotony of the jungled shoreline. Some folks dozed; the energy level of our group had definitely dropped a notch or two.

The bus was waiting to drive us back to San José, although several of us got off at Siquirres to await the bus connection to Limon. Jaime checked to see that we were secure in our ability to find our way, which we appreciated. We went to the bus station window and bought our tickets, then waited for the bus.

We reached Limon around two o'clock, finding a crowded station. Some watched the baggage while others bought tickets for the ride to Cahuita and then a few small snacks. We felt we had to be careful in the press of people or we could lose bags or cameras, maybe even wallets. It was another squeeze to get on the bus and find a seat.

The ride to Cahuita was hot, dirty, and rough. The road was terrible, just what we were used to. Some spots were so bad that we wondered if the bus could get through. Still, in a little over an hour we were disgorged in a quaint little town nestled against the Caribbean Sea, wondering where to go next.

Skip spied a blond-bearded young gringo, and we walked over to ask about the place where we had reservations, Cabinas Tito. The young man had a vacant look in his eyes, we found, as we got closer, and also couldn't speak English, as we had presumed. (We had read that Cahuita was a hangout for young folks backpacking around the country and that a drug-using subculture was part of the scene.) Still, Skip understood enough of the man's Spanish to head down to the end of the street we were on and turn left. There we checked for directions again and we were soon at Cabinas Tito, several cabins along one side of a well-tended lot surrounded by flowers.

The main house, also not very large, was on the same side of the gardened area as the cabins. We seemed to be approaching from the rear side of the lot, so we dropped our bags, which I watched as Skip walked on across to the main house. As he approached the house, a thin, barefoot black man clad in tattered shorts and T-shirt stepped from behind a blossoming red hibiscus bush and greeted him.

Skip asked if this was Cabinas Tito, and the man said, "Yes."

Skip assumed he was the gardener and asked with whom to speak to in order to check in.

The young man said, with modest dignity, "I am Tito," in English with a Caribbean lilt.

Looking impressed, Skip told him who we were and that we had a reservation.

Tito replied, "Oh, yes," and pointed to a nearby cabin. "Take that one there. I'll help with your bags."

With that he walked over to me, said hello, grabbed the bags, and took them to the cabina. That was that; no signing-in, in fact no office at all, it seemed. We had paid Alexis at the Cacts Hotel in San José, and she would forward a share of the money to Tito. We had paid twenty-seven dollars per day, and Tito's wife later complained to Skip, when he had spied her on her porch and stopped to chat, that the commission was too high. She would have let us have the cabin for fifteen dollars. But I reminded Skip that this way we at least had a reservation to count on.

As we were settling in, Tito popped back over with a key. The cabin was nice and new, with louvered windows surrounded by colorful print curtains and fresh varnish on those beautiful tropical woods. It was still hot, but there was a light breeze ruffling the curtains, and we were glad to have a satisfactory home for a couple of days as we explored Cahuita.

After resting and freshening up a bit, we started walking about town. It was different here from the Pacific coast. The Caribbean surf was much milder, more of a murmur than a roar, but more than that, the atmosphere was much less Tico, more Caribbean. Cahuita was a funky little town, full of quaint eateries and bars. There were more young people hanging out, more of the backpack crowd, more obvious presence of drug use. It had a little of the flavor of a European youth hangout, a more cosmopolitan flavor than its counterparts on the Pacific side. There was less gringo influence, including the fact that the water was not potable, as it was in Nosara. We even reminded each other to use bottled water to brush our teeth.

We strolled most of the streets, winding up back where most of the action was happening toward nightfall. We selected a little eatery and tried their tropical pizza with a cold beer, enjoying people-watching as we ate. There were numerous interesting, colorful characters to observe, most but not all of them young. We felt like the oddballs, actually, seeming to be the only standard (colorless?) middle-aged gringos around.

We strolled a bit longer after dinner, until the mosquitoes drove us back to our cabin. There were lots more mosquitoes here than around Nosara. We found a flaw in our accommodations we had failed to notice before: no screens on the windows. That limited our usual bedtime reading, since the lights drew the pests into our room. We soon shut off the lights and went to sleep.

The next morning we were up so early that we had to talk a young woman who was mopping the restaurant floors into making breakfast for us. It was a hole-in-the-wall place, and she may have been part of the family who ran it; anyway, she set her mop aside and fixed us eggs, toast, and coffee. We tipped a little extra for her kindness and headed off in the direction she indicated to find Cahuita National Park.

It wasn't far to the edge of town, where we saw a little wooden building, not much more than a shack, on the other side of a small gully. We wondered if this was it. If so, it certainly was not impressive, not in a class with what we considered a national park. We crossed the gully on a log that had been hewn to partial flatness on the top and looked at a few notices that had been tacked on the shed. They seemed to be related to park topics, so we looked around and found a path leading away from behind the building into the jungle. We shrugged and laughed, then walked on down the path, wearing our knapsacks stocked with bottled water and snacks.

It turned out to be a long walk, perhaps six miles or more, and not too different from jungles on the opposite coast. This area was clearly better-watered and more lush. Perhaps some of the vegetation was different and maybe a few of the bird species, but we felt pretty much at home here.

162

The day grew hot as we hiked, and we were glad for our bottled water, although it grew warmer right along with the day. We enjoyed some large troops of howler monkeys and the abundant bird life. At one point we came out on the shore of the Caribbean, where we could see a few fishing boats some distance out. A series of rock reefs jutted a couple hundred yards out into the sea, and we walked out a little way, going from shelf to shelf. From out there we could look back to our left and see the village, a quiet, picturesque scene. It felt like being on a remote tropical island.

We proceeded back into the jungle and on along the path we were following. At one point we had to leap across a little inlet of water. Skip was filming something with the camcorder when I noticed a lizard a little over a foot long at the edge of the inlet. I called, "Hey, Skip, here it is, I think!"

Sure enough, he swung the camera in time to catch a blur of motion as the Jesus Christ lizard ran across the top of the water to the other side. We had really seen it! After reading about it and seeing it on a National Geographic program on television, here it was in real life in the Costa Rican jungle. We felt very lucky to stumble upon such a creature. Such experiences keep us motivated to travel and explore and learn, and we feel especially fortunate that we both take pleasure in sharing such adventures.

We moseyed on along the path, beginning to realize that this was a perimeter trail and the park was mostly a peninsula jutting out into the Caribbean. The shelf of reef that we had walked on was the tip of the peninsula. We guessed that we would come out just across the neck of the peninsula from where we had begun our hike. Hiking without any advice or information just added to the adventure, we told ourselves. It was reassuring, though, when we passed a couple more buildings that seemed to belong to the park, especially a small outhouse. Outhouses are always reassuring.

It wasn't the same spot where we'd entered the park, but there was a dirt road that soon led us to the main highway. We thought about waiting for a bus, but it was so hot in the sun that we decided to just keep on walking. It couldn't be too far to Cahuita, since we had walked in a loop.

Near the bus stop sign we began hearing a noise, like a big flock of birds. Moving toward the sound, just down the dusty road, we found a huge tropical tree loaded with *oropendola* nests. This was at least the third colony of *oropendolas* we had seen during our ramblings in Costa Rica, but this one was by far the largest. Some seemed to argue and scold while others acted "twitterpated," as if they were conducting loud romances.

The tree was heavily hung with woven nests, resembling oversize oriole nests. In fact, there really was an oriole in the tree, but it was dwarfed by the great *oropendolas* which appeared to be about the size of a large pigeon, only half again longer. We also saw a long-tailed mandarin stop in the tree for a minute or two, an exotic creature with two very long, curved tail feathers and blue patches on its wings. Adding to the color of the scene were the tree's bright yellow blossoms and the background of cloudless blue sky.

We could barely drag ourselves away from the scene, but the sun was hot and we were out of water. Skip shot another picture, and we forced ourselves to move on down the road. In another minute or so the bus came by, passing us as we trudged through the heat. But now we could see the bus turn off to the right only a half-mile farther on. That had to be the entrance into Cahuita.

It was. In another fifteen minutes we were headed down the main drag toward our *cabina,* tired and thirsty. We bought another bottle of water and headed straight for our cabin and a shower. Then we adjusted the windows to best take advantage of what breezes were available and stretched out to read and rest until the day cooled.

Hungry as bears, we searched out Edyth's, a funky little restaurant in a shacky low-roofed building run by an elderly black lady who was famous for her Caribbean-style cooking. Her specialty was the use of coconut milk as a cooking medium for several entrées and vegetable specialties. We enjoyed the food but not the mosquitoes, which tried to consume us in spite of numerous smoke pots placed around the room, open on two sides to let in the air along with the mosquitoes.

We strolled Cahuita again that evening, but not for long because of the mosquitoes. We returned to Tito's and packed to leave early the next morning.

The bus left at six, as crowded as it had been when we came. It bounced us back to Limon, where we purchased tickets for our return to San José. We'd allowed enough time to explore Limon a little. We didn't want to do too much here, since we had our bags to tote around, but we had read of the sloths in the park near the bay and wanted to see if we could get a close look.

It wasn't far to the park. There were a few people seated on benches and some more walking through as if on errands or going to work. We didn't notice anything else at first, but then we saw a branch move and a few leaves drop to the ground, almost falling on a man sitting under the tree. He looked up and said something in Spanish, and we moved around, positioning for a better view.

There, just barely out of reach, was a furry, sleepy-looking creature that reminded us of a disfigured koala. It looked like something Walt Disney might have created or maybe a stuffed toy for on our granddaughter's bed. Technically, it was a two-toed sloth, although we counted three toes on its hind feet and two on the front. It definitely moved slowly when it moved at all and looked as though it was either asleep or eating at any point in time.

Skip conjectured that there must have been some evolutionary survival advantage to the sloth's slow movement, allowing the slow individuals to outlive and reproduce better than the quicker individuals. Perhaps fast movement in the branches attracted predators. Skip puzzles a lot over things like that.

We were mesmerized by the homely little guys munching their leaves. Their brown fur looked very soft. There was no enclosure at all. People either ignored the sloths or gave them (and us) a smiling glance as they passed. We watched and filmed for half an hour or so, then walked on out to the water's edge to look at the bay.

There were a couple of ships tied up on the other side of the bay, but not much seemed to be happening. The view was pleasant, but this seemed to be an old, unused part of the bay. We wondered about its history, maybe involving pirates or slavers in its obscure past. What wonderful or gruesome scenes had we missed by being too late in time at this spot? Possibly even Columbus had stopped here.

But we had to catch our bus at 9:30, so we headed back to the station to locate the one for San José. Another crowded bus. Ticos certainly make good use of their mass transit system. Soon we were climbing the *Cordillera Central*, the mountain backbone of the country, passing through Braulio Corrillo National Park in the cloud forest, through Zurqui Tunnel, and on over the top toward the city. By noon we were back in the Hotel Cacts, resting a bit and deciding what to do next.

We had a few more days to spend before departing the country, so we opted first for a visit to Sarchi, the little hill town west of San José that is famous for their handcrafted wood products. We located the appropriate bus connections and stops in our hard-used *Key to Costa Rica* guidebook, spurning the guided tours for something this nearby.

Sarchi is approached through the steep hills beyond Alajuela and is an old-fashioned town, except for the number of craft shops that have sprung up in response to the burgeoning tourist traffic. The hilly streets seem to have a woodwork shop and several outlets on each block.

Sarchi's specialty is ox carts of all sizes for the souvenir trade. You can buy tiny ones right up through quite large ones, all wonderfully painted with traditional fancy patterns and colors. They come knocked down and boxed for shipping, which they will gladly do for you. This flourishing souvenir business is a spinoff from the original trade in real working ox carts. They probably still make a few, but we didn't see any. We would like to go back sometime and see if we can locate a shop that still constructs working ox carts. All Costa Rican ox carts are works of art and remain the premier national symbol.

Sarchi craftspeople also make furniture, mostly on order. Their tradition seems not to have evolved much standardization, perhaps due to lack of mass production methods. Pieces are individually handcrafted to specification. You can get odd-sized pieces as easily as standard sizes. It isn't unusual to see a huge chair or an extra-high bed or a low sofa. Then, of course, you would have to custom order a mattress or chair pad to fit the odd size. But that's the way it works in Costa Rica.

Another Sarchi specialty is a folding wood-and-leather rocking chair. Many tourists have these shipped home after rocking away a few pleasant evenings watching those Pacific sunsets or mountain views. They are pretty comfortable, as we know from enjoying them at Martha's and at numerous other homes in Nosara. Leather and wood combine to creak a little, but I guess that's part of their charm, and after a while it becomes associated with the mellow result of rum and Coke on ice.

The next day, March 30, we signed up for a bus excursion to Irazu Volcano for the following morning. Having nothing scheduled for this day, we decided to hop a bus and take another trip on our own. Using our trusty guidebook, we located the proper bus stop for Cartago, an old city that was once the capital of Central America. It is the home of Costa Rica's most famous cathedral, the Basilica of Our Lady of the Angels, which houses *La Negrita*, the little Black Virgin, who appeared to a peasant girl in 1635. La Negrita is a small, crude figurine of the Virgin and her child. A poor peasant girl found it on a rock while she was gathering firewood and took it home. It disappeared during the night, but the little girl, Juana, found it the next day on the same rock where she had first discovered it.

When it happened once more, the mystified Juana told her story to her priest. The priest took the tiny statue and locked it away, but to his amazement, the same thing happened again; La Negrita was back on her rock. The priest interpreted this to mean that God wanted a church built on the site of the rock, which resulted in this beautiful basilica.

La Negrita has been the source of endless miracles and blessings and is the motivation for large yearly pilgrimages from all over Costa Rica. Believers walk tremendous distances to reach the church every August 2 to honor La Negrita and seek her blessings. Many of them accomplish the last segment, from the church doorway to the altar, on their knees.

We walked through this inspiring cathedral, gazing in wonder at all the showcases overflowing with symbols of healings and other miracles, then on downstairs to a cryptlike cellar where we could touch the rock where the Virgin appeared. Even though it was no special day, there were numerous other people lined up to parade past the rock. We agreed that this spot must truly be the heart of Costa Rica.

Some distance from the basilica are the ruins of a church that had been destroyed by an earthquake in 1910. Walls still standing, it was now used as a city garden, and heavily used, it appeared. Its paths were lined with lovely flowers and blossoming trees. People strolled the paths and picnicked here and there, quietly, as if absorbing its serenity. We enjoyed its shade and color, feeling refreshed as we left to travel on to Paraiso to locate Lankester Gardens. You may recall that we tried once before with Chet and Martha to see the gardens, but they were closed.

At our request, the bus driver deposited us at the end of a dirt lane marked by a small sign. We walked the half-mile or so to the buildings and then waited and knocked, fearing that the gardens were closed again, until someone came to collect the small admission and admit us. Happily, this time they were open.

Spring is the poorest season to see the gardens, since it is the driest time of the year. Still, we enjoyed walking the paths and locating the blooms hanging from the trees. Some were extremely small, others very large. The variety was amazing, in color, pattern, shape, and size, though they clearly were not at their peak.

We learned that the garden was established by an Englishman named Lankester but had been turned over to the University of Costa Rica. Probably it was suffering from the same lack of funds as the university does, and it was showing. The buildings and grounds both needed attention, but we nonetheless enjoyed our visit.

We hiked out to the main road to catch the next bus back to Cartago, ate a light lunch, and then made the return trip to San José, tired but happy.

The following day was clear, perfect for the trip to Irazu Volcano, which we had scheduled through the hotel. Much of the bus ride followed yesterday's route until we turned north just at the edge of Cartago. Then we began the upgrade on the flanks of the mountain, watching the panorama of Cartago Valley unfold off to our right as we passed through fields of onions, flowers, and other crops on Irazu's fertile slopes. Over the centuries volcanic ash and decomposed lava flows have created a deep, productive soil, which the Tico farmers have learned to till quite effectively.

Our driver stopped a couple of times for photos, and near the top he halted for a break at a scenic bar-restaurant that, at over seven thousand feet, they claimed was the highest eatery in Central America. Who knows? We enjoyed a few snacks and some strong coffee. Our guide passed the word that the bartender had a bottle of *guaro*, Costa Rican sugarcane moonshine, so of course Skip had to sneak over and get a sample. He said it was no different from the bottle he had at home in the closet, which was the *Casique* brand from the national distillery, and not much different from vodka.

Next stop was the summit. We could look right down into the muddy cone, which was peaceful at the moment, emitting only a little steam. Irazu hadn't erupted since the 1960s, when President Kennedy made his historic visit to the country. The Ticos remember that visit better than we do; they felt it gave them some long-awaited recognition. That volcanic eruption inundated a large section of the country with ash. Some folks claim they still find some of that ash in hidden places.

Most impressive, however, was the fact that we could see both the Pacific and Atlantic Oceans from that one spot. Actually, we could barely make out the Atlantic side, and it was really the Caribbean Sea, an arm of the Atlantic Ocean, and most of the water we saw on the Pacific side was the Gulf of Nicoya, though we could see a patch of the actual Pacific. Still, we were impressed and delighted.

168

On the way back the bus stopped briefly at the basilica in Cartago for pictures. We were able to boast that we had been there only yesterday and had toured the inside, something that some of our tourmates wished they had time for.

We used our final two days in Costa Rica to shop, which Skip calls my main sport, and to visit the public zoo, a butterfly garden, and the serpentarium, all of which are in the city.

The San José Zoological Gardens are a small, poorly funded, poorly maintained project. We love zoos and visit them frequently, but this one, while the mammals and birds were fascinating, was dirty and shoddy and made us feel sorry for the creatures. There have been occasional movements to upgrade the zoo, letters to the editor, fund drives, and such, but it doesn't seem to change much.

The butterfly garden was pretty new, small but well managed. It was a private enterprise, producing cocoons for sale while bolstering their income by charging admission to visitors like us. This one was located not far up the street from the Hotel Villa Tournon and was much smaller than the butterfly farm out beyond the airport. They gave us a nice, informative tour with a personal guide. It was apparently just across the ravine from the zoo, because we could hear a lion roar above the rush of the dirty little river that flows through this section of the city.

The serpentarium is right downtown, not far from the old Hotel Amstel, so we walked there, as we had to the zoo and butterfly garden. A few miles of walking will take you all over San José, and we like that.

The serpentarium is located on the second floor of an old city building, so we climbed the stairs and paid a few dollars' admission to see if we could learn the names of some of our Nosara jungle residents. We hate to just describe a snake we have seen; we like to know the names. Skip grabbed a booklet on reptiles of Costa Rica and went over to pay for it. He had been wanting one for a long time. Handing over his money, he began to leaf through the booklet, then realized that it was entirely in Spanish, technical language at that. So, embarrassed, he apologized and asked for his money back, returning the booklet to the shelf.

We enjoyed an extended hour trying to recognize snakes we had seen in Nosara and gazing in awe at some of the legends of which we had heard: the bushmaster; the fer-de-lance, which we had seen in miniature at Tortuguero; the banana viper; the coral snake; and our old acquaintance from home, the rattlesnake. We remembered the old southern verse to distinguish a coral, cousin to the cobra, from a harmless lookalike. "Red and yeller kill a feller; red and black, put 'im back.'' It refers to adjacent bands of color around the snake's body, and we recalled having need to recite it on a couple of occasions.

We walked all the way back to the Cacts Hotel at the opposite end of town, stopping to buy a few gifts on the way. We bought little cakes of blue soap to share with our friends; they remove stains when rubbed on spots before laundering. We picked up a heavy, coarse sugar cake called *tapa dulce,* which we cook in water to make pancake syrup. We also like to get some dried exotic fruits and Monte Verde cheese to pass around at home. As you see, much of our souvenir shopping was done in a supermarket, this time in a *Mas X Menos*, which translates (we think) to ''More for less.''

That evening we showered and packed and went out to a favorite restaurant, *Antojos*, about four blocks from the Cacts, on *Paseo Colon*. It is located below street level and specializes in Mexican food. We enjoy the music and atmosphere as well as the food. We talked over our experiences of the past three months and felt mixed emotions about departing the country. It is always good to return home and see our children and grandchildren and to catch up on our obligations to our parents and older siblings. But we knew it would be cold, and we would find a boxful of mail to review, plus our income tax forms would surely be waiting. Yes, definitely mixed emotions.

We flew back to Pennsylvania on April 3, our thirty-eighth wedding anniversary—not the best way to celebrate, being en route from 5:00 A.M. until 10:00 P.M. But then we had been enjoying the good life and had no room to complain. Still, in the backs of our minds constantly lurked our worries about Chet and how Martha was holding up caring for him. We had been in regular contact with Martha and knew that she had enlisted the assistance of Hospice, but Chet must certainly be near the end. What would we find?

14

1994, Martha Returns without Chet

The past year had been one of funerals. When we returned home from Costa Rica in early April we made a quick visit to my brother's home near Donegal in western Pennsylvania to check on my ninety-three-year-old mother. Oscar and his wife had been keeping her for the past four years as she deteriorated, needing constant care. (Skip and I took care of her business affairs, taxes and the like.) Within two weeks of my return she was dead, as if she had been waiting for me.

That was our welcome home, the first funeral of the year. I had been made executrix of her will, and while we had disposed of her home and personal property four years earlier, there was still the old farm to dispose of. This meant numerous trips to the lawyer and a realtor, all nearly three hours' travel from our home.

We buried Mom in late April; then Chet died in May. We accompanied Martha to the family viewing, along with her sons and their wives, Louise Lytle, Chet's longtime secretary, and her husband, Glenn. It was very sad, since we all had so many memories involving Chet, and all felt indebted to him for the many ways he had enriched our lives over so many years.

Chet's funeral was very large. He and Martha had been involved with many people over the years and had a special way of impacting people and maintaining longtime relationships. The clergyman who spoke emphasized the building of the church in Nosara and numerous other ways Chet's life had had positive effects. We knew and admired Chet for all that, but mostly we felt sorry for ourselves that Chet would be missing from our lives. *"Ask not for whom the bell tolls . . . ,"* I thought. *It tolls for ourselves. We're the ones hurting today, not Chet.*

After we saw Chet laid to rest under the big pine trees in the old Middle Spring Church cemetery near Shippensburg, we gathered at Martha's house, where her bridge club served a buffet lunch. Many old acquaintances were renewed, but basically we supported one another through this sad time, distracting ourselves with conversation as folks probably do the world over.

Both Randy and Tom, Martha's sons, came to Skip and me to thank us for helping Martha through Chet's death, especially during those final weeks in Nosara. This was very gratifying to us, and we told them of the esteem in which we held Chet—that we would always be glad we had the opportunity to provide the support we gave freely. We were very touched by the sincerity of their appreciation.

Jack Hargleroad was there, and sure enough, he pulled out his old Swiss Army knife to cut a piece of cheese. Skip commented wryly, "I hope you've washed that old knife," reminding Jack that it was that very same knife he had used to lance the carbuncle on Arepa's butt at Chet's house down in Nosara, causing several of us to laugh quietly until we cried.

We sold our Orrstown home in June, a nice little farmette with orchard, gardens, and barn on five acres. We had put a lot of work and money into that place, and we loved it, but it was becoming too much for us to take care of, especially since we traveled so much. We bought a large house next to our daughter. It needed a lot of work, but at least it didn't have all the grounds and fruit trees requiring constant care.

In addition, we had been signed up for a trip to Europe during August with our friends Glenn and Louise Lytle. We were worried that Skip's mother might die at any time, and we had been helping his dad cope with pancreatic cancer. We felt we would be lucky to squeeze in the trip to Europe before something else happened.

We did get to enjoy the tour of Europe, but Skip's mother died in September. After the funeral we tried to provide some support for his dad through the fall. Skip's sister, "Toosie," who lived just across the field from their father, had thankfully provided regular assistance over the years, allowing us the freedom to travel. But we felt guilty about dumping too much in her lap and made an effort to do the mowing and take care of basic maintenance requirements around the old farmstead.

Then Skip's dad died in early December. One more funeral: one too many, it seemed. Skip and Toosie were co-executors, so after the funeral they made arrangements for the auction sale of both the personal property and the real estate during the following May. Again, his sister managed details while we were gone, enabling us to return to Costa Rica in early January. Thank goodness for Toosie.

172

We had one more funeral to attend later that December. Don Powell, our good neighbor in Orrstown, died suddenly. Since he had retired two years earlier, Don had been our chauffeur when we needed to be driven to or from the airport for our travels to Costa Rica. He loved to hear of our travels. We paid him a nominal fee for the service, which he always protested. Don was scheduled not only to drive us again but also to be Santa Claus for our grandchildren, another duty he regularly performed for us. His funeral was especially sad, since he was only around sixty, while our parents had been much older. He would be missing a rewarding part of his life, we felt, and it was sad to ponder that. Also, his children were younger and more vulnerable to the loss.

Martha and Chet normally departed for Costa Rica in November, but since Chet's death she had waited and matched her schedule to ours. She met us in the Miami Airport in early January after dividing the prior two months' time between her sons in Maryland and Florida. We were happy to see one another.

As we chatted, Martha would occasionally break into tears at the mention of Chet or even at some hidden thought that happened to remind her of Chet. She would usually get past the tears pretty quickly, by sheer force of will, it seemed. Between the short episodes of crying she was cheerful as usual and talked sociably with us and with anyone else she happened to meet.

They checked our bags this time as we went through customs at Aeropuerto Juan Santamaria. When I unzipped my large bag, some sanitary napkins, which I had stuffed in every remaining space, popped out like popcorn onto the table. Everyone around seemed to be grinning and snickering as the inspector waved me on. I laughed, too, but I know I was blushing as I scrambled to grab the packets and stuff them back into the suitcase and struggled to reclose it.

Martha had made our reservations at the Villa Tournon and suggested that we share one room with two beds, one for her and one for us, each to pay half. When we checked out, she divided the bill into thirds. Oh, well, that's Martha. You never know what's coming next—frugal about this, generous about that.

After attending to some business and shopping in San José and the hard drive out to Nosara, we spent the usual week getting the place back into shape. Skip and Antonio moved the heavier furniture and the automatic washer into place while Martha and I moved the lighter stuff, cleaned, and got the beds and kitchens ready. There were water leaks, electric line breaks, holes in roofs, appliance problems, insect problems, and so forth, all requiring Skip's attention. Then there was all the washing and scrubbing for Martha and me and airing out nearly every item made of cloth.

Chini never showed up to greet us with Antonio. In response to our questioning, he told us that Chini was working in San José. She had been living there since November, working as a maid for someone, he thought. She had sold their household goods and major appliances to relatives for money to use for traveling and getting started. He had come home from fishing to find his house stripped and Chini gone.

"Is she coming back?" Skip asked. Antonio didn't know.

"Is she with another guy?" Maybe, he shrugged; he wasn't sure.

We were surprised. We had never expected anything like this. Antonio and Chini had seemed like friends as well as lovers. True, they had never married, but that's not unusual here. The only problem we had seen was their lack of children. We knew that Antonio wanted children but had no idea as to why they had none or its effects on their relationship.

Then Antonio told Skip that he was seeing a pretty young girl named Betty, who had "very light skin." He began bringing her around to visit and introduced her to all of us. He talked with Skip about Chini and his ambivalence regarding her. He wasn't sure about dismissing her entirely, but we could see he was in conflict.

On the other hand, he certainly was enjoying Betty's company; there was no ambivalence about that. And she seemed to reciprocate, beaming with pleasure in his company. After all, Antonio had some status in the community, a nice little house, a regular job, even a television set. A real romance was blooming here, but we couldn't believe that Chini was out of the picture entirely.

Gradually, we took time to watch the birds and mammals, then fit in a couple of hours at the beach. When we walked out on that beach with the sun shining and the "Costa Rican Air Force" (pelicans) in formation overhead and waded into the tide pools, we knew it had all been worth it; we knew why we came. Martha says, "Isn't this wonderful?" as she does again and again nearly every time we go to the pools, everyone laughs, and the world is bright. We're glad to be alive as we float and splash and soak up the beauty of the day.

We arranged the usual birthday party for Antonio after our dinner. We waited half an hour, but he never showed up, so we had his cake and ice cream ourselves for desert. Martha grumps about his unreliability

174

but usually forgives him the instant he arrives. An hour later Antonio popped in. He had gone fishing, probably with Betty as company, and put the party out of his mind until he returned home. We sang "Happy Birthday" and watched him eat his cake and ice cream, shoveling it into his mouth through a big grin. Then we gave him his presents, always a pleasure, because he receives them joyously as a child.

Jack and Helen Hargleroad arrived for a two-week stay at Casa de las Flores. We picked them up at the airstrip in Nosara and chatted about last year's ordeal with Chet, then gradually drifted into inconsequentials as they began to wind down from their trip. Soon things seemed relatively normal, given Chet's absence. We again watched the birds from the back deck during happy hour, trying to ignore that empty chair.

Skip sometimes helps Antonio when he gets behind in his work. This time Skip was using a machete to prune some thorny dwarf poincianas that Chet had planted as a hedge along a path below the main porch. One of the limbs fell onto his right arm. A big thorn stabbed straight into a large vessel, and instead of bleeding outwardly, it rose up into a lump the size of half an orange. Puzzled, Skip came up on the porch to show it to Jack Hargleroad, who happened to be there at the time.

Jack said, "That's a helluva hematoma you have there! Let me clean that and wrap it for you." Then he hurried off for some medical supplies.

Helen came over and commented, reassuringly, "Ugh! That looks awful."

Skip asked, "What's the problem with this? Why is it puffing up? It's not hurting much."

Jack came limping back on his artificial hip joint, explaining, "That puncture caused internal bleeding into the tissue. The problem is that all the blood in that lump creates an ideal medium for infection. That's the only real danger. We've got to get it cleansed with this peroxide and hope that thorn didn't inoculate you with something nasty."

It was reassuring to have the old doctor at hand; in fact, we've been reassured many times by his presence. Skip's lump disappeared in a few days, causing him no problem beyond a little discomfort, at least as he told it.

Soon the monkeys were back overhead at happy hour. They put on one of their best shows ever, totally distracting us from our reading. I don't know if there was a connection to the big show, but the winds came up later that night. We had never noticed a pattern, so I suppose it was a coincidence.

175

Chini visited one evening. Martha invited her to join us for dinner. We learned that she wanted to come back to Antonio, but he wasn't ready to take her back. She seemed sad as she talked of Antonio and his new woman, Betty. Chini returned to San José on the bus the next morning.

We decided to attend the big fiesta in Nosara that Saturday partly for fun and partly to support the ambulance fund, to which all the proceeds were supposed to go. We went at midday in order to see the bullfights, but the sun was awfully hot. Hats were the order of the day, especially for us gringos. Some of the Ticas were hatless, but they are born to the tropical sun, and besides, they have such thick hair to protect them.

We parked on the dusty roadside some distance from the grounds, since they were crowded with cars, trucks, people, and horses all the way into the village. There were buses, too, discharging loads of people from other villages who had ridden an hour or so to get here, maybe more.

The arena was surrounded by rustic booths thrown up during the past week, where food, drinks, trinkets, and other wares were being sold. Loudspeakers blared music all around, mostly Mexican, it seemed to us, with guitars and trumpets predominating. It was a truly colorful spectacle.

Some of the show riders were warming up their gaited horses, and we stepped aside to watch them prance by. They were beautiful to see, with their necks arched as they stepped high, seeming to dance a tango or a hesitation waltz. Their riders sat on them as if they were glued to their fancy saddles, not bouncing as I always seemed to do in my riding days. We could tell the riders were very proud men, and they seemed to be pleased when Skip took their pictures.

We chatted with friends from the development whom we hadn't seen very often, catching up on the latest gossip. We said, ''Buenas tardes,'' to Ticos we knew, enjoying the lovely smiles we got in return. Skip eyed the lissome senoritas as we strolled around, especially the queen and her court. One of our neighbors, Né, a dark-eyed beauty, was a member of the queen's group, so he took her picture. It's a macho society, so the young ladies are used to flirting and being ogled. Skip seems to like that.

After checking out the vendors to our satisfaction, we bought our tickets and entered the stands. I was a little uneasy about it, because they were made entirely of poles lashed and nailed together, with rough lumber for the steps, walkways, and seats. I could visualize the whole conglomeration caving in, us with it. But Skip pointed out that they'd been doing this for years, that they were good at it. Still, I think he had his fingers crossed, too.

We climbed up into the stands on the left side and immediately realized we were in the wrong section. The sun was glaring directly on the folks seated there. Back down we went, looped around to the right-hand section, and climbed up the steep stairs again. This was better, with blessed shade from some palm thatch installed behind and above us, although more crowded.

The stands didn't have much room for our long gringo legs and the seats were narrow and hard, but at least we were sitting and in the shade. Now we concentrated on the scenes before and around us, although the loud music was a little overpowering.

Some announcements were made in Spanish and were difficult for us to interpret. I have enough trouble understanding loudspeakers even in English. Soon a truckload of huge bulls was being backed up to the release chute, and the level of excitement rose a notch. More announcements.

Then the queens were paraded around the arena in a mixture of trucks and cars. We recognized Roger's old white Mercedes, and there was Rick and Bobbi Johnson's old red Toyota pickup. Bobbi had a bare foot propped up on the dashboard and was sipping beer from a can as Rick drove while the smiling beauty queen stood in the truck bed, all decked out in a frilly red gown, wearing red hibiscus flowers in her dark hair. Fortunately, the thickest dust stayed close to the ground. There was comparatively little dust hanging in the rest of the atmosphere. We could smell it in our nostrils, along with a mild perfume of horse and bull manure.

After the queen and her court were introduced and applauded, they left the ring. Then began the introductions of the featured bullfighters, who came from all over the country, although most were Guanacaste men, since Guanacaste is Costa Rica's Wild West. The cheering crescendoed when a couple of local names were called. These boys were heroes hereabouts, no doubt about that.

Finally the bullfighters were in place, backed up by some expert ropers. There were also some *barrachos* (drunks) in the ring along with some brave but scared youngsters trying to prove their manhood. Young people of both sexes lined the top rail of the fence, anticipating the terror

A bull rider holds both hands aloft at the fiesta in Nosara.

of being close to the bulls as they charged around the ring. Excitement reached a fever pitch.

The bull in the chute was being mounted by the first rider, much like our American rodeo bull riders do, hanging onto a single cinch rope as the agitated beast is released into the ring. Here, instead of one or two rodeo clowns, the ring was full of distractions. Several bullfighters with red or yellow blankets faced the bull in a crude version of the old Spanish style, trying to attract a charge and then sidestep as the bull passed with the rider on his back, if the rider was skilled enough to still be there.

The bull may ignore the official bullfighters and charge the kids or the drunks, who then either flee in terror, some scrambling ignominiously out under the fence, or, in the case of a few, display rather admirable evasive capabilities. Usually the bull makes at least one sweep along the fence, routing those sitting on or under the fence in a fluid wave, off the fence, then back again, reminding us of those flowing stadium waves at our pro football games. These people love it! They obviously get a high from that moment of terror.

During one "fence cleaning" a couple of youths became tangled. One tripped and fell in front of the bull and was hooked aside by the animal's blunted horns. The professionals and the ropers quickly distracted the bull while the youth's friends and others nearby speedily carried him to a place where the fence had a large red "+" sign painted in a white circle, a Red Cross emblem. To our surprise the emblem was on a trapdoor, which flopped open as they arrived at the spot. They zipped the injured youth through the slot right into the hands of the health workers on the other side. Slick! Not high tech, but quite functional.

We soon saw the young man walking gingerly about on the other side of the fence, and that was the only injury we observed that day. Not bad considering the potential for harm in that arena.

One of the highlights, in addition to the skills of the bullfighters, the beauty queens, and the fancy riding, was the amazing skill of the ropers. These men had the duty of clearing a tired bull from the ring before the next one could be released. Once a bull quit charging or responding to taunts, he had to be removed from the ring. The ropers used this moment to demonstrate their remarkable skills.

One roper rode at a gallop past a bull in the opposite direction of the bull's travel while twirling a wide loop over his own head. He threw the loop down and behind him so that it rolled on the ground in front of the bull as the bull ran directly into the noose, then pivoted his horse in time to brace for the jolt when the bull hit the end of the rope. Another rider roped only the horns of the bull from a distance of thirty feet or so. One roper received a huge ovation when he threw a loop in front of his own horse so large that he rode through it and then rolled it behind him, straight over in front of the bull in time to noose it, all in one fluid motion. I'd never seen anything like that. Skip commented, "Wow! I wonder how many times he had to practice *that* to get it to work."

We applauded until our hands hurt, riders, ropers, bullfighters, amateurs who got lucky, even the little boy in the big sombrero who stood alone in the center of the ring to sing the national anthem. We applauded the bulls, too, huge, snorting, slobbering creatures with loose, floppy skin, bucking and charging gamely until they were tired (but rarely hurt). We applauded the queen and her court in their colorful costumes. We even applauded Arepa when he commandeered the microphone to make a lame, unnecessary speech after the little boy sang. Everything was wonderful and colorful to us *Norteamericanos* who were fortunate enough to be there at the big *Fiesta de Nosara*.

179

We heard later that someone had absconded with the money collected for the ambulance. Then we heard that the money was recovered. We never found out who the culprits were or even if they were apprehended. Truth is, we never learned if any of the foregoing tales were true. The only thing we know for certain is that Nosara does have an ambulance, described in an earlier chapter as a hard-riding old four-wheel-drive Toyota with worn tires, itself capable of causing internal injuries on those rough jungle roads.

During the next hiatus from any momentous activity, Skip enjoyed a spider bite on the right side of his abdomen, which caused a tingling numbness that increased and decreased in cycles until after we returned home. The sensations never crossed the median line of his abdomen, which he interpreted as a sign that the poison had affected the nervous system. But the symptoms apparently never became painful or severe enough to frighten him into going to a doctor, although he discussed it with me. (Jack and Helen had by this time departed.) I think Skip really hated to take the time.

He also endured a bee sting during this period, which he said was more painful but less puzzling than the spider bite. Its effects disappeared in two or three days instead of lasting for weeks. He observes such things as if he were his own guinea pig.

Antonio's fling with Betty had been progressing for over a month. Betty would appear at Antonio's side as he painted the fence, or we would see them together at the beach. She would bring him a snack during work hours, watching adoringly as he ate. Both would grin happily when we came upon them together.

Then, about midseason, Chini returned, pregnant. She got off the bus and went to Antonio's house as if nothing had happened. She claimed that the baby was Antonio's. We had our doubts, but Antonio had been wanting a baby so badly that he just decided to accept it.

Antonio borrowed money from Martha to buy his appliances back and then asked Skip to haul them home in the jeep. Skip said, ''Thank goodness they have small appliances here. We had to carry them out of the damnedest places.''

We heard through the grapevine that Antonio's *casa* had become a love nest again; he and Chini were behaving like honeymooners. In a small village in the tropics, little privacy exists. Neighbors know what is going on, and gossip is cherished. But what about Betty? There were unconfirmed rumors that Betty was pregnant. Where would it all lead?

Betty's father showed up one morning to have a talk with Antonio. We could see them down near the gate looking serious, gesturing and debating. We never learned what was said, but we seldom saw Betty after that, and never with Antonio. Chini had obviously reclaimed her position with Antonio.

We later learned, to our relief and probably more so to Antonio's, that Betty was not pregnant. That knowledge closed this chapter of Antonio's life nicely, it seemed.

The latest gossip reported that flights to the local airport had been suspended because the fences had been cut and some young Ticos were racing motorcycles on the strip. After all, it was the only pavement around. Our development manager, Michael Sandweg, along with Arepa as Nosara's representative, had to meet with officials from the civil aviation board and convince them that such atrocious behavior would cease. Meanwhile, the nearest access to air transportation was the dirt strip at Carillo, and the inconvenience cost Nosara some tourist dollars as well as difficulty transporting guests in and out.

Rumors flew about the cost of meeting the aviation board's demands and how long we would be without our air connection to the outside world. But within a week and a half the commuter planes were making their approach passes over Martha's bungalow and the jungled hill behind it to bring her guests on time. Well, as close to on time as it gets in Costa Rica. The gringo association kicked in some money to help the town rebuild the fence and hire a part-time guard. The guard was supposed to chase kids and cattle off the runway prior to arrival time, but we rarely saw it happen. Things were back to normal.

It was getting late in the season, so Martha decided she had better call another beach party before everyone pulled out. She passed the word to everyone she saw at the beach and at the store, asking those to relay the message to others. The jungle grapevine really works here.

Martha began to plan her beach party food, which generally turned out to be the same as last time and the time before and the time before that. Then she commented, ''I know what Beverly will bring. She always brings deviled eggs. And Bob Bauer brings that potato salad made from plantains. He's always trying those jungle recipes. But then I nearly always have a cake and potato salad.'' Then she laugh hilariously at herself, and we joined in.

We loaded the jeep and tried to arrive half an hour early in order to police the area, cover the concrete tables, and set up the torches. Most

A *ranchito* on the beach, provided by the Playas de Nosara Civic Association. A dandy place for a beach party.

folks brought portable chairs, table service, and their own drinks, plus a dish or two. The result reminded us of our family reunions, with a wonderful variety of homemade specialties, largely hors d'oeuvres, casseroles, salads, and desserts. People loved the opportunity to get together and chat, to meet newcomers and renew acquaintances. Gossip was reviewed for validity or maybe just for pleasure, depending on the personalities involved. Most paused to admire the sunset with nothing between the eye and that essential star but the empty ocean.

The Sweelys arrived in time for the big party, happily so, because they enjoy such gatherings immensely. Things were going well, nothing unusual happening, when Ginny Sweely grabbed me and said with subdued excitement, "Isn't that Woody Harrelson over there?"

I replied, "I don't know. It does look like him."

"Oh, it has to be!"

Skip chimed in, "I doubt it."

"Oh, I'm sure of it."

It was. He was visiting our next-door neighbors, the Hendersons, whose daughter had operated a yoga studio somewhere around Hollywood, we were told.

Many of the group pressed in to meet Woody, but we couldn't make ourselves do it. Skip later noticed a woman standing on the fringes with a baby and edged over to chat with her. Her name was Laura, and she appeared to be Asian-American. She was quiet, modest, very pleasant, and friendly. She turned out to be Woody's woman, so to speak, and inquired what there was to do around here.

After explaining our Nosara lifestyle, Skip moseyed back to me to report. We wondered what Laura's life must be like living in the shadow of a superstar, especially one with Woody's reputation for short-fused violence. We decided we wouldn't want to trade places, although she seemed to be doing all right.

We saw them occasionally after that, on the road or at a store or restaurant, and would smile and wave. Laura responded in kind, and Woody . . . maybe. We also followed the stories about Woody's escapades. He attacked a parked bus in Nosara because the driver failed to shut off the engine and Woody objected to the fumes. He beat on the side of the bus with a rock, broke a window, and cursed the driver. Woody failed to return a rental car on time, and the police were sent to retrieve it. He drove at dangerous speeds on the local roads, and so forth. Maybe it's his calling to relieve boredom wherever he goes. At any rate, we can't say we know them personally or even that the rumors are true, but we see them around and they may portend a change in the quiet nature of Nosara.

One morning as we were making the short drive to the beach we came upon an unusual sight: monkeys on the ground. They avoid much contact with the ground since they are more vulnerable there. We stopped and they retreated to a safer level, all except one. It was dead. Apparently it had jumped onto the electric wire overhead without letting go of the limb with its tail and had gotten electrocuted. Its family and companions were obviously agitated and distressed by its demise. The scene gave us pause, making us think of the fragility of life in the jungle, . . . anywhere. I thought of Chet, and I suppose the others did, too.

With the guests gone again, we watched from Martha's deck as the new crop of monkeys developed and practiced their acrobatics, an ongoing pleasure. Beneath them, an iguana had taken to getting a drink from the birdbath (a concrete pool in the ground). A couple of purple-black grackles tried to chase him away. He was a small dragon and had to be some three feet long, including his tremendous tail.

As the season became even drier, we saw an old one-eyed coatimundi daily. We called him Pete the Pizote and threw him all the table scraps. He obviously enjoyed cleaning off the melon rinds, smacking his lips over the sweet juices. We tried to get close-up photos of Pete, but he's pretty cautious. We had to be quiet and sneaky to get near enough for a good shot.

As people departed for the season, there was less disturbance in the tide pools, and Skip got to see a greater variety of underwater critters as he snorkeled. Today he caught a sea horse, hardly more than two inches long. He read that the males bear the young, a practice Martha and I strongly endorsed. It propels itself very awkwardly by small clicks of fins in the middle of its back. Pretty vulnerable, it seemed to me. He also saw a small octopus and watched it ease across the floor of the pool. When he touched it, he received a squirt of ink in the face. Using the ink as a blind and diversion, the octopus scooted abruptly about three feet away, where it attached to the side of a rock, enjoying near-perfect camouflage. Skip said if he hadn't been prepared for its sudden departure after the ink squirt, he would have missed it entirely.

We watched an osprey catch a fish. It hovered, then swooped, hitting the water with a splash. Getting airborne again is a challenge, and it struggled valiantly with the large fish to get free of the water. It held the fish in its talons, in line with its body, not crossways, as might be expected. This way of carrying the fish is streamlined, and the piercing talons apparently paralyze the fish, for it didn't struggle. Once aloft, the osprey hesitates in midair as it shakes the water from its feathers. It looks like it is shivering silver drops in the sunlight. Nature is endlessly fascinating to us; we are always learning something new.

Banners flying, pickup trucks carrying loads of people, and blaring loudspeakers shatter the peace of the jungle as they drive up and down the dusty road promoting political candidates. It's election time again, and Ticos take their brand of democracy seriously. In true Spanish style, Ticos often choose a candidate based upon family. Perhaps my grandfather hated the candidate's great-grandfather when he was vice president fifty years ago. That determines my choice; otherwise I might be considered a family traitor. Grandsons of political heroes of prior years have a strong edge over their opponents. Party affiliations play a part, but clearly secondary to family history and preferences.

Many homes fly the banner of one party or another. If the home is too small and humble, then a tall bamboo pole is erected to elevate the distinctive colors of the esteemed party. Individuals vehemently defend their candidates and vilify their opponents. Arepa told Skip that his pick, Castillo, with the green-and-white banner, would win easily. His strongest opponent was grandson to a politician who had been found to be crooked. No contest.

Arepa's candidate lost. Skip commented wryly, "Now I know how to pick a winner here."

On election day we visited the Esperanza schoolhouse, which served as election hall, same as our local elementary school at home. Many folks were hanging around wherever there was shade, sitting on a low wall, standing with arms folded or behind their backs, or leaning against a mango tree, all enjoying a holiday atmosphere. As usual, the event called for decking oneself out in colorful clothes, especially for the children, who were present in goodly numbers. Kids here learn by participation and observation.

Antonio was present and involved in the proceedings, as usual. He's a member of the school board and water committee as well, an active citizen despite the boyish behavior we observed so much. Probably we apply our cultural expectations inappropriately, even unfairly. It's difficult for us to see things as they do.

Antonio and another man showed us the process inside the schoolhouse. There was a committee of observers and overseers, much like what we encounter in our small-town elections. Voters entered and were noted by the committee, then dipped a thumb in ink to mark their ballot. The actual marking was completed behind a large cardboard refrigerator carton cut down one side to form a booth. Choices were made by carefully pressing the inked thumb beside the chosen name. The inked thumb prevented attempts at repeat voting, here or elsewhere, since it wouldn't wash off for a day or two.

The illiteracy problem was solved by party workers who made sure that those who couldn't read knew the position of their candidate's name on the ballot, such as first or third. Some rural folks were hauled in on trucks and then hung around to visit until someone headed back in their direction. We were watching democracy in action, and they obviously took pride in it.

Things then slowed down at Martha's, so we left early one morning to see if there was any turtle action at Ostional. The drive is always special, following the deserted back-country roads in the predawn darkness. We still expected it to be jacket-cool at this time of day, but it never

185

was. The temperature, even at 5:00 A.M. was usually in the low seventies, so shorts and T-shirts do fine. We carried a plastic two-liter Coke bottle filled with water, plus cameras and binoculars. The moon and stars were still fairly bright, and we passed horses and cattle here and there where pasture fences bordered the narrow dirt track. Now and then we saw a light in a little farmhouse where some *campesino* had risen for early chore duty. Later we passed a worker here or there walking or biking, probably to reach a job some distance from home.

Ostional seemed like a ghost town as we motored around the turn and then made a left past the dark, rustic buildings of the turtle research station. We parked the jeep and locked it as our eyes adjusted to the darkness. Martha led the way toward the beach on the well-used sandy path.

Out on the open beach we saw the first signs of dawn to our left. A fisherman already had a large fish lying on the sand, well back from the water line. From down the beach there was a horseman approaching. As he passed us, we saw that he was carrying an old burlap sack. That indicated that he was searching for turtle eggs, an age-old practice here, though now partially controlled by the government.

We headed on down the beach to look for turtles and soon came across tracks, but no turtles. As the sky lightened, we could see farther down the beach but were disappointed by the emptiness. The turtles had been here not long ago, leaving only their ATV-like tracks and mostly empty nests. Dozens of vultures scratched and pecked at the last fragments of eggs. Here and there a dog hunted for breakfast, but the pickings were slim.

Skip shot a few photographs of the picturesque scenes and of birds when he could get close enough. This was a good day for tiger herons and hawks, but not much else. We decided to leave and return earlier tomorrow, since the signs indicated that we were too late.

Precisely! We spotted turtles the next morning as soon as we stepped out onto the beach, even in the scant moonlight. We avoided using artificial light, since that is supposed to confuse the turtles. We were able to watch them ride the surf to shore, fight their way through the backwash, and struggle up the incline to get above the high-tide level, where they could lay their eggs without having them wash back into the sea. They dug holes awkwardly with their back flippers, a laborious process. Then they backed into the hole to expel large numbers of eggs, often a hundred,

A sea turtle at the Ostional Wildlife Preserve in the process of laying her eggs. Dogs, vultures, raccoons and people steal most of the eggs, but some are saved here by people dedicated to their preservation.

more or less. Finally they covered the eggs using their back flippers, again awkwardly, and made their exhausted retreat to the ocean.

The whole process may take upward of an hour, a vulnerable hour, since they are out of their element the whole time. We watched one as it was harassed by black vultures, which pecked at its eyes and neck, stealing eggs as they emerged, making life extremely miserable for her. I couldn't resist running to her and chasing the vultures away. Then I saw that her right eye was hanging out of its socket, dangling grotesquely on a thread of tissue. Her carapace had been partly crushed, a big dent in her left side, probably from hitting a reef on her way in through the surf. The poor old girl was in terrible shape. I stayed until she completed her egg laying and returned to the water, with barely enough energy to make it. But those vultures merely waited until I left to finish their raid on her nest. I'm sure not an egg remained by the time we were halfway back to Nosara. Nature is pitiless.

When we ambled over the high path to Martha's porch for breakfast one morning, Martha said, "I don't know what was going on last night, but there were a lot of chomping and tearing noises that sounded like they were just outside my bedroom. What could it be? I don't think I was dreaming.''

Skip immediately headed down the lower path to the banana patch and called back, "You weren't dreaming, Martha! The neighbor's cows got into the bananas and tore the stalks all to shreds.''

As he came back up the path, he said to us as we leaned over the porch rail, "Well, we won't need to thin the banana stalks this year. We won't have to fertilize it, either. The cows left plenty of evidence.''

Martha replied with a worried look, "Do you think you can fix the fence so they won't come back in? Good Heavens, I'll never get any sleep the way it was last night!''

Skip promised to fix the fence after breakfast. Fortunately, Antonio arrived for work that morning and helped him. They got awfully dirty and sweaty working on that hillside fence, not to mention scratched and bleeding from the barb wire and thorns. Those Brahma cattle must have pretty tough hides, because it doesn't seem to bother them.

The local monkey troop has increased to twenty. They must be getting enough moisture from the shoots and blossoms they eat, for they never come down to the birdbath to drink even in the dry weather. The coatimundi is still coming to drink regularly, and an armadillo has also begun frequenting our little oasis as the season becomes drier. It seems such a stupid creature, rustling noisily down the bank to the low wall along the path, where it just stumbles over the edge and falls helter skelter into the pathway. Then, without any sign of consternation or pause, it continues on over to the birdbath.

While resting and reading in the hammock after lunch, Skip heard some terrible growling and crackling of brush behind our house. He hopped up and sneaked across the porch to see what was happening. There, not ten feet from the house, were a pair of male coatimundis having a tussle, probably over territory. After a snarling battle in the undergrowth, one chased the other up a tree, where they rested and cussed at each other. Then they tore off again, up and down the trees, until they disappeared into the jungle. Such spontaneous happenings as this made us love our proximity to the jungle. We never knew what was coming next.

The beach was littered with dime-sized jellyfish for a couple of days this week. They were brilliant blue and had stringy appendages, so thin as to be nearly invisible, two or three inches long around their perimeters. Kathy Benish and I received minor stings on our arms while soaking in the tide pools. They left small pink welts, especially on our softer areas. We therefore spent more time walking and beachcombing. Skip counted over fifty of the little blue biting buggers in one space of about twenty paces. We were happy when they disappeared, however interesting they had been. We did find a huge stingray and a baby one as we walked. They were dead on the beach, and the large one was over six feet long. Its stinger was huge, bigger than my index finger.

We drove around by the post office to check our mail, only to find that they had closed again in order to ride the bus to Nicoya for their paychecks. Someone must be stealing mail again. Martha was disappointed at getting no letters. Darn it!

March 4, 1994, brought an unforgettable scene to Guiones Beach. As we walked from Baker's Landing toward our favorite tide pools, we began to notice dead fish strung along the high-tide line. The farther we went, the more fish we saw, so we went on past the pools toward Guiones Village. The increase in the numbers of dead fish continued until there was a solid line of them. The line of fish grew wider until it reached six feet or so at places and nearly a foot deep, with fish at the center. Vultures and pelicans were circling all about. Some already sat, sated, in nearby trees or on the beach near the trees. They had probably been the first on the scene.

We were now a mile from where we had begun to see them. They varied from less than eight to over ten inches long and were attractive, graceful fish with deep blue backs. Ahead we began to see people and activity. Ticos were gathering fish into plastic bags and burlap bags. Some had wheelbarrows full and were struggling through the sand, perspiring profusely. Two trucks were being loaded with fish near the access road. There were tons of fish, only a small portion of which would be gathered and used. The poorer families would now have plenty to eat for a while.

Near the few houses comprising the village of Guiones, we came upon Antonio, grinning widely. He giggled boyishly as he made a great show of pretending to wipe his fish-smeared hands on us and explained to Skip that the doctor who owned a summer home there had hired him and a friend to haul fish away and burn them.

Skip asked, "How do you burn fish?"

Antonio explained with a shrug, "Use gasoline or kerosene."

We thought that a waste, but then we didn't have a home right next to tons of soon-to-be-rotting fish.

189

Tons of fish scattered along Guiones Beach, possibly chased there by larger fish feeding on them at high tide. A party atmosphere prevails as local folks share fish with neighbors, friends, and relatives, especially the elderly and needy.

Antonio was always happy to be in the midst of the action and was obviously pleased that we had seen him there, playing an important role as usual. He couldn't fully explain, though, why the fish had seemingly committed suicide. Perhaps a change in wind or tide had left them high and dry, or maybe a large collection of game fish had chased them up on the beach. Possibly it was a combination of events that had caused it. No one had a single satisfactory explanation. We continued to ponder the phenomenon.

Other Ticos were taking advantage of the game fish that had followed this bountiful migration, using the small fish for bait to catch large jacks and rooster fish. They already had several ten-to-twenty pounders tossed out on the shore. Skip photographed a pair of small boys lugging a single large fish. They posed with huge smiles for the picture. All in all, it was an unusual and magnificent scene. We felt greatly privileged to be there.

The next excitement came with Joyce and Patrick Lebel, a younger couple, Canadians from Montreal, who reported that a young German woman had been raped on the beach at gunpoint. This news created a stir and wringing of hands in the community, naturally. Patrick reported the incident, but law enforcement in the Nosara area left a lot to be desired. No one was apprehended, and the investigation didn't seem very extensive. In fact, rape seemed not to be taken as seriously in Costa Rica as in the States, though that may be different in the urban areas.

During the second week of March, workers arrived to replace the floors in the guest cabinas. The old wooden floors were becoming unsafe due to rot and termite damage, and Chet had arranged for their replacement during his final visit. After the workmen tore the old floors out and went home for the day, I got the shovel out of the bodega and climbed down into the newly opened area to dig for artifacts. I had heard Chet tell of rumors about that being an old burial ground, and this seemed a unique opportunity to check it out. I was after treasure!

Skip and Antonio apparently thought it was the most hilarious thing they had ever seen, because they stood in the doorways looking down upon my labors, grinning and haw-hawing with great glee as I dug and sweated.

My labors went for naught; I found absolutely nothing. I emerged dirty and drenched with sweat, though well photographed for posterity. If there ever were any artifacts, they either had been removed before my time or were deeper than I was prepared to go. More than likely the rumors were just that: rumors.

That night, as I tried to rest my weary body, there arose a clatter outside our bedroom window. It stopped. Then it began again and changed locations. Skip said, "What the hell is that?" as he dragged himself out of bed, slipped his feet into his sandals, and grabbed the flashlight.

I followed him outside, where we found an odd sight in the beam of our rechargeable flashlight. There was an armadillo—well, half an armadillo—protruding from a large, four-pound-size, peanut butter can that we had set out for the birds to clean. He had thrust his head into the can, then apparently developed a lust for the taste of peanut butter, for he had shoved his whole front half into the can with great force. His segmented shell-like covering locked tightly into the seam of the can where the top had been removed with a can opener.

The clatter that had awakened us resulted from the armadillo's panicked attempts to free himself, which of course only drove the can onto his shell more tightly. Only his back end protruded, so he blindly bounced himself into foundation walls, fence posts, and trees until he was nearly exhausted.

Skip grabbed him by the tail, avoiding his formidable digging claws, and tried to extricate the poor creature while I held the flashlight. The can was so tight that Skip could only get his fingernails under the rim, not enough grip to budge it in the least. It seemed we had found the perfect armadillo trap.

He handed the armadillo to me to hold while he took the flashlight and jogged over the high path to the bodega to get the tin snips. I stood there in the pale moonlight, holding the poor animal by its scaly tail as its hind feet slowly treaded the air. I thought, *Who would believe what I'm doing right now, in the middle of the night?*

The smelly critter was becoming heavy, but Skip soon returned with the snips. It's a good thing that the snips were small, because even so he had to push hard to get the tip between the can and the shell. Once that was accomplished, the can cut easily. When it fell off, Skip released the tail, and that armadillo hit the ground running. He circled us with his ears laid back, fast as a rabbit. We had never seen an armadillo move so fast. We could barely follow him with the flashlight beam as he recovered his bearings and tore into the jungle. We stood there in the darkness in our scanty sleeping attire and laughed quietly at yet another magical moment in the jungle. We hugged and then returned to bed, still smiling.

The beach, always changing, was thick with sand dollars today. There were big old ones, nearly four inches across, and smaller ones, still alive just under the wet sand. The live ones show a distinctive mark on the surface of the sand, which allows those who know the secret to find hundreds. Trouble is, who would want them? They average only two inches across and stink terribly until fully dry.

As we walked and marveled at nature's abundance, we came upon our friend Kathy Benish and stopped to chat. She invited us to their house for movie night and popcorn, something of a tradition when things got quiet in the development.

That night's movie was *City Slickers,* the Billy Crystal comedy, and it suited our mood. We laughed and added some of our own comedy, enjoying one another's company immensely. Other than an occasional video movie, we lived without television for our three months in the jungle. The more important thing, though, was how these get-togethers filled a social hunger that seemed to develop when we were away from home this long.

Kathy and Bob served fresh lemonade, made from their own fruit, and bowls of hot, buttered popcorn, which is often all Bob has for his final meal of the day. Of course, for us, it was in addition to our dinner, creating a concern for waistlines.

Evening visits like "movie nights" are about the only times we drive after dark, allowing us to occasionally see some of the more nocturnal animals. This time we lucked into seeing a deer, a first for us. We had been told that deer abounded in the area, that they were small, nocturnal, and shy. Antonio had told Skip that the local men often poached them for food. Now we were finally seeing one for ourselves, and it was definitely small compared with our Pennsylvania deer. It reminded us of the Florida Key deer, except perhaps a bit larger, but not much. Antonio had said that the bucks were larger, which would be typical. This was apparently a doe, and she quickly faded into the jungle.

As we did the shopping at the Super la Paloma, we bumped into our old friend Mary Yost. Her face was badly lacerated and swollen. Skip blurted out, "Oh, Mary, were you in a wreck?"

Mary told us she had been walking her dog, Mr. Yost, early the prior day when she had caught her foot on a tree root and fallen flat on her face. Later that same day we came upon her, snorkeling in her favorite tide pool. Skip commented admiringly, "She is one tough cookie." He and Mary enjoyed snorkeling together, and he has learned much reef lore from her.

The animals seemed to be more active this week. Besides the troop of monkeys and the armadillos, we noticed coatimundis sneaking mangoes from the big tree that hangs over the jeep. I predicted a siege of strong winds because of this. Skip laughs at my weather prognostications, and I tell him I learned it from my dad, who worked for years on the Pennsylvania Turnpike, besides farming.

I had the last laugh this time, because the winds blew that night and the next two nights as well. Actually, it's not funny, because I had to clean the whole house again. With so much screened area and leaky louvered windows, I can literally track Skip across the floors. A strong wind demands at least one whole day of housecleaning.

Saturdays required early rising in order to compete for the better quality fresh fruits and veggies at the store. We bought them directly from Orlando's truck as it was unloaded at a little plank stand beside La Paloma. Martha took a number, and when it was her turn she said, "*Tres tomates.*" Three tomatoes were handed down from the canvas-covered

Isuzu truck and placed in front of Martha on the waist-high plank. Then Martha said, "*Lechuga, grande*," and a large head of lettuce appeared from the depths of the blue truck. Martha inspected it and shrugged; "Their lettuce is never very good, is it?" Then, "*Sandia, grande*," and a watermelon was relayed to the plank, passed on for weighing, then returned. The process was repeated, occasionally requiring an intermediate interpretation from Skip or some other bystander when Martha's vegetable Spanish failed her. Once in a while she used the wrong word and laughed hilariously when she got a radish instead of a cucumber, or some other such confusion. The Tico clerks grinned and patiently rectified the mistake.

Finally the bill was tallied, and Martha dug into the special purse harboring our grocery kitty as Skip began lugging the heavily stretched plastic *bolsas* to the jeep. We all enjoyed the friendly smiles and greetings that accompanied "veggie mornings," in spite of the early hour. Gossip, if there happened to be anything new, was passed around during the process. By the time we had our purchases loaded, the store was open, and we picked up a few items, this time some toilet paper and rum and Coke. The tropical jungle is no place to run out of important basics.

The gossip item for the day was that the *National Enquirer* had called the Gilded Iguana to get the scoop on Woody Harrelson and the bus incident. We had heard that he was required to pay for the damage he did with the rock that day in front of the Bamboo Bar, but no more news since that. Jan Buferd, owner and manager of the Iguana, supposedly had told them that she knew nothing about it, thereby gaining the approval of most of the community for keeping Nosara out of the "slime-light."

It's generally pretty quiet during our happy hour on Martha's back deck, overlooking the birdbath. This evening it was noisy. Monkeys were howling, *chachalakas* were calling, and parrots were arguing noisily as they zigzagged overhead. That alone wouldn't be considered unduly noisy, but the neighbor boys added to it with a larger-than-usual soccer game immediately beyond the fence, and one of Franco's daughters had a baby who was unhappy about something, for it was crying lustily. This was no evening for reading; there was too much going on to allow us to concentrate. Actually, it was interesting to try to sort out all the different sounds.

An oil palm in front of Martha's main porch held a huge cluster of palm nuts this year. As they ripened, they drew the attention of numerous parrots, squirrels, and iguanas. As we worked around the kitchen and the dining table on the porch, we continually checked to see what was happening on the palm tree. Generally there was one kind of critter or another struggling to loosen a nut, about the size of a Brazil nut, but without the hard shell. Once in a while they would clash briefly and we would hear a squawk or chatter and quickly look up, but mostly it was a peaceful co-existence.

Car problems. Drat. We rely on the old jeep for transportation to the store, the beach, the telephone and post office, and to visit friends, and any problem with it is a minor crisis. This time we noticed steam when we stopped at the store, and Skip found a hole in the radiator where a stone had kicked up from the road and punctured it. He said it was pretty large to be fixed by that old standby, a can of Stop-Leak, but that's the first step. After checking a couple of places, we found a can at Gerry's hardware store. Skip loves that store, and Gerry even speaks English. The Stop-Leak worked! By the time we reached home, the trickle had stopped. Skip topped up the water, saying, "I sure hope that holds on our trip back to San Jose." Another crisis solved, at least for now.

On the way home from Nosara we stopped for a large snake in the roadway. Skip said it was a rainbow boa, like the one the bus had run over a couple of years ago. It has a base pattern of pale gray shapes overlaid with iridescent rose, which flashes bits of violet and other colors as it changes position relative to the eye and the source of light. It is truly a beautiful serpent and beneficial as well, dieting largely on rodents, according to our readings.

How exciting! Another beach wedding has been announced, this time for the daughter of our good friends Jim and Mary Rasmussen. Their house fronts right on the beach, a wonderful setting for a wedding. It is scheduled for late afternoon, with a reception before the service, allowing the nuptials to be concluded just at sunset.

Martha was excited, energized by the idea that she might play some part in the preparations. She suggested several possible roles she might fulfill and finally negotiated the duty of chief ice supplier, which she attacked with a vengeance. She added the job of supplying lemons and limes for the drinks and then insisted upon their using her refrigerators for cooling the soft drinks. She decided she would prepare an extra appetizer or two and just sneak them in. She was supremely happy as she involved herself in the preparations, babbling conjectures about who would be invited and where the out-of-town guests would stay, wishing that she might put up a few of them in her guest rooms.

Disappointingly, I caught a dose of *el grippe* the day before the big event, probably from my chief infector, Antonio, and was unable to even consider attending the wedding. Skip and Martha loaded the jeep with Martha's contributions to the big celebration, and off they went, Martha in her best sandals and tropical dress and Skip in his best white shorts and Hawaiian shirt, as I glumly watched.

Skip gave me a thorough run-down on the festivities after they returned. He began, naturally, with how drop-dead gorgeous the bride was, a glowing California blonde with figure to match. The groom was dark and handsome, though not tall. They were both very outgoing, welcoming the guests to the flower-bedecked home as though all were family. Numerous Ticos had been invited as well as many of the gringo residents of the development, although complete intermingling is always difficult due to the language barrier.

Everyone enjoyed drinks and *bocas* and socializing until time for the ceremony, when Roger led the way to the beach. He stood with his back to the ocean, facing the bride and groom, who were backed up by a large semicircle of family and guests, the red-orange sun low over the Pacific beyond his left shoulder. It was low tide and the breakers rolled in unthreateningly beyond Roger's bare feet as he intoned the rites of marriage. The sky was clear, the weather warm—good omens for a wedding?

Skip laughed as he told me of the surprise ending. After the groom kissed the bride in true Hollywood style, they both suddenly stripped off their clothing to reveal—what? Swimsuits! They ran straight into the surf and "took the plunge"—a rather apt metaphor, don't you think?

After more eating and socializing, Skip and Martha returned to find me asleep in bed, the best place to be with the flu. The next day I enviously pumped the foregoing report from Skip, with a woman's point of view provided by Martha. Happily, Skip had some videotape footage of the event for me to see after we returned home and had access to a television set. We've attended many weddings, but those in Costa Rica have certainly provided us with unique and special memories.

196

15

1995, Martha and Friends

Good friends joined us for the trip to Costa Rica this year. We had mentioned earlier that Louise Lytle had long been departmental secretary for Chet and Skip at Shippensburg University; additionally, she handled the Easteps' household business when they were away, often six months out of a year. Her husband, Glenn, checked on the Easteps' house and picked up their mail during those prolonged absences as well. This year the Lytles had accepted Martha's invitation to Nosara but could get away for only two weeks because of the responsibilities of caring for Louise's aging mother.

Due to our travel agent's efforts to obtain the cheapest airplane tickets, we were routed through Mexico City, strange as it may seem. This put us in our hotel in San José about 2:00 A.M., after a long time in the air, plus over an hour on the ground in Mexico City. In addition, the rules changed in Mexico and smoking was permitted. Skip and I were seated in the very last nonsmoking row, and the couple behind us smoked like fiends. I was nearly sick by the time we deplaned in San José. We should have complained and requested a seating change, but that's not our nature, so we endured it. Fortunately, Glenn and Louise were seated farther forward, away from the smoke.

Martha and a longtime friend, Jane Bauer, had flown another airline and were already at the hotel, asleep by the time we arrived. Martha, being well rested, had us up for an early breakfast, then dragged us off for an active day of shopping and business stops. Francisco Vives drove us around San José in the old jeep.

It was always interesting to watch Martha's guests negotiate the jeep. The jeep was pretty basic, showing some rust, and with a high step from the ground to get your foot inside. Jane, nearly eighty years old and not too tall to begin with, had some problems walking, much less climbing. Her pure white hair was thinning, but she kept herself immaculate and well dressed. She seemed somehow out of place struggling into the

Chipper, Jane and Martha with Martha's beloved "jeep," a well-used Toyota Land Cruiser.

rusty, often-dirty work vehicle, even with the always-ready hand that Skip gallantly offers. Martha herself, a year older, buxom, dark-haired, and with regal bearing, struggled with the climb into the back of the jeep, despite her never-say-die independence. I guess they see it as part of a great exotic adventure.

Again we marveled about the difference from yesterday's world; we sweated under a bright sun in a crowded city, surrounded by tall, forested mountains. The temperature was only in the upper seventies, but we had just arrived from our usual cold, dull January weather. Despite the air pollution from myriad buses and cars, it seemed a wonderful improvement.

Skip couldn't ignore the pretty, well-dressed senoritas as they strutted to work or did their shopping. Francisco pointed out an especially eye-catching young lady wearing a supershort skirt, and the men paused for a moment's silence to honor her presence. Her skirt was shorter in the rear than even she realized, I supposed, revealing things not usually revealed. Wow! We all grinned, then went on, driven by Martha's heavy schedule. I'm sure the men felt their lives had been somehow enriched.

Bedtime came early that night. Even Martha was in bed by 9:00 P.M., and the rest of us felt sleep-deprived after our long flights the night before. We were relieved that we didn't have to play games that evening, since we had to hit the road early the next morning.

Glenn and Skip loaded the jeep, and I mean loaded! It was crammed full of luggage, groceries, household items, and such, behind the front seats, with some more tied on top. They drove the jeep while we four women took a taxi to the Alfaro station and boarded the bus for Nosara. The men got a head start, but the bus caught them before we reached the Tempisque Ferry. We waved as we passed them, and they tooted the horn at us. We caught the same ferry and sat together during the crossing to admire the scenery.

They got a head start off the ferry, only to have us pass them again before we reached Nicoya. We arrived at Casa de las Flores first, where Antonio was waiting to help us open the house, and were on the porch when the men drove in. Then we worked like beavers to get beds ready and have something to eat by sunset. No time to prepare for company; they were with us. We were back in the jungle for another season.

We all worked hard for the next two days to get things livable, but the third day we headed for the beach. Any longer and Martha would have had a rebellion on her hands. Suddenly all the travel hassles and work felt worthwhile. This scene of sun, beach, and ocean made up for it all, and then some. What a relief! After this point, we gave priority to the beach and squeezed our chores into the remaining time, at least for the two weeks that the Lytles remained with us.

During one of our excursions to Nosara Village that first week, we heard of the death of a fourteen-year-old Tico who was killed when a large wave knocked him off a rock where he was fishing, not far from the hotel. Those waves sweep in from the open Pacific with great force, and they battered him to death against the rocks. He came from a well-respected family, and the whole community was sobered by his death. The phrase "there but for the grace of God go I" struck home, for Skip, Antonio, and Will Scarlet had fished from those rocks, along with many others. They had all probably slipped, too, at one time or another but had simply been more fortunate. I know I had dabbed antiseptic on numerous scrapes on Skip's legs derived from being battered against rocks while fishing. He had told me of a few narrow escapes, and I suspect it happens more often than they admit.

The funeral was a sad one, as is always true when elders have to bury their children. We watched the long line following the pallbearers, the whole procession on foot, as they trod the low road to the little cemetery just out of reach of high tide in the middle of our main beach. We stopped by the lonely gravesite at a later time to pay our respects and, in return, feel humbled by our place in the scheme of things.

Martha soon had us playing cards in the evenings, reveling in her games. Since there were six of us, she could organize her favorite game, Pennies from Heaven, making great rituals out of mixing and dealing the required five decks of cards. At one point during the game she became incensed because I was coaching Louise, a beginner at the game, too much for her liking. She protested, "Well, if Louise does what you tell her, I won't be able to get *my* pennies!"

Jane added, "Yes, Chipper, keep your mouth shut."

I know I should be above such silliness, but still, my feelings were hurt, partly because Louise was made to feel stupid and partly because I was put in my place as a sort of second-class citizen. Louise refused to play that particular game anymore, and our spirits were dampened for a while. We were pretty used to heeding and even anticipating Martha's wishes, but sometimes I got "full up."

Two days later Jane and I were fastening up the clothesline back of the main house when Martha came striding out of the back door saying, "No, no, no! You're putting it up backward. That end goes over there on the bodega. Then you tie *this* end over here at the guest house."

We dutifully reversed the rope, end for end. It certainly wouldn't do to have the clothesline backward. This time Jane was on the receiving end, too, but maybe because it was still morning and we were in good spirits we were able to just grin conspiratorially at each other like school-girls when Martha returned to the kitchen.

A few minutes later, as we proceeded to hang the laundry, Martha burst onto the scene again, regaling us about further deficits in our laundry-hanging skills. Some items were upside down and some were reversed, front to back. Some items had to be on the left end of the line and others on the right. When Martha again returned to the kitchen, Jane and I discussed our dire lack of clothes-hanging accomplishment. Somehow our mothers had apparently omitted a crucial part of our education in the finer points of laundering.

Later that day we made a run to Nosara for some needed groceries and stopped to pick up a young woman who was hiking in the dust along the road. She was clad like a streetwalker and had a tough sort of beauty and a demeanor to go with it. She told us in accented English that she was from France. We never saw her again, but we did get to tease the guys about the type of hitchhikers they stop for. Indeed, we do meet some interesting types here.

The Lytles' two weeks of sunning, swimming, and snorkeling passed all too quickly, and soon Skip and I were driving them to the Alfaro bus stop in Nosara. We got to hear the church bells ring while we waited for the bus, which started us on a discussion of the time we had shipping our old bell down here. It also reminded us that the church dedication was imminent, finally about to really happen. We received fierce hugs from our friends as they prepared to climb on board for the long, hard ride back to San José.

The dedication of the church was described in chapter 9, but the morning leading up to it had its own interesting moments. As I hung the laundry, by now with minimal interruption, I watched one of those committee-designed squirrels build a nest not far uphill from the house. It used leaves that it had nipped from the tree to tuck carefully into a fork in the limbs until it had a nice, round, compact home. Somehow the nest holds together as the squirrel crawls completely inside, where it will later hide its babies. Occasionally a windstorm destroys one of these nests, but not often. I don't see how in the world such a delicate-looking structure can survive the gales we regularly experience here.

A little later I saw a tarantula, dark and hairy, looking forever more menacing than it really is. He went his way and I went mine. Then the *chachalakas* crossed above the house, just inside the edge of the jungle, squawking as though in competition for a raucousness prize. I absolutely love days like this in the jungle.

We left for the big dedication ceremony late that morning and found the village crowded with buses, trucks, cars, and people. We had to park at some distance from the church and walk in the hot sun, only to find the church not only filled but also totally surrounded by interested visitors. We pushed in close enough to see inside but then backed off to allow others in. Martha was offered a seat inside, and we encouraged her to take advantage of it; she deserved it.

After the great fiesta that followed the dedication, we returned home, too full to even think of supper. Martha was on cloud nine anyway and, despite her usually voracious appetite, was content with a few *bocas* and some games. We had to play games later than usual that night in order

201

to get her calmed down. Even so, she told us the next morning that she had difficulty sleeping, with reruns of the dedication flitting through her head.

Soon after dedication day, Martha announced that she wanted to drive to Nicoya to go to the bank. That drive again! Once we reached the bank it took over two hours to transact her business. But we made the most of the day by visiting Albert and Nora Muller and having lunch at the Restaurant Nicoya.

After lunch Martha remembered that Antonio needed some cough syrup. When she learned the price of it at the drugstore, she decided that Jane and I should help pay for it. That puzzled us, but we cooperated. We also bought a watermelon and some cantaloupes from a street vendor before heading back toward Nosara.

On the way home, we rounded a sharp bend to find the Alfaro bus swinging across our lane, nearly broadside to us. Skip jammed on the so-so brakes, sliding in the loose gravel of the dirt road. The bus went on across our lane to enter a pull-off on our side of the road, allowing us to coast safely on through, albeit scared out of our wits. It is always a relief to make it back home in that old jeep.

Kathy and Bob Benish stopped by to chat and see if we were getting settled in satisfactorily. As we sat on Martha's porch sipping iced tea, the subject came up of the boy who had drowned while fishing. They told us that the boy's family and some close friends had been conducting a seance on the beach near the mouth of the river, trying to contact his spirit, even hoping to get him to come back. This had been going on for ten days, and they had carried chairs from the church to sit on out near the water since they had been spending so much time there.

His parents were apparently feeling a great deal of remorse for never having married, something for which their son had often wished. Now it was rumored that the boy's mother was nearly hysterical and the whole family was upset, grasping at straws, such as the seance idea. Finally, as their grief gradually subsided, they had Father Victor, the priest at the new church, unite them in the eyes of God. This apparently provided them with a measure of peace, for thereafter we heard no more about it.

We had noticed a large new *ranchito* being constructed in a hollow to the left of the main road on our way to Nosara. Skip marveled at the way the workmen climbed the long poles that they used as rafters, as high as twenty-five or thirty feet above the ground, to tie on other poles and then thatch them with palm fronds.

Martha asked, "Why do they go so high?"

Skip replied, glancing out the window as he steered the jeep, "For ventilation, I guess. The hot air probably draws up through the thatch similar to smoke up a chimney."

Then we soon noticed that they had stopped work on the *ranchito*. We puzzled over it but accepted it as inconsequential, until George Miller told us that one of the young men who had been working on the structure had fallen to his death from those very high poles that we had discussed only a few days earlier. We hated to hear that. Death comes so easily here.

About a week later we saw that the *ranchito* was demolished, totally torn down. We mentioned it and let it pass. Then, after another week or so, another structure was begun, very similar to the first. A different group of workmen went on to complete the *ranchito*, a very attractive one, tall and graceful as the first. Someone told us that the Tico workers refused to complete a *ranchito* that had killed a man; that one had to be totally removed, in spite of the waste of good materials. We wondered: *How much do we really know these people? How much do we falsely presume their beliefs to be similar to ours? How many other of our presumptions are erroneous?*

One evening we left Martha's driveway, turned left on the dirt road through Esperanza, went another three miles to the village of Garza (Heron), and pulled off at a little inn and beach restaurant called Casa Pacifica. The place is owned by George Miller, Martha's friend from near Harrisburg, but is operated by Bert and Paulina, a tall, beautiful young couple from the Netherlands.

We were ushered to a table set directly in the sand on the beach, under some almond trees. We sat there enjoying gourmet food within fifty feet of the soft surf of Garza Bay as the sun set over the Pacific. A few fishing boats and sailboats rocked easily out on the bay. A fisherman slipped over the side of his boat and swam ashore. The scene rivaled anything in a Hawaiian tour promotional, and the price of the meal was less than ten dollars each, all fresh seafood or chicken, salads, and fruit. (We usually have our rum and Coke on Martha's deck before leaving home, so we can watch the birds and mammals. Besides, it's much cheaper, and stretches the evening out longer.)

Around dusk a flock of birds flew into the trees overhead, clucking and chattering noisily. Except for Jane, we thought it fascinating, but Jane was ready to panic and run for cover. She has a phobia where birds are concerned, but we were able to calm her, and the birds cooperated by quieting down very soon, as darkness settled in.

We sang some old songs on the way home, feeling contented and at peace with the world, as well as fortunate to be here. Skip guided Jane up the pathway with a flashlight. Her vision is diminishing, especially in poor light. Martha required us to play games to complete the evening, so we proceeded directly to the game room, where we found a scorpion awaiting us. Jane was ready to do an about-face, but Skip stomped it and reassured her that she would be safe.

The game for the night was Rummikub, which requires matching tiles by colors and numbers in certain ways. Each player is to select fourteen tiles to begin, and winning requires getting rid of them. Jane was winning steadily this evening, causing Martha to grump about her luck and even intimate that we should switch to a different game. (Martha does hate to lose too much.) We kept commenting on Jane's good fortune, whereupon Jane stated emphatically, her thin white hair glowing above her sun-reddened face, "Oh, this is my game! I always was good at Rummikub."

Skip, becoming suspicious, watched a bit more closely as we drew our next round of tiles and then exclaimed, mischieviously, "Martha, look there! Jane only took seven tiles instead of fourteen. No wonder she's been beating you!"

Martha was struck nearly speechless and spluttered, "Why, Jane! You know better than that! You've had only half as many tiles as us to get rid of. . . . no wonder you've been winning . . . Good Heavens!"

Another hot afternoon as we puttered along at our chores we noticed Martha and Jane playing various types of solitaire in a competitive manner. As we prepared dinner that evening I asked Martha how the competition had gone. She explained confidentially that Jane had been cheating a little, so she had to cheat a little to stay even. These old gals play hardball.

The next day Joyce Lebel, our lively, jovial tennis companion from Montreal, came for lunch. She brought her guitar and entertained us after lunch with some truly fine music. After her fingers tired, she cajoled Skip into playing her guitar for a singalong, and we had a fine time. George Miller's companion, LaRue Snyder, had joined us as well, and Martha asked her for a haircut after the festivities were over. Such little diversions add spice to our jungle routine.

The next time we headed to Nosara for groceries, we stopped to pick up LaRue. She came out and asked Skip to come into the house to see what kind of animal had invaded her bathroom. Of course Skip was delighted to see if it might be something new to him, and I was equally interested.

Behind her commode we found the cutest little critter with large round, shiny eyes and soft reddish-brown fur peeping fearfully at us. We had never seen this kind of animal before, and racked our brains to recall any pictures or readings that might apply, all to no avail. Also, we had no idea if it might attack or even merely bite in self-defense, so I cautioned Skip to be careful, as did LaRue.

He found a bucket and broom outside the house that he thought might do the trick and soon had the frightened little thing in the bucket. He covered the bucket with the broom and took the animal outside to release it. The animal immediately scrambled up the nearest tree, a rather small one, and wrapped its legs tightly around the slim trunk. It appeared to go into a terror-induced trance, for it never moved as we all jockeyed for a better view and wondered what it was.

The little creature was still there, sound asleep, when we returned from the village. Skip took a couple of pictures, hoping to sometime identify it. The way it was sleeping, we presumed that it might be nocturnal.

On our next movie night at the Benish house, we described the animal to Bob and Kathy. They couldn't identify it from our description, but Bob is an information nut and has a large library. He and Skip searched until they concluded that we had come upon a honey possum. That name sounded sweet enough to describe such a pretty little guy. We were satisfied. Skip commented, "It looked like something Dr. Seuss might have created, absolutely charming."

One morning the howler monkeys woke us especially early. I rolled over and said to Skip, "They surely are hollering up a storm!" That's exactly what they did. That night the winds came, awakening us with ferocious blasts, bouncing limbs and palm fronds off our tin roof like thunder.

The next morning Martha and Jane declined going to the beach since the winds were still pretty strong. Skip and I were getting cabin fever and decided to walk to the beach anyway. We squinted against the dust and wind until we reached the beach and then squinted against the blowing sand that bit into our skin like sleet. Still we enjoyed being out. It always seems odd to us northerners that such a strong wind can be warm.

The wind blew the top of the surf back over itself, sending the foam flying. I spotted a wentletrap, a special type of white shell shaped like a common sea auger and sporting a lacy pattern that endows it with a delicate beauty. It is rather rare and sometimes valuable. Martha first taught us about them. She was good at spotting them, but we had great difficulty finding one. She told us that once we caught on it would seem easy, and she was right.

Ann Scarlet, our local shell artist, makes lovely earrings, necklaces, and pendants from them, along with many other pretty shells found here.

As we walked, we found three more wentletraps, a record find. I said, "Boy, Skip, wouldn't Ann be envious?" to which he replied, "Sure would, and so would Beverly Baumunk." Beverly makes a few jewelry items from shells also and wishes so much that her old eyes were better at spotting the precious wentletraps. So many of our friends here were aging past their prime, but we treasured their friendship and consider them to be good role models as we enter our "golden years."

Farther up the beach toward the hotel point we came upon a sea turtle laying her eggs. A couple of other people came to watch. Finally the old girl finished her job, covered the clutch with her back flippers, and struggled back into the water. We bystanders went on our way. When we looked back, we saw a Tico uncovering the eggs and putting them in a sack. We were angered by the sight, but as we discussed it, we came to grips with the fact that this was their country and their tradition, and we would be overstepping our bounds to try to act as police officers. Certain areas are protected to ensure survival of the turtles, and that boy may earn a week's wages from the sale of those eggs. We decided we wanted no part of the "ugly American" image and continued our walk, although disappointed that the eggs would never hatch.

The following week our local water supply was interrupted for a few hours, so we scrapped our scheduled chores and went straight to the beach. We swam and walked as usual but began to notice growing bird activity over the water. Soon we realized that those huge schools of *sardinas*, the Pacific anchovies, were coming in. The pelicans and terns were diving rapidly. Some of the magnificent frigatebirds were appearing, making passes at the minnows in great swoops with their seven-foot wingspans. Native fishermen appeared here and there, as if by magic.

Skip was snorkeling in the upper tide pool and got an underwater view of the big creval jacks actually devouring the anchovies before his eyes. Their lightning slashing attacks sometimes left numerous chunks of the anchovies floating around in the swirling water like so many bits of silvery confetti. What razorlike teeth those jacks must have!

He called me over to stand in the entrance of the tide pool, where the water drifts in and out with the surge of the surf. The fish also surge through this sluice as their access to the pool. We watched the minnows come by, swimming in perfect unison, as if all were guided by the same brain, a still-unexplained mystery. Then several of the great jacks zipped by into the tide pool, where, protected from the turmoil of the surf, we could watch them tear into the anchovies. They acted very much like a wolf pack attacking sheep, and we had a great place to observe them, our very own fish bowl! After they left we found numerous pieces of the unfortunate anchovies washed up on the beach, fast food for the vultures.

We made another strange find on the beach, a drowned porcupine. We had glimpsed no more than one of these strange critters during all of our visits to Costa Rica. I guess they are mostly nocturnal and rather secretive. This was our first chance to really inspect one. It had a yellow-ish cast to its coarse hair and long quills, which seemed sparse compared with those of our northern variety of porcupine. Perhaps that is one of its adaptations to the tropics, but it gave the porcupine a ragged, unkempt look. All in all, it was a pretty ugly animal, but then it would probably have thought the same of us, had it been capable.

Heading back toward Baker's Landing, our beach-access point, we found a green vine snake, less than four feet long and skinny enough to use as binder twine. It's a common snake but rarely seen on the beach. Maybe the high winds had something to do with these oddities.

"Valentine's Day is week after next," Martha said as we did the dishes after lunch. "What should we do?"

Jane's ears perked up. "Oh, let's have a party!"

Skip whispered to me, "It sounds like something from a Dick and Jane reader, doesn't it?"

We suppressed our chuckles as Martha and Jane jumped on the idea with both feet. They were soon seated at the dinner table, happily design-ing heart-shaped invitations, discussing the guest list, and planning *bocas*. Things went well until they had to select a starting time to print on the invitations. Such a heavy decision required lengthy debate.

They laid aside the nearly completed prototype for the invitations, retired to the rocking chairs on the porch with grunts and heavy plops, and discussed pros and cons. Jane favored five o'clock at the earliest. Any earlier just wouldn't have any class, and Jane clearly would not have anything to do with a common sort of event. Martha leaned toward four-thirty, since folks might want to drive home before dark. I had the temerity to comment that no one would leave before dark, even if the party began at three.

Nonetheless, the vacillation continued for the rest of the afternoon. Finally, Martha pronounced that, despite misgivings, five o'clock would be printed on the announcements. Jane could now complete her task. The flowery valentine-shaped invitations emerged one-by-one, ornately printed by her skilled hand, only a little less steady than it once was. We complimented Jane on her creations. Even Martha was pleased, although she still frowned when she focused on the starting time.

The next day, about midmorning, Martha headed to the kitchen to get some hard candy, Jane in tow. By now Jane's face was pretty red from the sun, which tended to enhance the whiteness of her hair. The sun and wind of our hours at the beach had taken their toll on her hair, making it frizzy, and because her hair was thin the sun had reached through to redden her scalp a bit. Antonio, big tease that he is, said it reminded him of possum hair.

When they reached the cupboard and grabbed the candy dish, they found it had been invaded by tiny ants. Of course by now their appetites had been whetted, so they decided to sit at the dining table on the porch and remove the ants. Jane could barely see the little creatures due to her vision problems, and Martha was due for removal of a cataract as well, but they squinted and toiled until they were satisfied that the last ant was gone. Candy is precious out here in the jungle, definitely worth the time invested.

By now the Valentine's Day party invitations had been delivered. Martha continued to stew, still vacillating back and forth between four-thirty and five o'clock. She couldn't let it rest. Skip rolled his eyes heavenward during happy hour when the topic came up again for the umpteenth time. Finally she decides to tell everyone personally to come at four-thirty, so they could get home before dark. Amazing.

Food preparations were under way. I contributed three cans of smoked oysters to place on crackers and a package of thinly sliced freeze-dried beef, which we spread with cream cheese, rolled up, then sliced for *bocas*. All those cans had been carried from Pennsylvania in our luggage. Martha had prepared French-fried yucca, chayote sliced into sticks to be dipped, and fruit chunks to be speared with toothpicks. She then decided we needed something more and told me to make some tortilla chips for a homemade chip and dip offering. I fried the tortillas a day early, but Jane found she had a taste for them, and I could barely keep ahead of her appetite. Finally Martha got on Jane's case, telling her there wouldn't be enough for the party, and if she didn't stop scarfing them, she would tell the guests that Jane ate them all. Problem solved.

Gradually more and more items were added until Martha was satisfied that it would make a good showing. Even red cloth napkins and tablecloth appeared from some musty footlocker to be aired in time for the big event. Skip was ordered to make sure there were enough bottles of spirits and sodas, with appropriate variety to fulfill individual tastes, most of which were well-known by now.

Of course the party was a success. Everyone was happy to be invited anywhere out here in the jungle, and all were already either comfortable together or easily able to bypass anyone they didn't want to spend time with. Little groups formed to catch up on mutual interests or gossip. Some floated from one area to another. A few just sat and listened as they sipped drinks and munched *bocas*. Skip acted as bartender and tried to keep drinks replenished as he involved himself in pieces of the various conversations. He also tended to take regular advantage of the *boca* table as he made his rounds, trying to be sneaky and avoid notice. I smiled and chatted as I passed boca trays to the clusters of guests, trying to make sure no one was being neglected.

Cooperatively, a full moon rose early, adding to the mellow ambience of the tropical night. Good food, plenty of drink, and warm companionship—what else could we ask for? I walked up to the game room to get another chair. From that small distance I gained enough detachment that I felt I was seeing something from an old movie or perhaps visualizing a scene from a romantic novel. I was standing back under a palm tree, looking down onto a comfortable, glowing social scene that was surrounded by darkness. I felt oddly as if I were in a theater watching a play enacted by friends. I mused, under my breath, "And they all deserve Oscars for such true-to-life performances." Then I carried the chair back into the circle of light, breaking the spell and becoming one of the cast myself.

Naturally it was long after dark before the guests began departing. So much for the long and painstaking debate over the starting time. Actually, the debate had been only between Martha and herself. While we'd all tossed in our two cents, we really never affected the outcome; that would have been the same regardless. While sometimes exasperating, it was nevertheless a fascinating process to watch. And it did turn out to be a fine party.

More winds came. This time they blew most of the day as well as all night. During a midafternoon break, it seemed that the mammals and birds rushed to enjoy some activity before the winds renewed their blowing. Tank, the armadillo, came to drink at the birdbath. A posse of coatimundis trooped past our house, seemingly heading somewhere important. Magpie jays hassled squirrels while parrots zigzagged noisily overhead. Most irregular, we spotted a caracara, a unique large, long-legged hawk that we had only ever seen here in Costa Rica, typically on the beach. Then the winds rose again.

The following week we met a newly retired couple, Dick and Boots Teach, from Buffalo, New York. There were so few people on the beach that we generally got to know anyone who stayed more than a week. These two were friendly and asked questions about where to eat and how to get here or there. They were totally enamored with Nosara, so taken that they were already contemplating the purchase of property.

A few days later we stopped in the middle of one of our long beach walks to see how Dick and Boots were getting along, only to find them terribly deflated. They had left their rental house to try a restaurant we had recommended and returned two hours later to find the place robbed. Nearly all their personal goods were simply gone, as well as some household items. They were short of clothing, toiletries, even food. Small appliances belonging to the home owner were missing as well. While these were not a large personal loss, the absence of those articles made for a less enjoyable vacation. Even their luggage had been taken, presumably used to carry away their own clothing and other goods.

The robbery had changed the Teaches' attitude toward Costa Rica immensely. They felt violated, unsafe, unable to enjoy those wonderful beaches with any peace of mind. They told us they probably would never return, although we wondered if they could resist Nosara's magnetism.

We sympathized and offered clothing and other items to help them enjoy the rest of their stay. But we understood how they felt. Such robberies are quite common. We have listened to many lamentations by friends who have had to come to grips with the same feelings of frustration and vulnerability. Most endure it and go on, but when it happens to newcomers, they often leave. We once again puzzled over our good fortune and at how little we had been troubled by robbery at Casa de las Flores.

Good humor got us over the impact of such troubles in paradise. That very day Martha and Jane were cooking and peeling beets. Soon Skip and I walked by and noticed bloody tracks all around the small kitchen area. Martha and Jane had dropped some beet peelings and tracked through the red juice. Their old eyes had betrayed them once again, and they hadn't noticed.

Skip inquired forcefully, "Where'd you hide the body?," which drew a long chorus of laughter once they caught on. In fact, needing a laugh at the moment, we overdid it and laughed until we were in tears.

Martha, not to be outdone, replied, "We have it on cooking! Just look at the blood in that pot."

Jane jumped on the bandwagon, too, with, "Hide it! Here comes the sheriff!"

We milked that situation for all it was worth, laughing until we were all exhausted and had to plop into the rocking chairs on the porch to catch our breath.

Rudy Boyer, Martha's old friend, came again to spend a few weeks with us. His motto is "celebrate early and often," and he lived up to it. He treated us regularly to dinners at our favorite restaurants and kept us supplied with his favorite brand of rum, a dark Nicaraguan variety called *Abuelo*, which translates to "Granddad." He had brought a supply of challenging crossword puzzles with him, which he and Skip teamed up to conquer. They spent much time during happy hour, while waiting for meals, and during odd rest periods working toward solving those puzzles. Rudy has a fine mind in spite of his age and loves to use it. He is retired from Dupont where he spent most of his life employed as an engineer. He often told us tales of his more challenging years as a plant trouble shooter and must have been quite a guy in his prime.

On Rudy's first morning at Martha's he asked if there was anything she wanted him to do. Martha said with a twinkle in her eye, "Well, Floyd Mains isn't here this year. He always said he was 'number two boy,' and he was responsible for sweeping the decks. I guess you're number two boy now, so if you can't sweep you can't stay." Rudy quickly grabbed the broom and thereafter swept the decks every morning before breakfast.

We popped over for breakfast the next morning just as Rudy finished his sweeping and headed for the table. Eagle-eyed Martha saw him and ordered, "Rudy, you've been sweeping. You'll have to wash your hands before you eat." Martha won't let an eighty-four-year-old kid get away with anything.

At happy hour Rudy told us a lot of stories. This time he related how he had watched a stalk of bananas ripen during his first year in Nosara when he and his wife were renting the Sperling house. The bananas had finally reached the desired color, so he called to his caretaker to get the machete while Rudy went to get the ladder, figuring one of them would climb up and hack off the bunch of bananas. When Rudy returned with the ladder, he found the caretaker had hacked the stalk off at the bottom, then chopped off the bananas and was already holding them in his hand. Rudy hadn't known that this was the standard method for cutting bananas, and he had missed it entirely!

Like Jane, Rudy has vision problems. He has difficulty spotting the birds and mammals as we discuss them and try to point them out to him, but he takes it in his stride, maintaining his good humor in spite of the problems of old age. One night as we returned from eating out, we followed our flashlights up the walks from the parking circle to the main house. By chance, Martha, Skip, and I took the upper path, while Jane and Rudy took the lower one. Jane was leading, since she had the flashlight, with Rudy following along, both trying hard to stay on the path. I imagine their surroundings were mostly a blur to them, for soon we noticed Jane's flashlight weaving off through the garden path away from the house.

Martha cried out, "Holy Heaven, Jane! Where are you taking Rudy?"

That was too much for Skip's ornery sense of humor. He called out, "Watch it, Rudy! Jane's leading you down the ol' garden path!"

When we finally led them back up to the porch, everyone laughing and half out of breath, Jane was blushing like a schoolgirl. Of course that didn't take much, since her face was constantly a deep pink from the sun, anyway.

One evening Martha and Skip had a tiff, a very rare thing. Some workers who were replacing louvers on Martha's windows had left their materials back of the main house where folks were used to walking. Tico workers seem to us to be careless about such things, probably due to lack of training and supervision. Skip happened to be watering some plants in the vicinity and had seen Jane trip and nearly fall over some boards as she approached the back door of the kitchen. He stopped what he was doing and began moving the slats and boards out of the way.

In a few moments Martha emerged from the kitchen door and asked, "What in the world are you doing?"

Skip replied, a bit grumpily, "I'm getting this stuff out of the way so people don't fall over it." Whatever he does, Martha tries to keep track of him, always wanting to maintain control, and that bugs Skip.

Martha said, "Well, they probably want it where it is. Let it alone."

Skip said, "No. Someone might get hurt. Jane and Rudy don't see well, and the lighting is poor back here," as he continued to work. "Jane already tripped."

Martha raised her voice to say, "Let it alone. You're causing more work. They can walk around it!"

Skip raised his voice in return, to respond, "Martha, quit ordering me around all the time! I'm moving it, and that's that!" He was getting pretty aggravated, a rarity for Skip.

Martha said loudly, "Don't you raise your voice to me!"

Skip finished the removal with a slam and a bang and walked away. Soon we were playing Oh, Hell, trying to act nonchalant after the unusual outburst, but I'm sure the name of the game expressed Skip's feelings.

One of Rudy's favorite lunches was *sopa de mariscos,* a hot bowl of mixed seafood chowder, shells and all. Skip liked it, too, and they ordered it at the Rancho Tico in Nosara every time we ate there.

The day we drove Rudy into Nosara to get the bus on his way home, we made it a point to stop at the Rancho Tico to treat him to one last savory bowl of soup. It was a sad departure for Rudy, since he expected this to be his final visit to Costa Rica. He had been coming here for nearly as many years as Martha, but now the trip was becoming too arduous for an old man traveling alone. He told us that he felt increasingly vulnerable due to his physical slowness and vision problems, plus his back was hurting constantly from an injury sustained in a recent auto accident. We saw to his luggage, kissed him good-bye, and helped him aboard the bus. We'd miss Rudy's enriching presence at Casa de las Flores.

Believe it or not, we were invited to a fashion show, right in Nosara! The whole community was invited. Models were coming from San José, in addition to some local amateurs who had been selected by tryout. It was scheduled for 7:30 on a Saturday night at a lovely little hotel on the way to Nosara, called the *Estancia.*

Roger Harrison's companion, Alfred, who does much of Roger's housekeeping and cooking, is also a designer of women's clothing. He had decided that a fashion show would be a good commercial endeavor, enabling him to advertise and sell his wares. The idea had started small but ballooned into a major community function.

Martha and Jane gradually became caught up in the idea. At first they debated whether to go or not, but as they discussed it with friends it became obvious that they would have to attend. Soon Martha became enthusiastic about it and invited more friends to accompany her to the event than the jeep could carry. This gave Skip and me an excuse to stay home and enjoy a peaceful evening together; no cards, no Scrabble, no Rummikub. Wow!

Martha rejected our plan; she wouldn't hear of it. She declaimed, "Oh, you'll fit into the jeep. I've had thirteen people in that jeep before! What would you do here alone?"

But we stuck to our guns and finally won out, after a low-key but extended battle for our civil rights. We had to explain to Martha what we were going to eat and how we would use our time. Finally Skip said with a twinkle in his eye, "Martha, we just may do something we don't want to tell you about."

Martha caught the twinkle and snorted, with a twinkle of her own. "Well, we'll have room if you change your minds."

Martha, Jane, and Rudy had happy hour with us on the evening of the fashion show. The girls were pretty excited. Jane loves her happy hour anyway, and the anticipation made her extra happy. She dropped her wineglass over the side of the deck and giggled hilariously when it rolled on down the steep hillside. Skip retrieved her glass for her, whereupon she went to the kitchen to refill it, babbling the whole time. Then she returned, set the glass on a wobbly stand, and promptly knocked it off again, giggling uproariously.

Skip commented, "At least I'm getting some exercise from all this. I'm glad I'm not going along; I'll be too tired to last the evening. And I hope you don't run out of wine, Jane."

I thought of Jane's attempt to buy a bottle of wine last week at the grocery store. She came home with a pretty bottle, opened it for a quick sample, and spit it out, making a terribly puckered face. Her old eyes had betrayed her, and she had bought vinegar instead of wine. Skip helped her return it on our next visit to La Paloma.

The old girls with Rudy in tow climbed into the jeep not long after seven that evening and drove off to pick up their guests. They were so late coming home that we were in bed, asleep, after a pleasant evening by ourselves.

The next morning we heard the story at breakfast. The setting for the show had been lovely. It was held at poolside, with a special walkway bridging the pool where the models strutted. Some of the costumes were so skimpy that one fellow fell into the pool, much to the delight of the crowd. And it was a large crowd, really too many for the available space. The main complaint, though, was that the show hadn't begun until nearly ten o'clock, as opposed to the advertised hour of 7:30. Martha felt they did that to entice folks to spend more for food and drink, which probably paid for the use of the grounds. The wait had been very tiring, but they did have friends to talk with, since nearly everyone was there, and the show itself was great fun. We were all still amazed that there had been a real fashion show out here in Nosara, in the middle of the jungle—*our* jungle.

Martha told Skip the next day that she had invited Mary Yost to come over for a haircut. Martha does that now and then, offering Skip's services to her friends and then mentioning it to him as an afterthought. He seems not to mind; at least he doesn't complain about it.

Then the following week she went to LaRue's for a haircut and returned to announce that we girls were all invited down for a drink and a swim in their pool. "But," she continued, "Chipper, you go with Skip to the beach. Jane and I will swim at LaRue's." I felt a little hurt by that rejection, Martha feeling free to control my life in spite of what I might wish to do. That control issue had always been there, but it seemed more and more blatant of late, especially since Chet's death.

Still, the beach somehow cleanses my mind; I know of no other way to put it. Finding it ever beautiful and interesting, I feel eased and comforted as we walk. Of course I clear my mind on Skip's broad shoulder as we walk, but soon we are distracted by our surroundings. This time we approach a flock of vultures to see what they are having for lunch and find two stingrays dead on the sand. The shrimp boat nets again?

During a quiet period at the house we noticed the *chachalakas* pecking at grit in the driveway. As they were very wary birds, we moved cautiously to observe them. Skip had been using a large basin to water some transplanted banana stalks below our house and had left the basin full of water in the center of the driveway circle, just in case some thirsty creature might use it. The jungle fowl did just that, dipping their beaks into the water, then tilting their heads back to swallow, checking for danger after each round. Then they flapped up into the big mango tree and ran through the branches, right out the other side, and into the next tree. They travel on foot through trees quite rapidly, more so than any other type of bird we have ever seen, flapping their wings only briefly when the space between the trees or limbs is too great to hop across.

Watching the *chachalakas* put us on the alert, and we spotted two huge woodpeckers above our house, chiseling chunks of bark onto our tin roof. In the process a reddish brown wood creeper caught our eye on the same tree; then we noticed several hummingbirds working on some blossoms farther up the hill. They were too far away to identify, but they surely were busy with those blossoms. Once in a while, one hummingbird would try to drive another away from the blossoms, just like our ruby-throats do back in Pennsylvania, reminding us of Snoopy and the Red Baron.

On our way up the mountain in the jeep one night, we were lucky enough to see one of the dark mountain cats cross the road in front of us. Again we checked with each other to assure ourselves that we really did see what we thought we saw. They are so illusive and fleeting that few people get to see them. I feel lucky to have seen them several times.

We know it's getting later in the season when Mary Yost invites us to dinner. She feeds us well, and we help her put it on the table. This time she served Costa Rican macadamia nuts and smoked oysters with crackers as appetizers, along with *Cuba Libre* drinks, mixed by Skip with Abuelo rum and Coke over ice. We discussed departure dates and forthcoming travel plans. Skip and I reviewed the latest additions to her lovely shell collection, oohing and ahhing appropriately at Mary's pride and joy. Chris, aka Mr. Yost, her Shetland sheepdog, barked noisily at a Tico riding by on a motorcycle, then at a visiting dog, then at a horse and rider. In fact, he yapped a goodly percentage of the time we were there.

After *bocas* Mary asked me to peel the beets. I winked at Skip; this has become a ritual. The beets were so hot that I had to hold them with a fork and still burned my fingers before I completed the job. Skip sliced the roast beef while Mary steamed the asparagus, her favorite veggie. As usual, it was a delicious meal, and when it was complete we waited with bated breath until Mary pronounced, "And don't stack the dishes! That way I won't have to wash the bottoms." Somehow, that pronouncement has become nearly as satisfying as dessert after a meal. Some things in this world can still be relied upon. Mary is certainly a delightful character.

After returning home we sat and rocked and chatted a bit before retiring. Jane commented, "It seems awfully hot and humid today. I can't do a thing with my hair." I had to look away from Skip, for we were thinking the same thing and nearly burst with laughter. Jane's hair, a pretty white but growing thin and frizzy, was no different from any other day. We thought of Antonio and his possum comment as we stifled our chuckles. By the same token, such moments endear the old girls to us. We truly are fond of them and respect their age and experience.

Franco, if you remember, Martha's onetime caretaker and next-door neighbor, had been working steadily for the Robertsons, down near the beach. His wife, Lou, was also employed, so they were doing well, with money for new clothes, bicycles, and then a motorcycle. One day we heard that Franco had wrecked his motorcycle while drinking and cavorting with a younger woman. They both wound up in the hospital, and Lou, along with their seven children, left him to stay with her mother. Esperanza was abuzz with speculation about what would happen next.

Some time later we heard by the grapevine that Franco had committed suicide. It took a while before we could piece together a reasonable "truth" from the fragments of fact and rumor being passed around.

A talented guy who had learned English from Chet along with how to deal with gringos, Franco was able to inspire confidence in his employers. Chet had trusted and valued Franco highly until the quarrel previously related. He had left Esperanza to work in the banana plantations for several years at Guapiles, then returned. The old-guard gringos, already knowing his history with Chet, wouldn't employ him. But the newcomers took Franco at face value, especially appreciating his ability to speak English. Subsequently, a man named Robertson hired Franco, saw that he was a very capable worker, and gave him more and more responsibility.

Just before returning to the States, Mr. Robertson gave Franco money to pay some bills and take care of the property, we were told. He handed over the keys to his car and told Franco to have things in good shape when he returned. Apparently Franco couldn't resist the chance to play big shot, something he was inclined to do anyway, so he took the money and the car and went on a spree. He spent the money on booze and women, got drunk, and demolished the car. He was so ashamed and depressed when he sobered up that he hitched a ride to town, bought some rat poison at the grocery store, returned to Robertson's, and ingested the poison. He was found dead in Robertson's house, after an apparently violent and painful ordeal.

I remember Chet relating Franco's statement when they parted company. Chet said Franco had told him that he and his children were Ticos and that they didn't want to be converted to gringos. Apparently he was feeling caught between two cultures, and it caused him enough distress to give up a good, secure job. I think he had difficulty thereafter feeling complete in either culture.

In addition to Franco's sad demise and unfulfilled life, his wife, Lou, was left alone with the responsibility for seven children. We all speculated on what would happen, whether their house was paid for, how they would survive, and the like.

It seems that after the shock and a period of adjustment, Lou is doing better than ever. She works steadily and has two of the older girls working part-time, too. Now she has control of the money and doesn't have to cater to Franco's macho whims or endure his drinking, womanizing and occasional abusiveness. The family dresses better now and seems to be healthy and prosperous. Who knows under what guise blessings may come?

Meanwhile, back at Casa de las Flores, Martha looked down from the back deck during happy hour and said, "My goodness, we haven't played any shuffleboard this year. I'll tell Antonio to paint the lines again, and we'll play some. Skip, you check and see if we have the right paint."

Within a week we had a big tournament under way. As the sun set, Skip turned on the lights, but they failed to illuminate the court very well. The surrounding plants had grown to the point where they shaded some of the lights. Skip had already repaired some rotted wires and rusted switches, results of the rainy season, but the lighting was still too weak for Jane's eyes.

Martha said, "I'll solve your problem," and climbed the steps back up to the house, returning with a flashlight. We finished the game with Jane holding the flashlight in one hand and her push-stick in the other.

Another afternoon, Jane walked down to the shuffleboard court to watch Antonio and a couple of village kids play. Martha, watching from the deck, blurted out with an amazed expression, "My God, Jane looks like a little old woman down there!"

Skip responded, not unkindly, "I hate to tell you this, Martha, but that pretty well describes her."

Martha made no reply. She seemed puzzled and perplexed by her observation and apparently needed to mull it over. Where do the years go?

These old jungle girls made us smile on a regular basis, if not out-right chuckle. I listened often to Jane's concern that someone might come into her room at night. "I sleep alone in the guest room, and there's nothing but screen around the top," she would say. "I can't get the windows closed tight enough to lock, and that old door lock isn't very strong. I worry about that."

I would comfort her on a regular basis, telling her that no one had ever done such a thing here at Casa de las Flores and that Skip would come running if he heard her call. Martha reassured her that the folks in the village, only a stone's throw away, would come, too. Still, Jane felt isolated and fearful, despite our reassurances.

One morning Jane told me at breakfast that there had been someone in her room last night. "There had to be," she claimed. "Last night when I went to bed I laid my flashlight on my nightstand where I always keep it, and it was gone this morning."

I asked if anything else was missing, and she said not that she knew of.

I explained that it was an unlikely thing for someone to break in and only take a flashlight. Still, she was unconvinced, so after breakfast, with her permission, I checked her room. I found her flashlight under the bed and tried to reassure her with as little embarrassment as possible. She was relieved but still never gave up her concern about someone entering her room while she was in bed. It seemed that the only time her fear fully left her was during happy hour, her favorite time of day.

One day Martha and Jane were in the kitchen preparing some tortilla chips for *bocas*. They were stationed side by side at the counter, cutting the tortillas into little pie shapes, ready for frying.

Martha, ever alert, looked over to check Jane's work, saying critically, "Jane, you're cutting those pieces too small."

Jane replied unremorsefully, "You're cutting them too big!"

Martha continued, "Well, they're too small. They'll fall apart."

Jane countered, "Well I'm dainty, and I'm going to stay that way!"

Martha walked out onto the porch where I was watering plants in hanging baskets and confided, "Jane's cutting her pieces too small, and they're all falling apart."

Another day, Martha was irritable about someone leaving a partially nibbled cracker on the kitchen counter, complaining, "That'll draw ants. It must have been Jane. It wasn't me. Was it you, Chipper?"

I replied, "No, Martha, it wasn't me. I thought I saw you eating a cracker a little while ago, though."

She looked puzzled for a moment, checked the cracker only to find traces of peanut butter, then burst out laughing. "It *was* me! I completely forgot about it." She tossed the cracker into her mouth and proceeded with her chores, her good humor completely restored. Since she was the culprit there was no problem. Thank goodness Jane and I were off the hook.

Martha was in a stew about peanut butter. She had a full jar of Peter Pan that she hated to open with less than two weeks before departure time, but she became obsessed with it to the point of drooling when she thought of it. The more she tried to dismiss it from her mind, the larger it loomed. She could smell it. She could taste it. It appeared in her dreams. She would awaken in the middle of the night and think of it.

Finally one day we returned from the beach, took our showers, and then walked across to Martha's for lunch. There she was, in the kitchen, stuffing peanut butter crackers into her mouth. She grinned sheepishly, explaining that we could probably empty the jar before we left, and if not, she could give it to Antonio and Chini. But she had been desperate for peanut butter and just couldn't let it alone.

I reassured her by saying, "Heck, yes, Martha. When you need peanut butter you need peanut butter. It would probably have spoiled by next year anyway."

I baked the last cake mix before we went to the beach and set it out to cool. When we returned, there were tiny ants all over it. This happens often enough that it is no longer a catastrophe. I carefully brushed the ants off the cake, covering any damage with icing. I, too, have become an experienced jungle girl.

Martha then began preparing potato salad for the final beach party of the season. Jane and I helped peel potatoes, wash and chop celery, and the like. Martha later seasoned it and mixed in the dressing, with Jane eyeing it hungrily.

As we set out dinner, Martha said, "Jane, why don't you give Skip and Chipper a sample of the potato salad?"

Jane responded, "I want some potato salad, too."

Skip chimed in, "Jane, haven't you had any potato salad yet?"

Jane said, "No!"

Martha said, "Yes, she did!"

Jane stood her ground. "But there is still some in the bowl."

Martha crumbled under the power of Jane's argument. "Well, go ahead and dish us all some."

As we chuckled over that exchange at bedtime, Skip reiterated his philosophy about food. "There are only a few forms of pleasure in life. As we get older, some of them fall by the wayside. No wonder food becomes more and more important."

I had to quote Martha again. "Yeah, Martha says these days the only sex she gets is by reading those romance novels."

Skip grinned. "They really are something, aren't they? The old jungle girls."

A few days later Martha had some friends scheduled for brunch at 9:30 A.M. She was pretty hyper about it, wanting to make a good impression. She had me doing home fries about eight-thirty, and before nine she told me to put ice in the glasses. I complained, "But, Martha, it's almost ninety degrees today. The ice will melt before they arrive. The potatoes will have to be reheated, too. Relax a little!"

She showed a restrained grin, responding, "Well, I guess we'll be ready on time." And of course, the guests were twenty minutes late.

During our final week we learned that our friend Mary Rasmussen had been attacked on the beach. This is a rather rare occurrence in Nosara and really puts a damper on the typically upbeat atmosphere. She was jogging when a Tico came up behind her, threw his shirt around her throat, and tried to drag her down. Mary fought him and escaped, after an all-out struggle.

When she stopped running and looked around, she saw the guy walking back up the beach. It happened that a truck hauling workers came down the beach, and Mary saw them wave at her assailant. She stopped the truck and asked the name of the man. This led to his arrest. He worked at Guiones, the little village at the southeast end of our beach. He tried to disguise himself by cutting his hair, but to no avail. His case was still pending when we left for home.

I had received word that my brother, Harold, was moved from the nursing home to a hospital due to problems with his feeding tube, so Skip and I left for home two weeks earlier than we had planned. That left Martha and Jane on their own for those two weeks. They were concerned, and so were we. Martha put up a brave front, but she was a little choked up when we left. Jane was obviously dismayed at our departure, but together they avowed they would be OK. They had Antonio on call and could always rely on George Miller and his main man, Bolivar, to bail them out in case of any difficulties.

Martha and Jane delivered us to the Alfaro bus stop in Nosara after an early lunch. Skip heaved our bags up on top of the bus to the man who stowed and secured the luggage, and we were soon aboard. We felt some pangs of emotion as we watched the old girls head off in the rusty old jeep, Martha at the wheel, clutching and shifting as if her life depended on it.

I said, "They probably won't sleep well with us gone."

Skip tried to reassure me, replying, "Martha's a tough old girl. She'll make it OK," but he wasn't any happier about leaving them alone than I was.

The bus driver took a few people on board who didn't have tickets, telling them they would have to get off if others along the way had tickets and he ran out of space. It happened. Two young Ticos had to exit the bus at a stop that seemed to us to be out in nowhere, because the bus was jammed full and a woman and her daughter were waiting with tickets in their hands. Tico buses are always an education.

At one point a policeman waved the bus to a stop. Those standing in the aisle hit the deck, trying to get out of sight, since it was illegal to haul standing passengers. The policeman, handsome, I noticed, talked to the driver briefly, then waved him on. Normality returned as people regained their original positions, smiling conspiratorially and chatting about the excitement.

Skip noticed some folks looking at him and picked up a few comments in Spanish about his hairy chest and legs. It was so hot that he was wearing shorts and his shirt was open in front. Ticos seem to be intrigued by hairy bodies, and a couple of young men were teasing the girl wedged in on the seat beside Skip. He just smiled and winked at them, getting some chuckles in response.

Our driver was a macho guy who drove fast and ignored the potholes, which were exceptionally bad for many miles on either side of the ferry. At times it seemed that we were hydroplaning over the gravel-and-washboard texture of the highway. Somehow we made it to San José, reminding ourselves that they made this run nearly every day. It was just after sundown, and we were standing with our bags in the Coca-Cola station with no hotel reservation.

I stood by the bags as Skip stepped into the street to hail a cab. The first cab was a clunker, and I saw Skip hesitate, could almost see him

222

say to himself, "Oh, what the hell," as he flagged it down. The driver loaded our bags but didn't seem to understand much of what Skip was trying to communicate. He immediately started off directly in the opposite direction from where we wanted to go. Street addresses seem to mean nothing to Tico cabdrivers, and we couldn't name a church or supermarket or McDonald's in the vicinity of the hotel. They drive by landmarks.

Skip got him turned around but couldn't get him to follow directions to the hotel we wanted to try, a different one that we had located on a prior visit in San José. We gave up and let him take us to another hotel, where he asked directions. Skip checked prices there, just in case, but it wasn't what we had in mind. We took off from there to find our old standby, the Cacts Hotel, but the driver messed up the directions again. By now we were near enough that things began to look familiar, so Skip leaned up over the back of the driver's seat and guided him by pointing.

We became lost again but rounded a bend in the street where we looked up a hill to the left, surprised to see the Cacts Hotel. That was a relief after such a hard day's travel and especially after Skip ran inside and found they had a room available. We checked in for two nights in order to have time to rearrange our flight tickets. The cabby charged us three dollars for nearly forty-five minutes of driving around in circles. A bargain (?).

We called the next morning and got our tickets exchanged for the following day. The agent said there would be a charge for the service, but we escaped without any extra fee, maybe because we said it was an emergency due to my brother's being hospitalized. We felt very relieved at this point and walked uptown for exercise and to do some shopping.

We try to stay alert to our surroundings when we knock about a city like San José, just to avoid trouble. We don't feel scared or tense, but we do keep our eyes open. Once on a prior visit to San José we spotted a couple of suspicious characters honing in on us, and the simple act of giving them a knowing look caused them to grin sheepishly and turn aside.

This day, someone crept up behind us and placed a hand on each of our shoulders, startling us. We jerked our heads around to stare into the grinning face of Jaime Alvarez, a friend and regular visitor at Casa de las Flores. Whew! We surely were glad it was Jaime at that point! We hugged him and exchanged a few words about what was going on, then continued with our shopping, a little abashed at having him sneak up on us like that. So much for our confident alertness.

223

We picked up some dried exotic fruits, some cheap rum, and a few colorful items from the Guatemala Shop as gifts, then returned to the hotel and repacked. We celebrated our departure with a nice, early dinner at Antojos, the quaint downstairs Mexican restaurant on Paseo Colon that features a bullfight decor and mariachi music.

The March winds were still blowing when we reached home, but we were there to give brother Harold some support and were glad to be reunited with our children and grandchildren. Still, Costa Rica was never far from our minds.

16

The Horselady of Nosara

Back when we made our first visit to Nosara, Martha stopped by a little *ranchito* that stood off the main road, down a sort of gully in the jungle. The owner wasn't home at the time, but Martha told us it belonged to a woman they called the Horselady. Her name was Polly Finley, and it was said that she cared more about her horses than anything else in the world.

Martha went on, "She rode her stallion all the way here from Alaska. They say that she was rescuing him from somebody, I don't really know. For some reason she decided to settle here and just lives for those horses. They are beautiful horses. They call them Arabians, and they say all the Ticos wanted to breed their mares to that stallion. She wouldn't let them, but they would sneak their mares in at night. Anyway, everybody says there are a lot of horses around now that look like that stallion."

It was an intriguing story. We began to wonder how much was true and how much was legend. If she had truly ridden here from Alaska, it should be entered in the *Guinness Book of World Records*, we thought. That would have been a prodigious feat. Skip was skeptical: "Could she really have done that? Could anyone?"

We only ever got to see Polly once during all our years here, but we kept hearing about her. We said hello to her in the store once, in 1995, I believe. Of course we were strangers to her, and she seemed shy, so we didn't press ourselves on her. She was petite, still attractive after seventy or eighty hard years of living, a freckled Irish girl grown old. She was dressed in tan riding britches and a white shirt, wearing a hat, and had good-humor wrinkles at the corners of her eyes and mouth. How I wish we could have known her.

Finally, in 1996, we heard that she had died. Now we wish we had made the effort to meet her and talk with her. Her story, if we could have gotten it out of her, would have been a keeper.

Maxine MacKay (see chapter 8) had the opportunity to talk with Polly and wrote some of her story in *Never in Nosara*, an unpublished manuscript of fascinating stories about people in the area as well as Maxine's own experiences. We learned part of Polly's story from that source as well as from word of mouth over the years. We can't claim much of what we report here as absolute truth, but we have done our best to keep it as close to the truth as possible.

Much mystery surrounds the Horselady of Nosara, but she is such a fascinating personality that we feel we must include her story. At first we wondered why Martha took us down that narrow two-track trail to Polly's *ranchito*. But then Maxine's short tale about the ride from Alaska caught our interest, although there were so many other new and fascinating things about Nosara that we hadn't focused on the Horselady enough to really grasp her story. We heard tidbits now and then, that she had been sick, starving, visited by her daughter, even that she had died. We had seen her horses many times running loose in the area, a fact that aroused complaints by some and concern by others. But to us she always remained more or less a mythical figure.

Now, with apologies for the secondhandedness of the story and credits to Maxine MacKay, here is the Horselady of Nosara.

As a girl, Polly Finley must have been a pretty little Irish colleen, but instead of being crazy about boys she was crazy about horses. She told Maxine that she had been married four times. Each marriage dissolved in the face of her first love, horses. She did have a daughter along the way who also learned to love horses. Together they performed in horse shows, some pretty classy shows at that.

Polly met the Arabian stallion Majuba at the Royal Dublin Horse Show. It was love at first sight, and Polly found a way to stay near him by getting a job with Majuba's owner. We could guess that she had applied some feminine wiles to get what she wanted; there's no doubt that she was attractive enough to do so. Working with Majuba and his owner took Polly to Alaska.

In time the owner found a replacement for Majuba because he was becoming cranky and uncooperative. When Majuba was put up for sale, Polly asked for first dibs on him but didn't have enough money to meet the price. She went to a bank, where she was turned down; livestock loans are bad investments.

Polly persisted and wangled a loan for some other purpose, then used the money to buy Majuba. She had three mares of her own prior to purchasing Majuba, and now she decided to take them and get away from whatever was complicating her life at the time—presumably a man, maybe debts, maybe both, who knows?

She pressed a friend into service to drive a truck pulling a horse trailer loaded with feed and equipment as she rode and led her precious horses down the Alcan Highway. It's hard to say exactly how this was accomplished, but one can imagine her riding one horse and leading others on a line. Perhaps the trailer could have held two horses or maybe all four. Perhaps Polly rode the horses only occasionally when they needed exercise. But Maxine says Polly rode all the way to Washington state. Sometimes she was hungry and sometimes the horses were hungry. Polly slept outdoors with her horses most of the time, and her face became cracked and reddened from the wind and weather.

Presumably Polly rested awhile in Washington and restocked her supplies, but whatever happened there, she decided to keep going. Possibly someone was trying to trace her, maybe the bank. We don't know where she got the money for provisions, either, but somehow she kept going with her "family" of horses, ending up way down in Central America, in Nosara.

My skeptical husband says, "All the way through Mexico and Guatemala? Without having her precious horses stolen? Crossing all those borders?"

I have no answers, except that this trek took place probably back in the sixties when things were different. Maybe they didn't need veterinarians' certificates then, or maybe she had them. Maybe she carried a gun. *Probably* she carried a gun. Anyway, she had been here for a long while; you couldn't deny that.

"But you have a point," I conceded. "That part or her trip in itself would probably make a good book."

For the first year or so in Nosara, Polly lived in her horse trailer not far from the grocery store, at that time Zambrana's store, which later became the SuperNosara. She would frequent the arrival of the veggie truck on its weekly run from San José and purchase or beg the leftover carrots, lettuce, and such for her four-legged family. Otherwise, her horses grazed on whatever vegetation they chose, which was plentiful in the rainy season. They roamed pretty much at will, returning to her for companionship, tidbits, and occasional grooming.

As she rode around the area on her horses, Polly kept an eye open for better quarters. One day she came upon an abandoned *ranchito* near the road to Section D, in the development. She checked on it from time

227

to time and finally decided it was deteriorating for lack of use; no one returned to it, and the trail was growing over with grass and weeds. She moved in, hoping no one would appear to evict her.

Using both the *ranchito* and the horse trailer, she made her home there in the jungle for the rest of her life, just a couple of miles from Bocas de Nosara Pueblo. She allowed her beloved horses free access to the *ranchito*, treating them as friends, almost as her children. She would skimp on her own food if necessary to take care of her horses.

Ever since she arrived with her blooded Arabian stallion the local *campesinos* and vaqueros had been excited. Aside from the few who had attended the big shows in Liberia or Alajuela, they had never seen this class of horseflesh before. And now here, right on their doorstep, was a world-class Arabian stud. At first they approached the Senora de los Caballos directly, but cautiously and politely. No, the senora did not want to breed her stallion to their mares. Polly was polite, too, but firm. After all, Majuba was a prince, not to be mated with mongrels and scrubs.

Actually, there are fine horses in Costa Rica, as well as great connoisseurs of horses and superb trainers and riders. We have watched them perform at the big fiestas, and they take a backseat to no one. But Polly was certain that her own beloved animals were incomparable aristocrats, not to be associated with the local stock. In short, she was a snob where her horses were concerned. No offer of a fee would entice her; no poor man's earnest plea could bend her.

So things happened in the night. Polly was often disturbed by noises in the jungle, even snorting and neighing. Obviously Majuba didn't know he was tainting his royal bloodlines on those restless nights. Those who are familiar with horses know that a stallion will move heaven and earth to do his duty when he smells the musk of a mare in heat. The local horsemen had only to get their mares a few hundred yards upwind of the great stallion; nothing could keep him from responding. It only made good sense to them. What could be more important than improving the bloodlines of their stock? Why, they were doing the world a service!

Polly could think of nothing to do but build a fence. She never saw the men who were taking advantage of her stallion, but she knew full well what was going on. In fact, Majuba was losing weight. She had to do something. Sometimes Majuba was gone when morning came, and that worried her. Sometime they might try to keep him.

Polly scraped together enough money to build a fence. She worked at it herself, along with some laborers she had hired. She hated to confine her babies; maybe just keeping them in at night would be enough.

It wasn't working. Polly learned that fences could be cut much more easily than they were built. All that money and work, down the drain. If she fixed the fence this week, it would be torn down again the next. It was very depressing. All she could do was keep trying, fixing the fence regularly and keeping track of her horses as best she could.

Then one night the thing she feared worst happened. Majuba disappeared. Polly was frantic, contacting everyone, following every lead and idea. Finally she offered a reward, and in time Majuba was located, but she had to pay highly to get him back.

Another year passed, and the situation eased up somewhat. Only occasionally was Polly awakened in the night, and Majuba regained most of his normal weight. Then one day in the village she noticed a foal trotting alongside as a vaquero rode its dam down the main street. The foal was a carbon copy of Majuba! Polly didn't know whether to laugh or cry. The foal was just beautiful, but those damned thieves! They had stolen the bloodlines of a great animal! So that was why her nights had been more peaceful of late. They had gotten what they wanted; enough high-quality foals to upgrade the local stock for years to come.

Polly's own mares bore fruit as well, replacing the occasional loss of one of the herd. She thought one of the older mares had been claimed by the sea, a thought that gave her much grief. But such things happen, and Polly was tough. She had endured lots of ups and downs during her long life and still was surrounded by her precious horses.

Polly once moved into a nice house in the development, mainly because one of her pregnant mares was ailing. She kept the mare in the house until the foal arrived. Then she kept the foal in the house with her because, she claimed, he had the purest bloodlines of any of her stock. He might possibly become a great stud and therefore deserved royal care. Polly's living arrangements caused some gossip, which would be revived every time someone passed the house and saw a horse looking out of a window or standing on the tiled porch, which sported three graceful arches.

Visitors reported that Polly's house also featured a boa constrictor in the rafters, up next to the roof. They said that it caused no problem for Polly; she had become used to living with nature. She claimed it took care of rodents better than a cat.

Once her precious foal reached maturity, Polly left the house and moved to a new *ranchito* which she had some Ticos build for her, away from the main road, where the old one was. Of course, the foal never became a famous stud, because by now Polly was neglecting registration papers, veterinary certificates, grooming and such details of approved horse management. Additionally, her scraggly *ranchito* in the jungle left much to be desired as a famous stud farm. Actually, Polly couldn't bring herself to sell even one of her family of mares and foals.

At one point her horses had done so much damage in the neighborhood that she received numerous complaints. The horses had been foraging in farmers' fields, trampling flowers and nibbling on landscape shrubbery. She tried to keep them under better control and even declared that she would move away, taking her horses up the coast to Ostional, the little village adjacent to the turtle sanctuary. That move never occurred. Polly was aging and at times ailing. By this time she had gradually lost control of her horses and probably was incapable of making such a move.

One thing is certain: the horses in the Nosara area are of better quality now than if Polly Finley had never made her famous ride from Alaska, no matter how much of that tale is true. Visit there and you may notice the refined heads and flowing manes and tails characteristic of the Arabian breed. There are still a few of Polly's own mares in the area. When we last departed Nosara, several were still wandering around the development, loved by some residents and cursed by others, as they have probably always been since her arrival.

Gordon and Charlotte Mills helped Polly at times, as did others in the development. They tried to make sure she had food when times were rough and medical attention when necessary. Sometimes when Polly was walking to town Mrs. Mills would stop and offer her a ride, but Polly usually had too many dogs with her, so Charlotte would say, "Just one dog, please, Polly." Even so, the Mills car needed a cleaning after such a trip.

In later years, after Gordon Mills died and Charlotte moved back to California, other residents occasionally checked on Polly. Bob and Kathy Benish gave her rides into town and provided some groceries, as did a few others. When someone expressed concern, Polly would reply wryly, "Oh, if you see the buzzards circling around my *ranchito*, you'll know what happened." The Horselady of Nosara didn't seem to worry about death, but it happened in September 1996, just about the way she had described it, leaving this old world a little poorer for her passing.

17

1997, Our Last Year in the Jungle

We were up at 2:30 A.M. to load our bags into Glenn's car and head for the airport. It was January 7, but the weather was decent, not the usual challenge that made it difficult getting to the airport most years. Glenn insists on being our airport chauffeur; he travels vicariously with us and loves when we provide him with a tour itinerary that he can follow day by day.

We watched for Martha as we checked in at the Aero Costa Rica counter. She had told us to meet her at Ticketing in the terminal, but Skip said it would be better to go straight to the boarding area, where we could sit and read without all the bustle. We didn't see her at Check-in, so we went on to the boarding area, assuming she was a little behind us. She wasn't there yet. As boarding time approached we became concerned. Skip said he would go look for her, but just as he was heading back down the long hallway, Martha appeared, hurrying in with her carry-on bags. She blurted out, "I was waiting for you at Ticketing. Where were you?"

Skip replied, "We told you we would meet you here, Martha. Anyway, we didn't see you at Check-in."

She said, "I was there. I was watching for you. But then I did get to talking to someone and must have missed you. And they made someone open his bags, so I got involved in watching what happened. Then it was getting late, so I thought I better come on through."

We laughed and hugged. By now the boarding call was issued, and we filed on down the ramp to the plane.

Our seats were about ten rows in front of Martha's. We waved to her as we settled in. Soon a stewardess stopped to tell us we could move back with Martha. She had found she had three seats to herself and requested our presence. We chuckled and followed orders. As we approached her, she pointed "Skip, you sit on the aisle. Chipper can sit here where we can talk." After a while she told me it was a good time for me to go to the bathroom. We were already back in familiar form and hadn't even reached Costa Rica yet.

I was carrying a doll in my flight bag for Antonio and Chini's new little girl and told Martha what happened as it went through the security check. The attendant watching the scope peered around the machine at me to comment, "I think she'll like the doll baby." As I was caught off guard, it took me a moment to realize that he had actually seen the shape of the doll in his scope. We all had a good laugh over that. Actually, it was reassuring to know that they really can scrutinize the contents of people's bags.

They also checked a small collapsible umbrella I had in my purse. Apparently it reminded someone of a bomb, with its compact canister shape, a new style.

We slept well that night at the Villa Tournon Hotel in San José, Martha's favorite. She was tired, having endured a mastectomy of her right breast only a month and a half before. And for that reason we took separate rooms this time. Skip commented after we parted from Martha, "She is amazing. She vacillates on so many trivial things, but she made that decision to have a breast removed and stuck with it. Now here she is, less than two months later, claiming no pain, carrying her own bags, and heading out to the jungle. You have to admire that." I agreed, wondering if I could be as decisive and upbeat in her situation.

Francisco Vives brought the jeep around right on schedule, receiving hugs and handshakes as well as monetary payment for taking care of the jeep, having it licensed and maintained. He drove us to Martha's lawyer's office, then on to his favorite supermarket, a fine, new one, of which he seemed proud. Martha led the shopping with great concentration, assisted by the rest of us in making decisions and reading labels. We left the market with a large stock of supplies to haul out to the jungle. Returning us to the hotel just in time for lunch, Francisco parked the jeep in the hotel basement garage and handed Skip the keys. After another round of hugs, handshakes, and good-byes, Francisco walked down to the corner to hail one of his old *compadres* from his cab-driving days for a free ride home.

Martha was ready to go to lunch in the hotel dining room, which is a bit expensive, so Skip invited her to join us in trying a lunch room beneath the bank building down the hill behind the hotel, his treat. She was a little apprehensive about it, as she often is regarding Tico food, but she conceded to try it, since Skip was buying.

232

We followed the short cafeteria line along the counter, pointing at whatever looked appetizing to us. We wound up with chicken and fried rice, a salad, fried plantain, and a drink, all for 300 *colones*, something less than a buck and a half each. Best of all, Martha was pleased.

We shopped for a while that afternoon, then returned to our rooms to read and take a siesta. Martha had friends coming in to meet us for dinner at the hotel that evening, so when they arrived we chatted and ate, enjoying the nicely presented white sea bass, a specialty of the house.

The next morning, after a big buffet breakfast, we were on the road before eight o'clock. The jeep rolled along as well as could be expected, and we reached Nicoya by midafternoon, after only one other stop for fruit at Martha's favorite market.

While in Nicoya we visited Albert and Nora Muller, who have a nice little house there. Albert sells real estate for Carico Realty and handles the church fund for Martha, as well as helping her with tax payments and such details. Martha checked on the church fund and asked Albert if any further progress had been made on the church. Skip and I asked Albert about the lawyer who had absconded with Carico's real estate documents and funds, which may have included the deed to a lot we had purchased through Albert. He told us he had been working on that and informed us of a different lawyer who was in charge of clearing up the mess. Albert told us to contact the new lawyer directly. We had hoped that the real estate office Albert worked for would take care of locating our deed, but that was apparently not to be.

We concluded our business with Albert and headed on toward Nosara, planning to stop for a late lunch at a new place Albert had told us about, called Matambu. We found it after fifteen or twenty minutes' travel and ordered the usual rice-and-chicken dish. Skip asked the owner if he knew our friend Jaime Alvarez, who lived not much farther down the road at Silencio, to which he replied, "Oh, he's my brother."

The "small world" truism applies doubly in Costa Rica, since the country is small and the families are large. We chatted with Jaime's brother Pinkai as best we could, given the language problem, as we ate what we could hold of the huge platefuls of *arroz con pollo* that his wife had set before us. Then we said, "Adios. Say hello to Jaime for us," and drove on toward Nosara.

At last Skip stopped the jeep under the big old mango tree not long after four o'clock. Antonio, grinning widely, came running to hug us and help unload the jeep. It is always a relief to finally arrive at Casa de las

Flores after the long, hard, dusty, hot, jolting trip, and it's always fun to see Antonio.

Antonio had the place looking pretty good this time. The paths and open areas had been raked, some of the bushes had been pruned, and things were still green from the rainy season. Numerous piles of fresh ashes gave evidence of Antonio's penchant for burning heaps of raked-up leaves and twigs. Martha would rather he would carry them into the jungle and let them rot, but that requires more work, so Antonio conveniently misunderstands her and does it his way. He seems very content to stand and watch those burning piles. If the smoke happens to drift up over the porch where Martha is sitting or working, so much the merrier. She'll lecture him and shake her finger as he stands grinning at her. If she gets angry and stamps her foot, he'll actually giggle at her. They have a unique relationship, fun to watch.

Right at this moment, though, everyone was happy to see one another and worked like beavers to get things prepared sufficiently that we would have beds ready to sleep in. No game playing tonight, not even a sit-down meal. The late lunch and a few snacks on the run kept us going until nearly nine o'clock, when we just said good night to one another and dropped into our musty-smelling beds.

Even with the smell of mothballs and mildew, it was wonderful to tune into the mysterious sounds of the jungle as we drifted off to sleep. It was even better to awaken to sounds of monkeys and jungle birds the next morning. I thought, as I luxuriated drowsily in the mellow coolness of dawn before arising, *This is priceless. Most people we know will never experience this. We are truly fortunate.* Then, of course, we hopped out of bed and shook out our clothes and sandals to make certain there were no scorpions or other such surprises in them.

Then it was over to Martha's for a light breakfast on her sunny porch. She said she hadn't slept well, that her refrigerator was making a weird noise. We were too busy to focus on it, though, since we had several days of cleaning and organizing to do before the place would be in ship shape. Our work was interrupted occasionally by friends dropping by to say hello, welcome us back, and share some bits of gossip or news.

Chini brought the new baby up for our approval. Little Juliana was very pretty with her big, dark eyes, and Chini had her dressed like a Christmas doll. I brought out the dolly that the airport security guard had spotted and told them the story. Antonio and Chini were delighted with the tale, which I suspect they have since retold many times to their friends and family. I had other gifts, mostly clothes, to give Juliana, and Skip had brought some toys and rattles, along with some fishing hooks and line for Antonio. The proud parents beamed, obviously doting on their long-awaited baby. Anyone could see that Antonio was absolutely and totally smitten. It was fun to watch them.

Friends related the story of Betty Kulp moving back to the States with her four big dogs and several cats. Michael Sandweg had been pressed into service to help her with the arrangements, including obtaining the necessary animal shots and certificates, the special travel arrangements, finding a hotel that accepted the animals, and managing her property while she was gone. It sounded to us like a difficult ordeal. Michael said he even had to "grease some palms" to make things work out. His wife, Paulina Anderson, took responsibility for renting the property, since she was in that business.

Will Scarlet dropped by to welcome us back. He related how his wife, Ann, had accompanied him to the grand opening of *La Luna*, a new little restaurant on the beach near the hotel. Ann had climbed upon a tall three-legged stool, to ease her tired, old feet. Someone called to her from behind, and when she swiveled about the stool toppled over. She tried to break her fall by putting out her hand and sprained her wrist badly, winding up wearing a brace and sling for several weeks. Will said the worst part was all the kidding she had to endure about getting drunk and falling off a barstool.

Skip jibed, "Yeah, you wouldn't contribute to that rumor, would you? Actually, you're pretty lucky, Will. Not many eighty-year-old women are lively enough to party like that!" Will grinned broadly.

There is some truth in that, I thought. We admire Ann and Will a lot and hope we can be as active in another twenty years.

We soon noticed that Martha's refrigerator wasn't cooling the food properly, so we had to carry much of it to her old refrigerator in the *bodega*. It happened that a large nest of stinging ants had been constructed under the floor during our absence. The vibration of any passage over the floor drew their soldiers up through the cracks between the boards. They moved us to dance quicker and livelier than any music. Lord, could they bite! It felt like red-hot pins in our flesh. We had to make numerous trips to get all the food moved from the kitchen, and each time, no matter how carefully we sneaked, they would feel the vibrations and boil up to bite us.

Skip and Antonio received immediate orders to get rid of those ants. It took a day or two, and we were lucky they didn't burn the place down, but they eliminated the ant problem. Some stragglers persisted, but even they finally disappeared, with the help of powdered insecticide, Baygon spray, mothballs, and some diesel fuel.

Problem number two: the old refrigerator wasn't working very well, either. Anything that had to be kept very cold was carried another sixty or so yards across to our small refrigerator. At least we were getting lots of exercise.

Skip had a list of supplies we needed in order to get the place back in shape, like lightbulbs, pipe fittings, PVC cement, paint, and the like. He told Martha he wanted to make a run to Nosara, so she decided it would be a good time to get some more food items, including veggies. Besides, we could try to locate the appliance repairman who was supposed to be living in the shed beside La Paloma Supermercado.

We were back by noon. Vernal, the repairman, said he would be here tomorrow. We'll see if that happens. Skip grabbed his plumbing supplies and immediately started on the seven water leaks he wanted to fix.

The next morning Martha finished her laundry and told me to start mine. Naturally the machine quit while my wash was in progress, so I got blamed for hexing it. Skip told me the belts and pulleys heated up after it ran for a while and that's what caused it to malfunction. "You're the second user. That's when it will happen, so you get the blame." It still bugs me, getting blamed like I'm doing something wrong.

Vernal showed up about noon, surprise of all surprises! He approached his task with good humor and some apparent skill. He was a chubby, jolly guy, very likable. His obese wife and daughter waited in his remnant of a pickup truck. It was truly a junkyard refugee, with no doors, no engine hood, and only two rusty fenders. We hoped it would get him and his family back to Nosara.

Vernal was so poorly equipped that Skip lent him some tools to make his job easier. His young son, a bright and willing little guy who grinned at Skip's teasing, acted as Vernal's assistant. Vernal checked some things and said he would have to order some parts for the refrigerator. Then he made some adjustments to the washing machine. It's hard to believe that we received service so quickly and competently. He expects the parts in a week. Who knows?

236

Martha thought the kitchen refrigerator was working better, so we moved the food back. Wrong. After a few hours we moved it all back to the bodega again. Only a few ants attacked us this time. Skip and Antonio were duly informed.

We checked with Vernal whenever we saw him, and one day he told us the parts had arrived. His wife's father acted as his supplier, getting the parts in San José and sending them by bus to Nosara, the usual family connection. The only problem was that now his truck was broken down, no big surprise; he would have to get it fixed before he could come to Martha's to install the parts. That took several more days, but he did show up. He replaced the defroster timer and thermostat control. After a few trial hours, we moved the food back again, this time successfully. What a relief, especially since we had company coming for dinner the following day.

The monkeys showed up to entertain our guests, along with an armadillo, who took a drink from the birdbath. By the time we finished our dinner, we found army ants streaming across the deck. They came from the garden below the house, up the pillar to the deck, across the deck to *cabina* #1, along its front wall, off into the back garden, then up the wall and off into the jungle again. We carefully stepped over them and let them do their thing. By the time our guests left, the ants had disappeared, but they had provided us with some additional jungle entertainment.

One day Martha lost her coffeepot cord. She popped in on us early in the morning to borrow mine, explaining that I was probably at fault. I found it later while doing the dishes at her house after breakfast. It was inside her electric skillet where she had put it away the past evening. Her comment was, "Now why would you put it in there?" Hmmm.

Skip habitually tossed the fruit peelings and scraps into the jungle just beyond our house, since we enjoyed watching the animals, including butterflies, which were drawn to them. We don't believe in hand feeding, a practice that endangers both the feeder and ultimately the animal, when it loses its fear of people. We observed from our bedroom windows and sneaked occasional photographs but tried to dissociate ourselves completely from the scraps.

Whenever we saw some interesting activity at our feeding area, we would tell Martha all about it, something she enjoyed quite a bit. I guess it began to sound too good to Martha, for she decided she wanted to try a feeding area of her own. We began dividing the scraps, throwing some

237

of them beside Antonio's pile of limbs and prunings, about twenty yards up the hill behind the house.

Martha didn't want the animals coming too close to the house and didn't want an unsightly pile of scraps in front of the house. This was a long and difficult decision. She finally settled on the spot beside the pile of limbs as the best location, and the animals cooperated by eating the scraps. But she then found the animals couldn't be seen from the house. After two days, the whole idea was forgotten. Skip returned to carrying the scraps across the high trail to the jungle beside our house, and we carried our tales of the animals back to Martha.

We had nothing planned one morning, so Martha decided it would be a good time to try the new banking service. Since last fall, one of the Nicoya banks had been offering banking services at the outdoor restaurant beside La Paloma Supermercado in Nosara. This was a good chance to see how it worked.

Jack and Helen were visiting, and we all hopped into the jeep and drove to Nosara to check out this big event. It was to open at 9:00 A.M. We were there early and did some shopping, then chatted with friends as we waited. Nine-thirty came and went. Folks wondered if we should give it up. Others said, "No, just give them time. You should know that by now. This isn't the United States."

Ten o'clock came and went. More doubts were expressed. Before long a car drove up and three business types in white shirts, ties, and long pants climbed out, carrying cardboard boxes and a briefcase. The bank had arrived.

After another ten minutes, numbers were distributed and a teller sat down at one of the restaurant tables. Ready for *numero uno*, the bank was open!

Martha held number five and was called before eleven o'clock. Helen Hargleroad had wanted to cash some traveler's checks, but we had persuaded her to go to the store manager, Antonio, instead of waiting for the bank. Antonio (not our caretaker) had cashed her check on the spot, long before the bank tellers had even arrived. We waited in the heat, hunting shade as Martha conducted her business, joking about the blinding speed of bank service in Costa Rica, then reminding ourselves to be more charitable and to take the country as it is. We *Norteamericanos* certainly are an impatient, spoiled lot.

By the time Martha had finished at the bank, the morning was nearly gone. We stopped to show Helen and Jack the church. Father Victor looked in on us and was embarrassed that he was wearing T-shirt, shorts and flip-flops. Of course we weren't dressed much better and allayed his concerns as best we could. None of us would have wanted to wear heavy black clerical robes in this weather. We complimented him on the beauty of the nativity scene remaining from Christmas and took a few snapshots, including one of him and Martha together.

It was lunchtime, but Martha wanted to show us the new condominiums. She was considering whether to sell Casa de las Flores and purchase a new condo or perhaps one of the older condos. The stop was brief. Jack and Skip got out of the jeep to take pictures, but the builder was out of town, so we didn't try to go inside.

Then we made another brief stop at the hotel, since it was on our way, to show how it was still torn up and incomplete. This was a ritual we repeated nearly every year, lamenting how it was a shame a hotel at such a beautiful location was never finished; it was forever torn up in one area before another section was completed. Now there was water in the pool, but the entrance was a total mess. Par for the course. Too bad; it could have been a world-class property.

As we left the hotel, still lamenting its ongoing mismanagement, Helen asked, "When are we going to see the new condominiums?"

We all guffawed, to Helen's puzzlement, when Martha replied, incredulously, "Helen! We just came from there! Were you sleeping?" Indeed she had been. The funny part was that no one had noticed. We had no inkling that Helen, sitting straight up in the back of the jeep, had been asleep behind her sunglasses and huge floppy straw hat, completely unaware that we had even stopped at the condos.

Martha said, "Well, we're not going back now. It's lunchtime. And then you'll need your nap." And that settled that.

Our first few trips to the beach this year were very pleasant. Of course we had missed the beach and its beauty while we were away, but this time we additionally enjoyed some unusual overcast skies, which made it safer for our untanned skins and a bit cooler for everyone. We are all prone to getting sunburnt on our first trips to the beach, excepting Martha, and she never fails to point that out.

"I never burn, and I've never had skin cancer," she says with a lordly flare as Skip stands there covered with a hat and T-shirt, following the recommendations of his dermatologist. He has precancerous skin spots removed nearly every year.

Hotel Playas de Nosara, a struggling hotel occupying a great location with gorgeous views of Pacific sunsets.

As we enjoyed the tide pools, I noticed an odd-looking stick of wood floating by and snatched it before it disappeared. To my surprise, it had a key attached, probably a hotel key. I showed Martha, and she immediately grabbed it from my hand and started trying to locate its owner. She queried those few folks nearby, with no success. Then Ed Wheeler, the cardiologist who had assisted us with Chet, came jogging down the beach, and Martha showed it to him. He said he would carry it further along and check with some others. Sure enough, he found the owner, who hadn't even realized it was missing. It was their hotel key, and it was a highly unusual thing to have it retrieved from the sea.

That evening we celebrated Antonio's twenty-ninth birthday with cake, candles and ice cream. Chini and Juliana were along, naturally, and the baby was delighted with the candles and singing. It was a first for her, and she seemed to think it was all performed just for her pleasure. Antonio acted as if it were for her, as well. He was seeing it all through her eyes, I think, and reveled in it.

Chini persuaded Juliana to give us all hugs and kisses, which she did very demurely, flashing those lovely dark, shining eyes. I think of my own grandchildren and how I miss them. What would the world be without little children? I can't imagine it. We think children lend purpose to life.

The weather became windy, but we still went to the beach. We came home to shower and have our happy hour, but not many animals showed up to entertain us, due to the wind. We squeezed in some reading as dinner cooked and then enjoyed chicken, cole slaw, French-fried yucca, and green beans, followed by chocolate cake and ice cream. Not bad for being stuck out in the jungle. We had to put up with some blinking lights and brief outages, common when the wind is strong, and kept our flashlights at hand as we tried to play cards.

During our Sunday walk I almost stepped on a snake on the trail past the cemetery. It had a pale bluish back and was fast as the wind. It practically sailed through the bunches of beach grass, zipping out of sight and into the jungle. We also came upon a small spider wrapping a large grasshopper in its web, reminding us of David and Goliath.

Martha took along a fresh pan of corn bread that afternoon when we drove up on the mountain for lunch and cards with George and Beverly Baumunk. The corn bread turned out to be so hard that we couldn't eat it. Martha was embarrassed, but we all made a joke of it. George said, "Just throw it over the rail and down the hill. The animals will eat it." But he couldn't resist adding, "They have strong teeth."

We came home late in the afternoon to find that Martha had locked her key in the house. When it happened before, Skip had located a spare key for her back door and attached it to the jeep keys. That enabled him to let her in without cutting the screen, as he normally had to do. Then, in spite of playing cards all afternoon, Martha insisted on another round that evening. Where did she get her energy?

The winds blew most of the week, knocking a big palm frond down onto our roof one night. It thundered like a cannon, rudely awakening us, although we tend to sleep fitfully during windstorms anyway. The whole house was filthy from the dirt blown through our screens, especially after they were torn by flying debris, and through the spaces at the comb of our roof. Cleaning serves little purpose until the winds stop, but I felt compelled to do some sweeping during the pauses. I hate wading through dirt.

The paths were littered with leaves and limbs. Antonio has to start his raking and burning anew after each windstorm. Skip generally has torn screens to restaple and other repairs and sometimes helps Antonio clean the grounds. We are all glad when the winds stop.

241

One day Lili Adams became entangled with an orange jellyfish, somehow getting it wrapped around her arm. She showed me the marks the next day at the beach and said it was still painful. We discussed remedies, including applying meat tenderizer and flushing the area with seawater. I prefer not to mess with such creatures, although I'm sure Lili felt the same. It's not done by choice. When we returned home we found a scorpion in our bedroom. Skip zapped him in a hurry and swept him outside.

Saturday, January 25, was the main day of the Nosara fiesta, the day of the bullfights. We decided to go again, in spite of the heat, and it was certainly bright and hot. Only a couple of incidents differed from the prior description of the fiesta in chapter 14. One was that while we sat in the bleachers, absorbed in the action in the ring, something in the boards and poles cracked. Fear shot through me like a thunderbolt. For an instant I expected to be lying on the ground in a heap of poles and people. But nothing happened . . . nothing. Skip and I exchanged grimaces and Kathy Benish looked alarmed, but no one else seemed bothered in the least.

Martha said, "Oh, don't worry." I worried, but nothing happened.

We always leave the fiesta before it is over. It gets a little repetitive after a couple of hours, and by doing so we also beat the final rush. We were told the next day that a bull had cavorted too energetically after we left and had broken his back. The cowboys had dragged him out of the ring; the owner cut the animal's throat and hauled the bull away to be butchered. It was not pretty to contemplate, but that's the way life is, sometimes.

Early in February, Skip had a good day snorkeling. He found a giant tun, which is a lovely round type of conch with a delicate lip that opens to a wide sort of grin. This one was over seven inches at its widest point and entirely intact, which is rare because the thin lip edge is usually broken by the pounding of the surf. It is a cousin to the grinning tun, or gaping tun, which is nearly identical except it has a thick lip, where the giant tun's lip is thin. We have a lovely collection of grinning tuns, which are less fragile.

He also came upon an unusual bright blue starfish that would have reached from edge to edge on a small dinner plate. He brings his discoveries to show me and beams like a schoolboy pleasing his mom. I am always duly impressed and enjoy his discoveries as much as he does.

We return the living specimens to the sea, though it is sometimes hard to give up such exquisite creatures. We at first treated this practice as a conservation issue but have since learned that there are laws in many countries, including Costa Rica, which specify the release of most living shellfish. A few species are listed as harvestable, with limits and restrictions similar to fishing regulations.

Some restaurants use locally harvested shellfish in soups and such specialties as ceviches, which feature thinly sliced fish and shellfish marinated in lime juice as *bocas*. They often use the shells as decorations, after the meaty part has been removed. One of the commonly used local conchs has a large pinkish-orange porcelain area at the opening, which makes it a real eye-catcher, especially when it is large and mature.

As I watched the washer one morning to make sure it would go into the spin cycle properly, I noticed smoke rising from the plug, at the outlet. I leaped forward and shut off the switch and yelled for Skip. He searched out a new receptacle and plug and replaced both, carefully. Darn that washing machine! Martha came around the corner and asked, "What did you do this time?" Aarrgh!

Skip and I dropped Martha at the civic association building, then went on to Nosara to pick up some items at the hardware store, La Paloma, and check for mail. The jeep's clutch began to malfunction, something Skip had been attuned to during the past few days. The gears made a racket, even with the clutch tramped clear to the floorboards. We decided to go straight to the garage. Yes, there is a garage. It had been open for some months now, located not far beyond La Paloma.

Skip explained the problem, and the head mechanic, Santiago, said he would be able to look at the jeep in about an hour. He had to tow another vehicle in first.

We decided to use the time to do the grocery shopping, so we retraced our route to La Paloma. That was not a great decision, for after getting the groceries Skip was barely able to get the jeep into gear for the return trip, short though it was. This time we stayed at the garage and waited.

After another half hour, Santiago brought a younger mechanic over to look at the jeep. Skip related the problem again and showed them the empty fluid container mounted under the hood on the firewall. They nodded knowingly, Santiago said a few things, and the young guy grabbed a few tools and got right to work. It was a hydraulic clutch, and the seals had deteriorated. They had the parts on hand to rebuild it and were done in less than an hour. The bill was less than ten dollars. We were delighted.

On January 29, we had friends for dinner, all oldtime Nosara winterers, including Mary Yost, Fran Super, and George Miller. This group had lots of stories to tell of the early days in Nosara, along with tales of other travels and experiences. Skip and I were prepared for some good listening out on the back deck, but unfortunately it was not to be. Mary had brought her Shetland sheepdog, Chris, and he spent the evening barking at the large troop of monkeys that happened to be overhead. When howler monkeys hear loud noises, they howl in return. And did they ever howl in response to Chris's barking! We had trouble hearing ourselves think, the noise was so loud and continuous. During occasional short interludes, we could hear the blaring of a televised soccer game just below us in the village. We shook our heads and laughed. We had never before nor since been exposed to so much noise here in the jungle.

Dinner was served just about dark, and things were beginning to quiet down to the point where we could hold a decent conversation. Mary still made feeble attempts to shush Chris when he heard something in the jungle, and he gradually settled himself, since he was nearly exhausted from chasing back and forth under the monkeys. He's like a spoiled child; he obeys Mary only when he feels like it. She fed him some of Martha's dinner food and set a dish of water for him on the porch.

The monkeys were still around the next day, so we watched them some more at various times. It's easy to attribute human qualities to them, due to both their humanlike appearance and some of their actions. I watched a male, female, and half-grown "teenager" for nearly half an hour, right above the deck where I was sitting, about midafternoon. They seemed to be a family group, although even that could be an erroneous assumption. I preferred to think of them in those terms, anyway. At one point, the youngster went straight over to the male (father?) and put its arms around him, seeming to give him a big hug. I swear Father had a surprised look on his face, but he made no nasty response. When they separated, the male made what seemed to me to be a "come-on" motion to the female, and they moved on as a unit, Dad, Mom, and youngster, in that order.

Bolivar, George Miller's main man, had sent his workers up to Martha's house to replace some of the old screening. They worked with the most basic tools, prying off strips with a screwdriver and fastening new screen with hammer and nails. Heresy! Skip couldn't stand to watch such uncraftsmanlike work, so he trotted over to his tool shelf to get his handy little pry bar and dug out Chet's staple gun. The Tico workers grinned when Skip handed them the tools. He watched for a little while, giving them pointers when they were unsure of proper technique.

Martha changed her mind several times about which screens she wanted replaced, and the Ticos looked puzzled each time. She would give them directions in English while using her hands to enhance her meaning. The young men understood very little English but tried to follow her incomplete gestures and sign language. Then Martha would change her mind and reverse her instructions, while the Ticos were still trying to sort out her first directions. Skip patiently waited until the ultimate moment to interpret her wishes, the point at which Martha could no longer change her mind. Then he tried to clarify her desires to the workers, not always successfully. Gradually the work got done. Then Martha would say, "Well, maybe I didn't need to replace that one, but now it's done. What do you think?"

I escaped to our house while the Ticos worked on Martha's, since mine needed a good cleaning, and I informed Martha of my intentions. About two hours later, I returned, telling Martha that I was going to do like the Ticos and take a break.

She said, "You don't need a break. You just came back from a break."

I replied, "Martha! I was working the whole time."

She responded stiffly, "Well, I want to know exactly what you were doing over there."

Feeling like a schoolgirl, I explained in detail everything I had done, but I was certainly not happy with that interaction.

On Tuesday, company was coming. The time was near at hand. Martha was terribly fidgety. Corky Adams, a descendant from the presidential line of Adamses, along with her daughter, son-in-law, and grandson, had been invited for brunch. Corky even has a granddaughter named Abigail Adams, although she was back home on Long Island, attending school.

Actually, the time was set at noon, but since the main dish was an egg casserole, Martha had decided to call it a brunch. She apparently wanted dearly to impress them and kept trying to improve the menu.

"We'll dice the fruit and serve it in bowls. It's always pretty that way." Pause. Think. "No. I think we'll slice it. Then we can arrange it on a platter. That might be nicer." Pause; rock faster. "I wish we had

245

some of those little sausages. It's almost too late to go to the store." Pause. Rock, rock. Think. "Oh, wouldn't it be awful if they had eggs for breakfast? After I made this egg casserole for lunch? . . . Brunch.

"It's too late to go get some little sausages, isn't it?" Rock, think, fret, fidget.

"Martha, I think it will be a lovely brunch. That egg casserole is so good, and the fruit is colorful and tasty. You have toast and coffee and Ruth Heiges's coffee cake. Wouldn't you be pleased to visit someone and have such a nice layout?" I tried to reassure her.

"Yes," she replied, "I guess I would. It's too late to change anything now . . . but I do wish I had some of those little sausages!"

Of course Corky and her family were delighted with the brunch.

Some time later, George and Beverly Baumunk graciously invited us to accompany them on a day trip to the Indian village of Guaitil, where the famous pottery is made. *Gracious* is an apt description of the Baumunks—what a lovely couple: white-haired and mannerly in the old tradition. They look like the ideal grandparents, although they lament the fact that they have no grandchildren. Of course we accepted their invitation, delighted for a day afield.

We spent a couple of hours moseying around the village square at Guaitil, examining the wares in the rustic booths. We compared and discussed the quality of their work, the colors we preferred, the various styles. We asked prices. Then we went around again, and George bought several pieces to decorate the new house they had built for their son, Creston, next door to their own house. Skip sneaked off to buy me a delightful vase that featured a very recognizable howler monkey in relief. These craftsmen really know their subjects in detail. Skip hid the vase and presented it to me on Valentine's Day. How romantic!

We treated George and Beverly to a Chinese lunch at the *Restaurante Nicoya* and made it home in time for happy hour. George was over eighty and drove like a teenager, which made for some exciting moments. Still, he always seems to arrive safely, at least so far.

Martha had told us about the new municipal dump, saying it was such an improvement, such a lovely dump. We wondered if there was such a thing as a lovely dump, but we obliged her and drove around the back road on our return from Nosara in order to see this phenomenon.

It was a mess. Trash was strewn everywhere. We could recognize their attempts to initiate recycling, since there were scattered piles of plastics here and glass bottles there. But weeds were growing up through the piles and litter was blown all over. It was obvious that hopeful plans had gone astray, probably for lack of overall organization and infrastructure. At any rate this dump was certainly a dump. Martha was disappointed.

Our old friend Rudy flew in on February 5 for one last visit to Costa Rica. He was eighty-four years old and still a bright and joyous person. He wondered if we had celebrated Groundhog Day. Since we hadn't, he said, "Well, I'll take you all out to eat."

Martha said, "But Groundhog Day is over," to which Rudy replied, "Well, we can celebrate next Groundhog Day!" He then repeated his theme: "I believe in celebrating early and often!" And he made sure we did just that. If anyone made any excuses, Rudy would say, "My treat!" How could we turn him down?

The next morning we were taking Rudy to the beach but stopped to see George Miller. As we pulled into George's driveway, Skip noticed the right rear tire was going flat. With so much dust and rust he had difficulty getting the jack to function. After some effort it became operable, but then the wheel lugs were frozen tight. George advised, "Pull on one side of the wrench and hit the other side with a hammer. That's how they do it here." Skip just kept struggling.

Skip was still trying to muscle the lugs loose to no avail when Bolivar arrived on the scene. Boli grabbed a hammer and beat on one side of the lug wrench as he pulled on the other. He had the wheel off in a few minutes. Skip said, a bit abashed, "Well, you can't beat youth, strength, and experience! And George did tell me to use that hammer."

We went on to the beach, but when we next drove to Nosara Skip made sure the tire was repaired. This is no place to be driving without a spare tire.

While we were at George's, he gave Martha a lemon as large as a grapefruit. His trees often bear more than he can use, and he is always generous with Martha. She decided to make a lemon pie, and that one lemon was sufficient for this pie with enough left over for two others. The pie was delicious. Of course, Martha's pies always are.

While we were eating breakfast one day, the neighbor's big rooster crowed loudly just below us in the banana grove. He was answered by one of his hens from a good distance away, over near the driveway. We watched as the rooster tore headlong all the way over to the hen and chased her back to his feeding ground in the banana patch. I guess he didn't want her wandering so far away, and it was obvious who was boss. They returned to contented scratching and feeding, but the hen now stayed within reach of her lord and master.

Fifteen monkeys showed up that afternoon. Two females got into a spat directly above the deck where we were sitting, craning our necks to watch. They hit and growled and whimpered, obviously agitated. Suddenly we jumped up and ran aside as we felt a shower of fine spray descending on us. We concluded that loss of bladder control may be associated with a high level of agitation. One of the females left the scene, and within minutes they were quietly munching away on the young shoots and blossoms. All was again well in paradise. We returned to our seats to watch and read, enjoying the peace of the hot afternoon. Showers—with water—would soon follow.

Rudy wanted to see the turtles once more, so we departed at 5:00 A.M. for Ostional Wildlife Preserve. The temperature was mellow, contradicting our inclination to use sweaters in the predawn darkness. What a quiet, peaceful time of day! The darkness and absence of people created a ghostly impression as we stared ahead into the vibrating headlight beams of the old jeep. Our own silence was broken only by occasional comments about the water level in the fords or the roughness of the road when Skip was unable to avoid one of the many chuckholes. A very few *campesinos* were up and about, tending to livestock or heading to the fields. They appeared as subdued as we were in the gray dawn.

We parked the jeep at the dilapidated ranger station and quietly walked directly out onto the beach. A few Tico fishermen were there ahead of us and had several large, shiny creval jacks flopping on the beach. Fish for breakfast, no doubt. In some households, no fish, no breakfast.

We asked if there were any turtles this morning. "Tortugas?"

"No," was the response, indicating with a mixture of gestures and Spanish that there remained only tracks on the beach. We were too late.

Still, we ambled south along the beach to take a look at the tracks and enjoy the beauty of dawn over the jungle and ocean. Although there were no turtles to be seen, the bird life was something to behold. Terns and pelicans were active over the ocean, while several kinds of herons and a few hawks populated the lagoon area. Black vultures were busy on the beach, making certain that no turtle eggs escaped destruction. We resented their persistent thoroughness. The sand was so full of bits of eggshell that every square inch must have contained some. There were a few dogs searching for eggs, but they could hardly have competed with the plethora of vultures.

Despite the absence of turtles, we were pleased with our morning's adventure. The ride back to Nosara was pleasant as we enjoyed the mellow breeze through the jeep's windows and watched for birds and mammals. Back at Casa de las Flores we enjoyed breakfast together and chatted about the trip. Antonio appeared for work while we were eating, and Martha gave him coffee. He grinned as he stirred in the usual two heaping spoonfuls of sugar. Skip commented, "Our day is really just beginning, but it feels as though we've already completed one." We all agreed; getting started so early makes the day seem long indeed.

That evening we watched a storm over the ocean from the Benishes' deck. It was lovely to see: great jagged loops of lighting illuminating dark clouds, augmented by a distorted reflection of the flashes in the choppy sea. Never a drop of rain reached us where we sat, barely half a mile inland.

The next time we played cards in the game room, the lights went off, leaving us in complete darkness, although we could see that the little table lamp on the front porch was still on. That meant the overall current was not interrupted, so Martha concluded that Antonio must have been playing tricks on us. She growled, "That darned Antonio!," then yelled for him to stop, but there was no response, not even a giggle or footfall to disclose anyone's presence.

Skip felt his way down the steps in the darkness and proceeded over toward the game room switch on the *cabina* wall. Before he reached it he exclaimed, "It's on fire!" and yanked out his big red handkerchief to slap the flames out. Actually, the flames were only tiny, but it's frightening to think of how rapidly they can grow.

The next day we made a run to Nosara for new switches and other supplies, including rum and cornflakes, the real necessities of life. We had tried other locally available boxed cereals, but nothing seemed as good as cornflakes. We joked about how tired we had become of cornflakes, and the possibility of finding a suicide note from Martha, saying, "I just couldn't take another bowl of corn flakes." But still we ate them, though practically never without a garnish of sliced bananas.

Skip replaced the burnt switch right away, but we thought of the similar occurrences at our house and wondered how often such things could happen before a serious fire resulted. We began to ponder the advisability of Martha's remaining here for many more years.

Martha's favorite game, Pennies from Heaven, requires five decks of cards. When she dug them out of her storage cupboard this year she found them somewhat mildewed and sticking together. This was certainly a serious problem. Her face was a study in concern. So I said, "Martha, after lunch I'll help you separate and clean those Pennies from Heaven cards."

It took the better part of two hours to complete the job, and then we powdered them with Johnson's baby powder. When Skip came over from a job he was working on at our house to join us on the deck, he commented, "Gee, is there a baby around here that you two have been hiding from me?"

On our next trip to the beach we were bobbing lazily in our favorite tide pool when we saw a dark horse galloping up the beach in our direction. It was really racing, flat out, and as it came closer we began to see that the rider's arms seemed to be held straight out on each side. When it passed in front of us we could see it was a beautiful black horse with long, flowing mane and tail. The rider was a shapely young woman with long blond hair, clad only in a bikini and boots, standing straight up in the stirrups with her arms straight out. Skip exclaimed, "Shades of Lady Godiva!"

What a wonderful sight! The lovely blond lady on the racing black horse, holding on with only her knees; truly a remarkable display of horsemanship and athletic grace and beauty. We laughed, then commented about the strange sights we have seen, wondering what we might see next.

Time to make another trip to Nicoya. Martha had some important banking to do, so we made that rough trip once more. Skip and I escorted Martha into the bank and then sat in the park while she waited in line. Every so often Skip went back into the bank to check on her. Each time she was in a different line. The third time he went in she looked worried and said with a touch of panic in her voice, "Skip, I just realized I don't have any identification with me!"

Skip helped her check again; no passport, no driver's license or Social Security card, no birth certificate. He stayed with her at that point. Then, after two hours' waiting, the teller took care of Martha's needs without any request for identification. Apparently they recognized her from her numerous prior visits. What a relief to be done with that and proceed with some shopping and a nice lunch break before the long, hot drive home.

Another *ranchito* under construction! Again we could watch its progress from Martha's deck. The large family next to the lower gate was still expanding, and a *ranchito* is the easiest way to add a room. Izabel's compound now housed fifteen, including his children's spouses and a couple of grandchildren. (Izabel, pronounced "EESS-a-bel," is a man's name; the feminine would be Izabela.)

As usual, the young men were sent to the other side of our compound, into the lower reaches of George Baumunk's property, a very thick jungle, to climb the oil palms for fronds. For several evenings they dragged fronds and poles down the road in front of us, but in less than two weeks they had their new sleeping quarters under roof. This one was tall enough to have a loft; they needed the extra sleeping space.

I commented as we watched their progress, "It must take a huge quantity of rice and beans to feed that clan." Martha and Skip nodded dutifully.

Still we admired the happy way they played together before suppertime. It was their backyard that became the community soccer field for the evening *fútbol* games we had watched so often. Izabel himself, clad only in a pair of red shorts, would sometimes play goalkeeper. It was a peaceful sight, in spite of the sounds of the hard-played game, as the village mothers cooked supper over wood fires and smoke hung in a soft cloud over the little collection of bungalows.

I wondered, *Do they know how poor they are? Does it matter?* They seem so contented and have such family togetherness. That's a different kind of wealth, I suppose.

It was mid-February before we saw the first turquoise-browed motmot. Skip spotted it just ten feet from our screened porch, in the jungle. It was later in the season than usual and therefore all the more welcome. We have become quite fond of these lovely creatures with feather colorings impossible to describe. As we watched, it flew a short loop to catch a large insect and return to its perch, then whacked the bug against the limb to kill it before swallowing, its characteristic practice.

Antonio came by with a large fish for Skip. That meant he had already supplied his uncle's family and his grandparents and probably some neighbors. It must have been quite a large catch. He stayed and related his "fish stories" with great animation as he watched Skip fillet the hefty creval jack. Then Antonio took the remaining carcass home with him to be cooked down into soup stock. Chini would probably use it as flavoring for a large pot of rice. They don't waste much.

251

Skip hefts a big crevalle jack provided from Antonio's surplus on a good day.

On February 21 Chini came up the hill to ask Skip to drive her father to Nosara to see the doctor. Chini accompanied her father, who looked very ill. The doctor was absent and a note on the door said he wouldn't return for seven more days. Why didn't that surprise us? Skip felt bad for their circumstances, but they took it very matter-of-factly. The next day Chini's father was so ill that she took him by bus to the hospital in Nicoya. They admitted him for three days because of pneumonia.

The following week we were invited to an open house. Terry and Amy Lewis had just finished their new home on a jungled knob less than half a mile from Casa de las Flores and were throwing a big bash to celebrate the fact. They were a handsome younger couple from Georgia. He had had the foresight to get into the cellular phone business at its outset and had done well enough to semiretire and build his dream house here with an unobstructed view of the Pacific Ocean.

We had been watching its progress each time we returned from the beach. Just before the junction of the beach road with the main road we could look right up at their house emerging on the hillside. The swimming pool seemed to hang right on the edge of the steep slope and made us wonder about earthquakes.

When we drove to the new house, we had to go the long way around—a couple of miles up the road, then hairpin back up the mountain, cross to the back side, then return over the top to the front and down a steep lane. When Skip began parking the jeep, Martha screamed, "Let me out! I don't want to roll down over that bank! You're going to kill us!" She got out, and Skip got the jeep turned around and parked.

The house was bigger than we had guessed, having seen it only from a distance. It was spacious and airy, with lots of openings facing that incomparable view of the Pacific. The furniture and ceiling beams were made of a lovely rich tropical wood, finished with the natural grain showing. Floors and countertops featured colorful tiles. Most entrancing of all was the swimming pool. It was positioned in front of the house, just below the main living veranda. The front edge of the pool hung right on the cliff side and featured a constant flow of water over that edge. Of course the water flowed into a tiled trough several feet below the rim, but the effect was great. To bathers in the pool the view was continuous, looking across the surface of the pool straight out into the ocean without a break.

Skip asked Terry about earthquake concerns. Terry assured him that the engineer had taken that into account, using deep pilings and such devices to anchor everything securely. Of course there were no guarantees, but Terry seemed secure in the belief that it had been well designed.

The food was excellent, prepared by Bill Lancaster and his wife, operators of the Bamboo Bar in Nosara. Martha was delighted with the party, calling it the social event of the year. She was concerned that the Baumunks had not been invited and admonished Skip and me not to mention it to them for fear that their feelings might be hurt.

We settled for a very light supper that evening, after such a tempting lunch at the party, but afterward Martha's sweet tooth was crying for chocolate. A frantic search revealed that the supply Rudy had brought her was gone, totally depleted. Disgruntled, she plopped down into a rocking chair, grumbling, "I could kill for a piece of chocolate!" Actually, I sometimes feel the same.

A few days later, as we were doing our regular tour of the beach, I found a starfish the like of which I didn't even know existed. Big enough to span a dinner plate, it was bright, almost electric blue, with spots of red and dark blue scattered sparingly across its front. It was rather heavy and seemed stiff. Perhaps it was dying, or maybe that was its nature. The other side was dark gray, almost black. I wondered if there was a way to preserve it to show to people, but we couldn't imagine how it could be done. Skip said it would be bound to stink terribly, so we gave up on that idea. Still, it seemed a shame that all we could do was look it over carefully and have no record of it but memory. Skip gave me his standard philosophy at such moments: "That's the way life is."

Bridge was the game of choice after dinner, since Rudy was aboard to make a foursome. Martha is a lifelong bridge enthusiast, having been trained by her mother in her childhood years. She goes by the book and loves to win, as she does with all her games. When the cards fall her way, her spirits soar; she is lively and happy. When her luck fades, so do her spirits, and she sometimes nods off in the midst of a game.

One night when Skip and Rudy were on a roll, Rudy took too long to sort his cards and make his bid. His old fingers were having difficulty separating the cards. Martha lost patience with him and said, "Holy Heaven, Rudy! How long is it going to take you to bid?" I felt sorry for Rudy, but losing does make Martha a little grumpy.

It was getting on into the latter part of February when Skip blurted out, "Hey, we're all starting to look sort of shaggy. We haven't had any haircuts since we arrived. I'd better check my clippers and see if they still work. That old rainy season makes them rusty."

He oiled the clippers and got them loosened up, then asked me to try them out on him. They worked adequately enough to get the job done, at least good enough for what he called a jungle haircut. Before the day was done he had talked Rudy into a haircut, too. Later in the week George Baumunk stopped in to ask Skip if he could make an appointment with the barbershop, so Skip cut both George's and Beverly's hair. They are always very appreciative, thanking Skip profusely and

The school bus, a pickup truck, returning kids from *colegio*, during the first month that high school was available in Nosara.

praising his work. That stimulated Martha to jump on the bandwagon, so Skip cut hers, too, as everyone else sat and rocked and drank iced tea, offering comments about bald spots and such. I hesitate to comment on style, but at least we all had shorter, cooler hair by the end of that week, in spite of the rust on the clippers. Besides, Beverly delivered a pan of chocolate brownies in payment for Skip's tonsorial services.

On the way back from our next trip to Nosara, we caught up to a flat-bed pickup truck loaded to the sideboards with young people on their way home from school. Most of them were wearing the blue-and-white uniforms required at the new secondary school that had recently opened. We snapped a picture of the truck as it stopped in a cloud of dust to drop off the Esperanza contingent, the youngsters in our neighborhood. They certainly looked happy as they joked and waved and smiled their good-byes. This was the first secondary school in the area, where they could finally get some further education without having to leave their families. We tried to imagine what that meant to kids in such a family-oriented culture and ultimately to the progress of the community!

The mangoes are beginning to ripen, and the monkeys seem to have acquired a taste for them. We had never noticed them eating mangoes

255

before, as much as we had watched them over the years. Perhaps there has been a shortage of certain blossoms and they are reverting to plan B, or perhaps mangoes are a newly acquired taste for this troop. At any rate, they are tearing into the mangoes as if they are addicted. Some of them race to a tree, and the winner will defend it as if it were a personal possession. They greedily strip trees, sometimes taking only one bite from a fruit before dropping it in order to grab another.

Skip salvages some of the riper fruits, cutting out the bitten areas and eating the remainder. When he gets too many, he fills his hat and brings them up onto Martha's porch. He places them in a bowl on the side table, hoping Martha will be tempted into converting them into a pie, which happens more often than not. Each time she recites, "If the mangoes are green, they taste like apple pie. If they're ripe, they make a peach pie." We are never unhappy with the results.

Mary Yost invited us for dinner again. I told Martha and Skip that Mary would have beets again and ask me to peel them. "That means I'll burn my fingers again, since she always takes the boiling pot off the stove and hands them to me. 'Here,' she says in her deep voice, 'you peel the beets, Chipper.' So I do it and burn my fingers."

Martha and Skip laughed, knowing the truth of my statement. Skip said, "Chipper, you've got to run some cold water over them, even if you do it behind her back." We all laughed again, but that was probably the best solution.

Sure enough, when we arrived at Mary's condominium I smelled beets the minute I walked through the door. I whispered to Skip as Martha occupied Mary, "Do you smell the beets?" We had to smother our laughter. After all, we do love the old girl.

After rum and Coke and some nice *bocas*, Mary growled, "Chipper, come peel the beets."

Martha, Skip, and I smiled secretively as I rose and marched to the kitchen. Martha even came to watch over my shoulder, and we snickered quietly as I sneaked the beets briefly under a stream of cold water. But they still stung my fingers as I stripped the skins off.

Mary's dinner was just great, and we enjoyed her company as usual. She told us of her travel plans, and we shared ours. She gave us some advice on our forthcoming trip to South America, and Martha promised to let us read her log book from her trip there with Chet many years ago. These old jungle girls have been around! We listened carefully to their tips.

256

Skip and Chipper with loads of bananas and mangoes,
standing on Chet's shuffleboard court at
Casa de las Flores.

Two days later Antonio clunked Skip on the head with a large plank as Skip was helping him load them onto the jeep. Skip was nearly decked and was a little wobbly for a short while but then seemed to recover OK. He continued to help Antonio move the planks to his house. Antonio planned to use them to add on an outside kitchen area. He uses most of the cast-off materials from Martha's place. If he doesn't need them, he passes them on to his neighbors.

Cornflakes! Every day cornflakes. Thank goodness for bananas. Those delicious little home-gown bursts of flavor seem to save our sanity when we have to face another cornflake breakfast. The other Central American cereals we have tried just don't seem to cut it, so we stick with old reliable. And Martha hasn't yet committed suicide over them, despite her threats.

This morning while we were eating breakfast we heard a baby howler cry for help. Its mother had hurried ahead to claim a spot in the mango tree, and baby had been left behind. The space between the trees was too long for it to leap, so it was trying to get Mom's attention. Mom greedily guzzled a few more mangoes before responding. Skip said, "That's a sure sign of addiction." Then she returned and pulled a limb down within reach of baby. It quickly leaped across the now manageable gap and ran up the limb onto Mother's back, wrapping its fingers tightly into her fur. Mom wasted no time hurrying back to her spot in the mango tree, but now baby obviously felt safe and secure.

The next morning the mango trees were full of monkeys by the time we gathered for breakfast. There were three mothers with small babies on their backs competing for the luscious fruits. It looks like we will have to settle for cast-off fruit this year. The monkeys have first pickings.

We noticed something today that we had missed before. When the smallest babies ride on their mothers' backs they wrap their tails around the base of Mother's tail, in addition to wrapping their little forepaws in her fur. After years of monkey watching, we were surprised and a bit abashed to realize this observation had escaped our notice for so long.

A coatimundi has been getting pretty brazen, sidling right down onto the back patio with us standing there watching from the doorway. Martha said, "We'll have to be careful where we put the bananas with this guy coming around so fearlessly." She repeated the story of the time one had quietly walked into her bedroom in midday, eaten two bananas and dropped the skins on the floor, then disappeared without anyone even seeing it. "The peelings gave him away. Nothing else peels bananas that way, just like we do, still fastened together at one end."

While we watched from Martha's deck Franco's daughters put the laundry out to dry. One or two of the younger girls climb the tree that leans over the upper corner of their house, jump over onto the roof, and catch the wet clothes and bedding as the others toss the items up to them. The laundry is then spread on the hot tin roof, where it dries in jig time. When the laundry is dry, they clear a space in the center and spread a sheet. The laundry is placed in a pile on the sheet, which is then gathered into a bundle and handed down to the tallest girl on the ground.

"Hmm. Solar heat. Pretty energy-efficient," commented Skip.

The girls do have a problem when a wind comes up, though, and dust from the road must also be a bother. But then again, they don't have to call the appliance repairman as we do. Their backup system on windy days is to hang the laundry on the fences, but I'd be afraid the barbwire would tear too many items.

Someone told us that Woody Harrelson was vacationing on the Osa Peninsula (southernmost Costa Rica) with his family and had cut his leg. He had tried to cure it with a natural remedy that included maple syrup, but it had developed into a serious staph infection. Finally he was flown out to San José, where he was treated with antibiotics. His lady, Laura, was expecting their second baby, and she was reportedly hoping to give birth in the ocean waves. The next issue of the *Tico Times* carried the story, pretty much as we had heard it.

About ten-thirty one evening in February, as we were just dozing off after a strenuous bout of cards with Martha, a loud diesel truck came through, traveling fast and blowing the horn repeatedly. That not only wakened us abruptly but started the monkeys howling, too. The troop above our house roared, then the troop across the road, then one down by the village, then ours again. They roared in volleys for several minutes, each one agitating the other. We grumbled to each other briefly, then began laughing at the absurdity of it. How were we ever to have guessed that we would find ourselves in this situation? We had been raised in rural western Pennsylvania in households of very moderate means. We had reached adulthood before we ever thought we might be able to afford to see the ocean or conceive of visiting another country. Now here we were, grumbling because monkeys in the jungle next to our house were disturbing our sleep! It did have its humorous side.

The next morning the monkeys began howling again at four-thirty. The squirrels were chasing one another around the Guanacaste tree, knocking twigs and seedpods down on the house roof—mating season, probably. Some insects must have come down with the limbs and leaves, for the rufous-naped wrens, a large, noisy variety, began pecking and feeding on the tin roof. Then that darned truck driver came back through again, blowing his horn, setting off the monkey chorus once more. That started the village roosters crowing in rotation, soon to be followed by the *chachalakas*. Lord, what a cacophony! It was impossible to sleep through. Still it was so ridiculous that we could only lie there and grin at each other, shaking our heads and reminding ourselves how unique and special it is to be in this place.

Just at daybreak we slipped on shorts, shirts, and sandals and stepped out onto the porch to survey the goings-on around us. Things had simmered down somewhat. The monkeys were working their way across toward Martha's, munching shoots as they traveled. The squirrels were so tired from chasing around that they stretched out on the limbs with all four feet hanging down, just like the monkeys do. The wren brigade was still busy cleaning up insects on and around the house. Other birds were scouring the trees for breakfast. One blossoming tree was inundated with hummingbirds; we couldn't tell what kind because they were too high up, but they certainly were busy. It was a wonderful morning, paradise, almost.

After lunch Skip was having his siesta in the hammock on the screen porch, which meant mostly reading a good book, along with an occasional doze, when he heard a familiar whistle and quiet call from a distance. "Eskip, Eskip!" Pause . . . whistle. . . . "Eskip, Eskip!" Antonio needed something. Skip rolled out of the hammock and stepped out onto the porch. Antonio waved for him to come follow him to the bodega workshop. He was carrying an old, heavy-looking board.

When Skip caught up with Antonio at the bodega, he explained and mimed until Skip understood that he wanted the board sawed into one-inch by one-inch strips to make handles for lobster hooks. *"Anzuelos para las langostas,"* he explained in Spanish.

Skip asked why this particular piece of wood; it was heavy as lead. Antonio replied that the weight made it easier to hold the hook down when he was swimming underwater. This wood would actually sink, while lighter wood would constantly pull toward the surface. It was hard enough to keep one's own buoyant body down while searching for lobsters without fighting with a floating hook handle that added to the problem.

Antonio held the piece and Skip sawed at it with the dull old Craftsman until the blade smoked; then they changed blades and repeated the process until they had two four-foot strips hacked out of the heavy old four-by-four. Skip, impressed with the dark red grain woven gracefully with black lines, said, "Wow! That's more beautiful than walnut wood."

Then they drilled a small hole in the end of each strip where hooks could be inserted. Antonio asked to borrow Skip's little block plane to smooth and round the strips. Satisfied, Antonio went trotting home with a grin on his face, probably imagining all the wonderful lobsters he would catch with his fine new gigs. Skip just grinned and shook his head as he watched him go. Then, his siesta disturbed, he went off to water some plants.

The next day at the beach, Lili Adams told us we had missed a big spectacle the day before. I said, "I knew we shouldn't skip a day. It's always bad luck to miss a day at the beach!"

Lili described how they had watched dozens, probably over a hundred, stingrays jumping and flipping in the waves. They had called a surfer to shore just to avoid trouble. It was a rare event, and we groaned and lamented because we had missed it. The ocean is full of surprises if you hang around long enough.

The army ants are back again. They have marched across the paths, up and down stairs, over Martha's porch, through the guest bathroom, and past the *cabinas.* Luckily, they have not disturbed Martha's main living areas (or the game room!), so all we have to do is be careful not to step on them as we move around the grounds and porches. They seem to clean up the nests of other ants, for we see them carrying eggs as they march, and the other ants seem to panic and run around hysterically at their approach.

One time we responded to an invitation to dinner with George Miller, arriving at the appointed time, punctual gringos that we are. He had his latest gardener, Kiko, helping him serve drinks and *bocas,* and we sat around in the leather rockers chatting and enjoying the refreshments until the three expected Ticos arrived.

Nearly an hour and a half later, the expected guests had still not arrived, but three other Ticos arrived in their place. The first three had been detained by other obligations but made sure their friend and employer would not be totally disappointed by sending substitutes in their place. George was not too surprised, saying casually, "It's more interesting this way."

George is about seventy-nine years old, but like Martha, he doesn't act his age. He is an excellent cook and had prepared the dinner himself. He experiments regularly with strange new tropical foods, which we thoroughly enjoy. This time, however, he served lasagna with garlic bread and that great old standby, three-bean salad. Martha provided dessert in the form of a mango pie, a bit runny but still delicious. The Tico guests smiled their pleasure when they tried it.

261

We learned that Antonio, the manager of the La Paloma supermarket, had just had a new baby son, so we toasted him and sort of dedicated the dinner to him. It was a very nice evening.

When we returned to Casa de las Flores it was after nine. Skip and I were ready to head to bed and read for a while, but Martha said, "I'm not tired yet; I'm still wound up. You have to stay and play with me awhile." So we accompanied her to the game room and played some Upwords, the three-dimensional Scrabble game.

Oh, heck, another wash day. The washer worked fine for Martha, but halfway through my wash it rebelled. Martha grumped at me again for having such a heavy wash. Skip tightened the belt again and we muddled through, but I'd just like to cancel wash days. He took me to the beach in the afternoon, and we walked and talked until the world looked brighter again. Boy, some days I need that beach badly!

One lazy afternoon as Martha and I were sitting on the back deck reading and keeping an eye out for wildlife, a bird caught my eye. I didn't recognize the bird but watched as it flew down to the ground to grab an insect and returned to its branch. I nudged Martha, pointed, and whispered for her to look. The bird whacked the bug against the tree limb a few times, loudly enough that we could hear it. Then it threw the stunned insect up into the air and caught it as it fell. We were amazed as we watched it repeat the process several times, much like a lonely child playing with a ball. I was glad I had alerted Martha because it was one of those things where you ask yourself, "Did I really see that?"

After the bird finished its game and departed, I got the Costa Rica bird guide out and looked it up. It was the dusky ant bird, and the book even described its behavior. We didn't dream the strange scene after all!

Another day we watched vultures circling and feeding on the far side of the shuffleboard court. I called Skip and we walked down to see what unlucky creature was serving as their dinner. It was a possum, stinking pretty badly. Thank goodness the cleanup crew was on the job. These were black vultures, which seem to predominate here. We have noticed them in Pennsylvania during the last twenty years or so, and their numbers seem to be increasing. Turkey vultures, the buzzards with the red heads, are our common type up north. They exist here, too, but in lesser numbers than the black-headed black vultures. Here in the tropics things could get pretty smelly if it weren't for the carrion eaters, so we are very glad to have them around.

On our way home from an evening of movies at the Benishes', we spotted a strange creature on the road just before we reached the gate at Casa de las Flores. Martha said, "Holy Heaven, what is that?" It had long reddish-brown hair and long but very bowed legs. Its gait was a mixture of awkwardness and grace as it hurried ahead of the jeep.

Skip said, "Wow, it's an anteater! Are we ever lucky to see it! I've only seen one since we've been coming here, and that was a brief glimpse in the middle of the night."

Martha responded, "I've never seen one before, and I've been coming here longer than you, about twenty years now."

The anteater turned into our driveway but then veered off to the right, up the hill toward Meditation Circle. Skip quickly drove the jeep on up to its parking place and grabbed a flashlight to see if he could get another look at the strange creature. I ran after him, and we did spot it, after first hearing the leaves rustle behind some snake plants on the edge of the hill. It was difficult to see among the plants and shadows, but we did get a fairly close look at it. Its head was long and narrow, a sort of continuation of the arch of its back, though it seemed too small relative to its body. It had bowed legs and was pigeon-toed—altogether a unique, ungainly, but wonderful creature. It sensed our presence and moved away down the hill, where we were reluctant to follow in the night.

We discussed the experience with quiet excitement as we wound our way back through the garden paths up to Martha's porch to tell her about it. What a delightful end to a nice evening, and again no pictures, only memories. (But that's the way life is.)

Maybe the anteater had been coming to dinner, since we had so many army ants around. Martha almost decided to come over to our house to sleep because there were so many ants. Her house was nearly surrounded by the marching columns, with one of them going right through her bedroom and out past the door of her bathroom. She pondered the situation as we sat and rocked on the porch. When Skip and I decided to go to bed, we took another look and found that the ants in her bedroom had passed on through. Just like that, silent as spirits, they had gone. We thought of Kipling's *Jungle Book*, where he writes that the insects are the rightful rulers of the world. Here in the jungle with army ants and killer bees, scorpions and tarantulas, it does become a thought-provoking premise.

I don't know if there was a relationship, but it rained that night, an unusual event in March, and that was the last of the army ants during our stay. We had over three inches of rain, and it thundered down on our sheet metal roofs like a herd of buffalo going overhead. But oh, what relief from dust! The air cleared; the plants turned green after the removal of their thick dust coat; birds sang as though their throats would burst. All people and animals seemed happier. And the ants were gone.

We occasionally noticed coatimundis checking out our bananas with larceny in mind. To avoid theft and sometimes to hurry their ripening, we cut the bunches just as they began to turn yellow. Then we laid them on the patio behind Martha's house to ripen in the sun. But they have to be hung inside before nightfall or the coatis will soon steal them. Martha prefers they be hung in her bedroom, where she can keep an eye on them. There is a long wire hook reaching down from a rafter inside her door just for that purpose.

It turned out that the coatimundi mentioned earlier that was described as "becoming too brazen" really became that. Martha found peelings on her bedroom floor in the morning but couldn't locate where he had entered. After a search, Skip found where a corner of a screen had been torn just enough to let the sneaky little guy slip through. Then the screen had flipped back into place, making the opening nearly invisible. Apparently he had gone out the same way. Without the peelings his passage might have gone entirely unnoticed.

Martha told Skip to move the hook and bananas to one of the guest *cabinas,* where the walls were higher and illicit entry would be more difficult. Also, it would be a new location where bananas were not customarily hung. Problem solved.

No. The next morning, not only were there peelings on the floor but also a pile of *pizote* poop. (*Pizote* is the Spanish name for the coatimundi, said "pea-SOH-tay.")

When Skip called her over to look, Martha exclaimed, "Holy Heavens! Where are we going to hide them now? Is there no place that is safe from that ornery little critter?"

The screen, though higher than our heads, had been torn just like the one in Martha's bedroom. Skip had to search carefully to find the opening. He decided to rig a booby trap for the next night, a concoction designed to frighten the animal when he jumped up to get at the bananas, letting the bananas hang where they were.

No luck. Friend *pizote* had no trouble at all getting at the bananas again in spite of the noisy booby trap. No matter where Skip would hang them, the critter's powerfully sensitive nose would lead him right to them.

After some discussion the only safe place we could think of was the old refrigerator in the bodega. So Skip would close the bananas in the refrigerator each evening and set them out again each morning. It was another chore, but those bananas were valuable. They made our cornflakes tolerable and kept Martha from reaching the end of her rope. There was peace in the valley once more.

One day an ultralight airplane kept circling and landing on the beach while we were enjoying the tide pool. We walked up the beach to see what was going on, learning that a young couple was taking people up for a fee. They were apparently working their way from beach to beach as a sort of working vacation. The pilot was able to take off and land in incredibly short distances. From our point of observation the little green-and-white craft was a pretty sight against the blue sky, with the ocean and jungled hills for a backdrop. Its noise was a detriment, but it didn't carry very far against the muffling sounds of the surf. One more surprise in an ordinary, though peaceful and beautiful, day.

We discussed bringing some money along on our next trip to the beach, finally deciding to do so. The next day we tucked several twenty-dollar bills in our beach bag and watched for the arrival of the ultralight. No luck. We had missed our chance.

There was soon much more action at the beach, though, because the *sardinas* were amassing close to shore and the big fish were following them. We first noticed the increased bird activity. Then determined-looking fishermen began passing on foot and on bicycles. After a while some came back past us carrying stringers of fish, some so heavy the men had to stop and rest. Two guys came by carrying a pole between them on their shoulders. The pole was so heavily laden that it sagged in the middle and the fish nearly dragged on the ground. They laid their burden down not far from us, and Skip had to go over for a closer look and to offer praise on the size as well as the number of fish. Those two were certainly proud of their catch.

Leaving Martha at the tide pool with a friend, Skip and I walked on down the beach toward the rocks at Guiones where all the action was happening. The frigatebirds had arrived to take advantage of the feast. They have wingspans reaching eight feet or more and are supposed to be the second-largest bird in the world in that regard. They rarely land but catch and eat fish literally "on the fly." Sometimes they grab a fisherman's bait and steal it or, worse, get hooked in the process.

We watched one man who had hooked a frigatebird land it and pull it to him. He had the bird by the neck, and we were afraid he might kill it. The big bird was beating the man with its wings. Skip ran over to help, folding its wings together in one hand as he tried to unhook it with the other. He got his finger in its bill, receiving a bad gash for his efforts. Together, they did get it freed and tossed it back into the air. After a couple of frantic flaps of those huge wings it was comfortably aloft again, sailing away on the air currents, looking much like a graceful paper airplane. Skip wrapped a salt water–soaked hanky around his finger to stem the bleeding.

Farther on we found a baby stingray, about the size of a fifty-cent piece and bright purple. At least we thought it was a stingray; it had a tiny tail, and we couldn't think of anything else it could have been.

Once we reached the rocks near where the fish were schooling, the activity made a great panorama. Anchovies and herring were scattered along the beach, where the fishermen grabbed those still alive to use as bait. Some fishermen netted fresh bait and shared it with others. Small pools were used to store individual catches and were sometimes red with the blood of large fish. We hopped from rock to rock, stopping to admire the larger fish. Most were jacks, strong and pugnacious-looking, but there were occasional rooster fish with long, flowing tips on their fins. Once in a while a streamlined snook was tugged ashore. All are powerful game fish, strong fighters.

Some of the old folks were satisfied to gather the larger of the herrings before they dried too much on the beach. They were about the size and build of the trout most anglers catch in Pennsylvania, eight to ten inches long and proportionately more slender than the jacks and roosters. The herring had followed the minnow-sized anchovies into the shallow water and fed on them; then the game fish chased and devoured the herring, apparently driving some of them up onto the beach. That helped explain why there were so many herring ashore.

The people were smiling and happy, enjoying the party, for that is what this was, a big block party where everyone knew each other and took pleasure in getting together. They bantered and teased about their success or lack of it, commiserated about the "one that got away" or cuts and abrasions received from the rocks, and generally behaved as families and neighbors everywhere. Well, maybe these folks were a little more cheerful and smiling; of course they all knew one another very well.

266

We were welcomed with smiles and even offers to fish, but we declined, fearing that we'd beat ourselves up on the rocks. We certainly would have lost our sandals in the waves, and our feet would have taken a tremendous beating without them. These folks were used to such activity. Their feet were tough, and they knew their way around the rocks; our feet were soft as marshmallows by comparison, and we didn't know where to step. But we surely envied their skill and camaraderie.

We stood among them and watched every phase of the process. Some were throwing lines with treble hooks across the protected tide pools, yanking fiercely in order to foul-hook herring or anchovies for bait. Once a good live bait was in hand, it was rehooked behind the rear dorsal fin as the fisherman hurried out toward deeper water at the outside edge of the rocks. There the bait was swung several times around the angler's head to gain momentum, then flung as far out as possible to reach the "big ones."

A baitfish on a line was slower than its free siblings, so it was usually snatched up quickly by one of the jacks in the middle of their feeding frenzy. Most casts produced hits, although sometimes the bait was flung off due to overzealous casting amid all the excitement and competition, and other times the bait would be stolen or bitten off behind the hook. Seeing a nine-inch herring bitten cleanly off in the middle elicited respect for the teeth of the quarry; the herring looked as though it had been slashed with a razor. Of course, as mentioned earlier, occasionally a frigatebird or pelican would nab the bait as it hit the water, only to be roundly cursed in Spanish for its interference in the fish-catching process.

But often a nice, strong fighting fish would be surging at the other end of the line, surely one of the most passion-evoking experiences in this life to those who have experienced it. Men's faces glow as they talk of fighting a big one. They brag about how long it had to be fought and about its length or how much it weighed, but those statistics only represent the fight, the battle that is felt through the hands and arms, back and legs, clear down to the soul. It must be that way. They will rise early, stay out late, endure intense sun, wind, cold, and heat, and still be supremely happy to have felt a big one surging on the line, even if it got away. True, for these Ticos it may mean food on an otherwise sparse table, but to watch their faces is to know that they are like fishermen everywhere: they love it beyond most of life's blessings.

I should mention that we have seen women fishing, but only a very few with that look in their eyes. Maybe they fish more for the food rather than the battle. But that's more serious grist to be discussed another time.

Once a fisherman fights his fish until it is tired enough to be dragged ashore, he backs up onto the rocks with it, still always in danger of losing it, and grabs it just ahead of the tail. Then he runs barefoot with his trophy across the terribly rough and sharp rocks to deposit it in one of the small pools of seawater remaining among the outcropping ledges that form the reef. Then the great prize is all but forgotten as he runs to the bait pool to begin again.

All the while the frigatebirds, pelicans, and terns are circling, diving, and calling; wives and family are watching, helping, and calling encouragement. Some children watch to chase off thieving birds; others try to get bait for fathers or older brothers. Pretty young maidens try fruitlessly to capture the attention of certain fishermen; better luck another time.

Sore feet, hands cut by fishing lines, scraped anklebones, fin punctures—so what! There are big fish and herrings for everyone! Every neighbor, friend, or relative, no matter how poor, can have fish on the table tonight. I guessed that was reason enough for the big smiles they wore.

As usual, Antonio was on the scene, accompanied this time by Candy, his uncle's son (Candy is also Chini's sister's son.) Yes, Antonio's woman, Chini, has a sister, Simona, who is married to Antonio's Uncle Rejeno, so I suppose Candy is Antonio's second cousin–nephew. Candy was fourteen years old and a quiet, charming little guy. He smiled broadly when we greeted him. Skip shook Candy's hand and I kissed him. He proudly showed us two nice jacks he had caught as Antonio, his mentor, beamed with pleasure. Antonio's presence always made us feel at home in a crowd of Ticos.

Skip asked Antonio where his fish were. Antonio replied with a careless wave of his hand that he had caught several at the beginning of the big run and had already delivered them to Chini and his grandfather and neighbors, then brought Candy back to catch some. He had apparently been the one who had alerted the community to the great event and was now proudly watching the results. What a guy!

We left the grand spectacle to walk back toward Martha at the tide pools. Before we reached her a noise behind us caused us to turn and look. There was a herd of cattle following us up the beach! Two vaqueros on horseback were guiding them, keeping them moving and holding them together. They whistled and slapped the cattle with their ropes, reminding us of movies about cowboys of the Old West. One rider was followed by a young foal that was apparently expected to learn good cowherding technique from watching its mother's performance.

But unlike earlier herds we had seen on the beach, this one was being pushed from behind by a modern herder in a jeep-type vehicle, which was "riding drag," as they called it in western lingo, but with a modern twist. We were a little disappointed by the intervention of this modern technology but were still delighted to see such a wonderful scene. There were probably fifty or sixty of the Brahma cattle of various colors parading along our beautiful beach with the blue Pacific on one side, jungle and palm trees on the other. Not many places in the world can such a sight be seen, and it came right on the heels of that wonderful fishing spectacle. We felt truly fortunate to have come to the beach this day.

Martha was just as delighted as we were to have seen the herd and mentioned the little foal chasing after its mother. We described the big fish run to her, but she said, "Oh, I've seen that before."

Skip wandered to the lower end of the tide pool and noticed some large fish cruising in and out of the inlet, so he ran back to get a few of the stranded herrings. Then he returned and tossed them into the pool in front of the jacks to see if they would hit them. They did. Some of the small fish even panicked so badly they swam clear out of the water, most of them returning with the next surge of surf.

He called to Martha and me to come watch, and we were able to see the big, aggressive jacks slash at the herrings in the clear, calm water of the tide pool. They struck so viciously that bits and pieces of herring shone in the sunlight after each strike. Martha said, "Holy Heaven, I'm not going back in there now!"

Skip talked me into getting some of the herrings and tossing them to the jacks, which was a memorable experience. We even talked Martha into throwing a couple of herrings to the jacks. They reminded us greatly of a pack of wolves in their hunting style. But soon they left for better hunting and we took a final swim before returning to Casa de las Flores. Back at the house I jotted down some notes so that I could remember the day in detail. What a day, and how I wish we had had a camera along!

Holy Week, the time between Palm Sunday and Easter Sunday, is called *Semana Santa* in Latin America and is the most important holiday of the year. Family members go to great lengths to be together at this

269

time. Nosara's beaches are crowded with Ticos, and beach houses that sit empty most of the year are alive with activity. Many people come from San José and elsewhere to enjoy the beaches, nearly always in large groups.

The collection of Tico vacation homes at Guiones is in full use during *Semana Santa,* and the tide pools there are often full of people sporting their best beachwear. We avoid using their pools at this time out of respect for their "space." But we enjoy walking the beach to catch a glimpse of all the activity, while maintaining a respectful distance.

The pool was crowded as usual, and the prosperity of the occupants was obvious. From a distance the rock-and-sand-rimmed pool resembled a nest of Easter eggs, it was so colorful. At a little closer range we could see, besides bright swimsuits, many of the ladies were wearing large, colorful hats. Probably the fashion caught on as a result of the skin cancer scare, but it made for a nifty scene from our point of view.

Some of the less affluent locals used plastic sheeting and tarpaulins tied between trees to shade their picnic areas. One of the large families had brought Grandma and placed her in a hammock tied between trees. Skip recognized Rozio, the pretty young lady who works at La Paloma as checkout clerk, and waved at her. Next time at the store he chatted with her about their Easter party and mentioned that she had a lot of family at the beach. She laughed and replied animatedly, *"Si, mucha familia!"*

People often ask what we do during our stay in Costa Rica, out in the jungle with no television or telephone. We have a canned reply to that, which Martha picked up from an earlier resident: "I don't know, but we're awfully busy doing it." And somehow it seems to work that way. We get up in the morning with nothing much on the agenda, and before we know it we have been busy the whole day.

Just today, Skip was sitting in a rocking chair, reading. First he swatted at his ankle. Then he began stomping. I started giggling and asked, "What in the world are you doing?"

He replied, "The damned ants are coming up between the floorboards. Every time I rock, some more pop up through. I can't stomp fast enough!" That started him on an extermination project, which led to cleaning out some waste boards and pipes from under the porch. As he carried the waste items away he noticed another bunch of bananas that had ripened and that the coatis had found, so he proceeded to cut the bananas off and then chop the stalk and carry it away.

By that time he was dirty and sweaty, so he hopped under his favorite outdoor shower to rinse off, just about the time Martha called loudly from her porch, *"Skip! Time to stop working. Come on over for happy hour."*

That sort of chain of events seems to be typical, and actually, it keeps us from becoming bored. And in spite of our comments about Martha's games, they help provide a little extra diversion, allowing us to appreciate quieter moments for reading, meditation, and watching the mammals and birds. At any rate, we seldom feel bored out here in the jungle.

Last evening Antonio popped in after dinner for a visit. He sat at the table on Martha's porch, chatting and fingering an Easter centerpiece that Martha had just set out. He chattered animatedly in Spanish, laughing and playing with the decoration until he broke it. His expression was priceless, a mixture of puzzlement and worry framed in a moment of silence until we all broke out laughing. Then he giggled sheepishly as he made a feeble attempt to fit the pieces back together. That's our Antonio, twenty-nine this year and still just a large boy.

We saw a pair of male howler monkeys fighting today, a rather rare thing. They growled and chased, grabbed and bit until they fell clear out of the tree. Even that didn't stop them; they hollered and fought on the ground, even more furiously. Finally they separated and climbed different trees, which seemed to give them the space they needed to withdraw with dignity.

One time, Becky, a visiting friend, had sat on the back deck alone and watched a monkey giving birth in one of the trees. She said a number of the troop hung around and observed as the lead male received the baby and then handed it to the mother. We jokingly asked her if he spanked it first, but she swore it happened that way and that the baby even began hollering right after it was born. I guess we'll keep on learning as long as we watch these creatures.

Lili told us an unusual story at the beach. She said her gardener had related to her that he had been riding his bicycle on the road one night last week and literally run into an anteater. Normally a shy creature, the anteater had apparently felt it was under attack. As it was rolled under the bicycle's wheels it lashed out with its formidable front claws and slashed the tire to ribbons. That was one we had never heard before!

Another day at the beach Skip and I were returning from our walk, chatting and looking for shells and such, when we noticed Martha standing up and moving around. There were two dogs that seemed to be pestering her. As we hurried nearer we also saw her *Tico Times* newspaper blowing away toward the water. At closer proximity we were able to discern that the dogs were not really harming Martha; it was more like they were being a playful nuisance, dragging her beach bag around as she tried to catch them.

As we ran to retrieve Martha's newspaper before it got doused we saw that there was a girl out in the water who seemed to be having difficulty getting back in to shore. Before we could think of anything to do, one of the dogs hanging around Martha spotted the girl and tore into the water. It swam all the way out to her. She grabbed onto the dog's tail, and it towed her in far enough that she could get her feet on the bottom and push in through the surf, unharmed.

I asked, "Martha, are you OK?" as I handed her the papers.

Martha replied as she retrieved her beach bag, "Oh, yes, I'm fine, but Holy Heaven, what a morning! Those crazy dogs, and then that girl . . . wasn't that wonderful, that dog pulling her in?"

We both nodded our agreement, and I repeated, "You never know what you're going to see in Nosara."

Skip said, "We keep saying that, but it surely is the truth."

Late that afternoon we retired to our favorite back deck at the far end of the guest cabins with icy drinks and good books, watching between paragraphs for wildlife. The big Tico rooster and one of his hens soon showed up for their drinks from the birdbath. Then a pair of large flycatchers appeared to wait their turn for a drink and perhaps a refreshing dip. But the rooster and hen took their good old time drinking, which evoked some impatience from the flycatchers. The male, sporting a bright golden-yellow vest, hopped down to the nearest croton bush and gave the two dawdlers a serious lecture about their manners. The rooster promptly left, but the hen wasn't about to be hurried. She drank and drank, dipping her beak and tossing her head back to throw the water down her throat. Such inconsiderate behavior earned the hen another dressing down by the impatient flycatcher. This time she took heed and departed, pretending it was her idea all the time. Both flycatchers immediately fluttered over into the birdbath to bathe and drink to their hearts' content. When satisfied, they returned to their favorite limb to shake off excess water and preen a bit before departing.

That night I was writing my notes on the day's events when I noticed something brown, about the hue of milk chocolate, in the spiral binding of my notebook. *Hmm,* I mused, *it looks like a dried leaf rolled up in there. How could that happen?*

I poked at it with my ball-point pen in an attempt to remove it. I'm glad I didn't use my finger, for I jumped as out ran a scorpion. It was very quick, and before I could swat it or even get hold of something to use to hit it, it zipped across the table, down to the floor, and disappeared into a crack in the corner. And I had my arm lying right across it as I was writing!

Another night we were sitting peacefully on the back deck when we heard an ominous buzzing sound growing louder and louder. Skip said, "Bees coming!"

Martha said, "Holy Heaven! Not more bees!"

When we had arrived in January, Antonio showed us where he had torn a panel off the back wall of guest *cabina* #2, right around the corner from where we were sitting, to remove a large nest of bees. Sure enough, they were returning.

Martha ran for the Baygon spray bomb and fly swatter and was soon spraying and swatting like a mad woman, babbling rapidly the whole time. Skip and I weren't sure whether the bees were as dangerous as Martha was at that moment. But wonder of wonders, the bees retreated!

It was a short-lived reprieve, for the whole swarm returned in a few short minutes. Martha was getting more upset ("Holy Heaven, what'll we do?!"), so Skip relieved her of the Baygon can and circled around to enter the door of the *cabina* and spray the bees through the screen, a position of closer proximity and much greater safety. He was inside, the bees outside. His strategy prevailed; he was persistent and the bees couldn't get at him. After a while they gave up and buzzed back up into the high limbs of the cassia tree above the deck, where they seemed to congeal into a great living, humming lump. After that only a few desultory explorers buzzed around, and they left the *cabina* wall alone, at least for the time being.

We checked after dark, and the bees were still there, clustered peacefully on the limb. But the next morning, to Martha's great relief, they were gone. Still, we wondered, would they return?

George and Beverly Baumunk stopped to tell us of their forthcoming trip to Lake Arenal and the volcano. They sounded excited, since their son, Creston, and three of his friends were going to accompany them. Creston would be driving a rental car, and they planned to travel in tandem. The dust would be a problem to the second vehicle, but they would have a backup if any car problems developed. Besides, trying to fit all six into one vehicle would be uncomfortable.

We wished them safe travel and thought about them on the morning they departed. We all agreed that it was nice for Beverly to get out to see some of the countryside; she stayed home a lot, albeit a lovely home with a beautiful view.

It wasn't long until we heard that George and Beverly had returned, never having reached Arenal. We soon got the story from them.

They started early in the morning, and everything went fine for all of an hour. Then George's car, a four-wheel-drive Isuzu Trooper, broke down. They hadn't even reached Nicoya yet. Creston drove on ahead to the nearest garage to arrange for a tow. The service was surprisingly prompt. They fastened a chain to George's car and had towed it a short way when the chain broke. They repaired the chain and went on, but it broke again. After another quick fix, they got the car into the garage and got right to work.

They decided a new clutch plate was in order, and everyone was pleased that they happened to have one on hand and could get right to it. The job was accomplished in jig time, since the Trooper was becoming a common type of vehicle here and the mechanics were familiar with it. The problem was, it didn't do the job; the engine was running, but George's car still wouldn't move. Something more was needed, but they would have to tow it on into Nicoya for that.

After they reached Nicoya, George insisted that Creston and his guests go on to Arenal without him and Beverly. They ate together at the Restaurant Nicoya before separating and happened to bump into Michael Sandweg, our former development manager, while they were there. Michael provided a ride home for George and Beverly, which made Creston feel a little better about going on with the trip.

George returned to Nicoya to pick up his car the next morning. The Trooper was working fine now, and it was on his way home that he stopped in to give us this report. We expressed our happiness that it all worked out OK, although we felt bad that Beverly still didn't get out for her vacation. But that's the way life is in Costa Rica.

Our departure time was nearing. If we wanted to have some final get-togethers with our friends we had better get them arranged. Kathy Benish had a birthday soon, followed closely by her wedding anniversary. We wanted the Baumunks involved, too, but their car was back in the garage and it was difficult to communicate with them. Martha's CB radio still wasn't working very well, and it's a long drive up the mountain just to deliver a message.

Skip suggested, "Let's deliver it on foot. We can walk up the hill behind the house in the morning before it gets hot. There's a path up the end of the hill that the natives use to go to work sometimes." He pointed over toward the east corner where the sky flower vine was blooming like morning glories. "It starts right over there."

Martha looked up. "Oh, my, that's awfully steep. Do you think you can find your way? There might be snakes. You'll get all sweated up."

Skip just grinned, asking, "What do you want us to tell them?"

Martha gave us precise instructions, and we exchanged our sandals for walking shoes. Skip put on a hat and grabbed a pair of broom handles from the bodega to serve as walking sticks, and off we went.

He held the barbwire for me to crawl through at the edge of the lot, and then we were on the path. Soon we were climbing a very steep hill through the jungle. At places we had to help one another when the dirt and gravel caused our shoes to slip. We were glad to have brought the walking sticks.

As we neared the top a man appeared, dragging a crooked pole down the hill. We said, *"Buenos días,"* as we stood aside to allow him to pass, but we didn't recognize him. We concluded that he was probably just sneaking a little firewood off George's hill.

We stopped to rest at intervals. Martha was right; we were sweating profusely as well as breathing heavily. The sun was glaring down through the trees and making itself felt already. I was glad we were longtime exercise walkers, or we would have had even more difficulty reaching the top of this hill.

We reached a shelf where the slope leveled off somewhat and the path became a jeep trail. Skip pointed on up the slope, saying, "There's George's fence. We're almost there."

Sure enough, another hundred yards and we were trudging up George's driveway past Creston's new house. When George opened the door at our knocking, we laughed at the surprised look on his face. He laughed in return at our sweat-drenched appearance but then expressed concern when he realized we had climbed the hill on foot. Beverly emerged from the kitchen, exclaiming, "My, oh, my! How did you ever climb that hill? Let me get you something to drink."

We sat a few minutes with them on their porch, the one with the grand view of the ocean, as we sipped ice water and arranged to pick them up for the big party. They were delighted to be included, thanked us profusely, and volunteered some items to add to the festivities.

The return trip down the mountain took less energy but seemed more trying on our legs. Mine were almost shaking by the time we reached the bottom and crawled back through the barbwire fence. Skip went straight to his favorite outdoor shower and persuaded me to do the same. We stood under the cool water as we undressed, rinsing our sweat-soaked clothes in the process. It made us feel a little like Adam and Eve, hidden from Martha's view by palm trees and croton bushes as we bathed and hung our clothing out to dry.

We put on clean clothing—only an item or two, remember, here in the tropics—and returned to Martha to answer her questions about our adventure. By the time we finished our report along with another glass of ice water, we realized it wasn't yet 11:00 A.M. It seemed like we had spent a whole day, and we still had an hour left for chores before lunchtime.

The night of the big party for the Benishes, Skip left an hour early to drive the jeep up the mountain to pick up George and Beverly. Beverly had to be helped into the front seat, beginning with a step stool to elevate her high enough to reach the seat. He and George both had to assist her. Then George had to climb through the back door to get into the rear side seats, another risky endeavor for a person over eighty years of age. The ride down the mountain is dusty and bouncy, not the most genteel thing for an elderly couple. In fact, back home it would have been considered an ordeal, but here in Nosara it is thought a small price to pay to spend an evening out with friends.

This night was easily worth every discomfort; it included cake and *ice cream,* not to mention playing Pennies from Heaven, all great favorites. Beverly brought a birthday gift to present to Kathy at some propitious moment and told Martha what it was. Martha was delighted, though a bit discomfited that it might outclass the small, though thoughtful, gifts she had found. After we all sang "Happy Birthday" and slurped down the cake and ice cream, Beverly reached under her chair for the gift to hand to Kathy.

Martha exclaimed, "Oh, yes! We have some surprises for you!" She grabbed for Beverly's package, intending to present it to Kathy along with her own bag of items.

There was a short tug-of-war as Martha tried to wrest Beverly's package from her grip. Beverly was not about to relinquish her treasure, though, and hung on for dear life, all the while doing a fine job of maintaining her usual composed, refined expression in spite of the effort required.

Martha apparently realized the scene she was creating and released her grip, recomposing herself enough to say graciously, "Beverly, you go ahead and give Kathy yours first." After a moment's appreciation of Beverly's gift, Martha set her bag in front of Kathy, diverting our attention pretty quickly to her gifts.

We soon got down to the important business of cards, but after a couple of hands the men's team forged ahead. Soon Martha was bored and she dozed between her turns. Sometimes we even had to awaken her when it was her turn. Then we would all laugh, Martha included. We all understood how much energy she typically expended during a day, easily enough to make any one of us lesser beings weary. As Skip says, "She is something!"

18

Out of Nosara

Private telephone service was coming to Nosara, but Martha had her mind made up not to apply; she didn't need a telephone. She had gotten along fine for nearly twenty years without one. Besides, now the lines at the public phones would be shorter. We heard this line of logic several times as we sat on the back deck watching the birds. George Miller and the Baumunks had both applied for phone service, though.

We could tell Martha was still thinking about it, but she was emphatic about her decision. We agreed with her, knowing that she was really still undecided and that our input wouldn't change anything.

Paulina Anderson, who supervises Antonio and pays Martha's bills during the off season, was going over the books with her at the table one day when Martha asked abruptly, "How do you apply for a telephone?"

Paulina replied, "You have to go to the bank in Nicoya and fill out an application. It costs seventy-five dollars."

Martha said, "When can you go with me? We're leaving pretty soon and I want a telephone. George Miller and the Baumunks have applied, so I think I should, too."

Surprise! Monday, April 1, Paulina drove Martha to Nicoya to submit the application. The die was cast. Now as we sat on the deck, we would hear the reasons that Martha needed a telephone. And we agreed with her; we learn slowly, but we do learn.

While Martha was away we realized again how peaceful it was here and how much control Martha exerted over our lives. I mused as I made lunch in the kitchen, *How will I ever get lunch without Martha telling me what to do?*

As I related this to Skip, he laughingly responded, "Yes, she runs the show, but she is a unique and special person, and we wouldn't be here without her."

I agreed, "Yes, I joke about it, but she has taught me an awful lot about Costa Rica and living in the jungle."

278

We went on to discuss the fact that this was probably our last year here in Nosara with Martha. We had thought about it a great deal and discussed it with Martha but still felt bad about it in some ways. We felt a little as though we were bailing out on Martha, but we had forewarned her two years ago, when we missed a winter in Costa Rica to tour Australia and the South Seas. We had promised to spend one more year with her in Nosara, and now it was coming to a close.

We needed to be somewhere where we could be more in control of our own lives. I had sole charge of my older brother, who had been incapacitated by strokes, unable to speak or eat, and I felt guilty about leaving the country with him in a nursing home and no one else to visit him or make required decisions.

Skip was bothered more and more by skin cancer, and although he was becoming better about covering up and using lotions, the tropics, especially the beach, were not a good place for him to be hanging out.

We hadn't rationalized this part to Martha, but her buildings were aging to the point where they posed constant problems. Roofs and decks had been replaced, as had the window louvers. Painting was a constant chore, and the water lines were patch upon patch. While all these things were a bother and expense, the electrical lines and connections were more than a headache; they were dangerous, as the numerous little fires at switches and outlets proved. Upkeep was pretty expensive for Martha, and just when she thought she had things caught up, another problem would develop. Even our house, the ''new'' house, had to have its deck replaced this year, after only five years of weather, and the floor joists were sagging. Wooden houses have a short life span in the jungle, due partly to insects but mostly to moisture. The wet season causes rapid deterioration.

The result is that we have been encouraging Martha to move to a condominium, where she has more people to fill her need for social contact in our absence, along with reduced caretaking problems. She vacillates during our discussions about this solution, one time desiring the change very much and the next time declaring that she could never leave this place. She gets sentimental over all the memories, the monkeys over the back deck, and. ''What about Antonio? If I sell, I want him to be guaranteed a job.''

We understand how she feels and even share many of her feelings, but we do have to make our move. We feel sad about departing this wonderful area, but then we'll have the adventure of finding another way to spend our winters. However, we sincerely want Martha to have a satisfactory transition and not feel stuck here. It's hard for us to get her prepared, though; she vacillates on her decision so much and sometimes tries to talk us into returning. We know that if we gave in, it would never end; she would stay on here, investing more and more in the old buildings, postponing her departure year after year. We conclude that it is best to stick with our decision, best for us and, we hope, best for Martha in the long haul.

So after a peaceful lunch, just Skip and I together, we began sorting our belongings, what to take home with us in two or three bags and what to leave with Martha or give away. Our final departure was becoming real; it had a tinge of sadness about it as we opened the footlockers we used for storage.

Our attention suddenly became more focused on the present when Skip slid his hand down under some clothing to lift it out of a dresser and was stabbed in the finger by a scorpion. It flew when he yanked his hand out of the dresser, and he cursed it as he rushed to stomp the scurrying critter before it dived into a crack under the baseboard. Then he asked wryly, "Do you think we'll miss these little surprises back in Pennsylvania? It's never this exciting at home when we do house-cleaning." We laughed as I went for the spirit of camphor bottle, an old-fashioned concoction we use regularly for stings and subcutaneous sores.

This time he experienced more reaction to the sting; he felt a little light-headed, and his lips became numb. Prior scorpion stings hadn't affected him very much at all. The symptoms lasted the rest of the day but were almost gone by the next morning. I asked him how he felt at noon, and he said he had forgotten about it.

Late the same afternoon that he had been stung by the scorpion, as we walked the beach together talking about what to do with some of our household items before we left, Skip stepped on a Venus shell. It has long needlelike protrusions from a quarter- to over a half-inch long and they stabbed into his foot. He sat down on the sand, and I plucked four of the pieces of shell out of the pad of his foot. He commented, "Maybe it's a good thing we're getting out of here." Still, we had to look around and think of the beauty we would surely miss.

The three of us went to the *Giardino Tropicale*, or Tropical Garden, Italian restaurant the next evening, since we were letting our larder deplete prior to our departure date. Pizza John, as some irreverently call him, is a vibrant, handsome man who was a published professor back in

Italy, or so they say. He'd made the Johnson home over into a quaint little hillside alfresco eatery. He'd landscaped it beautifully with tropical flowers that peeped over your shoulder as you dined. One dining area, elevated on posts, offered a limited view of the sunset over the ocean, while the lower area featured tables arranged around the large wood-fired beehive pizza oven. The tantalizing smells of baking pizza mingled with wood smoke and scents from tropical blossoms. With John's Latin charm as an attentive host, it adds up to a nifty way to spend a dinner hour.

While we ate we chatted with neighbors who told us that it was not so peaceful at John's last Saturday evening. A woman unfamiliar to us was having dinner with a man who lived nearby, whose wife happened to be in San José for a couple of days, they said. His wife returned unexpectedly and spotted her husband's car in John's parking lot. She stopped to join her husband for dinner, finding him happily entertaining the "other woman." They said the wife flew into a towering rage, grabbed a beer bottle, smashed off its base like marines do in barroom brawls in the movies, and attacked the other woman, cutting her up pretty badly.

I asked, "Why would she attack the woman instead of her husband?"

Skip quipped, "The way you ask that question reminds me of why I never eat out with other women."

Martha just said, "Holy Heavens!," then tried to find out who they all were.

Time is running out. It is April 2, our last full day in Nosara, and we have many things do do. Martha is a little more hyper than usual and a little more bossy. I have so much to do that I escape into my own chores, but Antonio and Skip are under the gun most of the morning. After lunch we make a run to Nosara to fuel the jeep, pay the bill at La Paloma, and check the post office one last time.

Martha also wanted to stop at the hardware store to buy a shovel and a large sheet of heavy plastic to cover her living room furniture. She had been set on these purchases for a week. When we went into the store, she bought the shovel—Antonio needed that badly—but changed her mind about the plastic sheeting. We could make do with what we had.

We stopped at George Miller's on the return trip to say our good-byes. He had been concocting a coconut pudding from his own coconuts, which he served to us topped with chocolate sauce, coffee on the side.

Not bad for a man approaching eighty years of age. George informed us that he and Bolivar were going to San José tomorrow and would probably see us on the way. Also, he said, "Boli took me to a place up on the mountain between San José and Cartago that I'd like you all to see. We're going to be gathering plant specimens day after tomorrow, but that evening I'll have Boli pick you up and we can enjoy an evening out together. Would that be OK?"

We all agreed, though the arrangements were vague and I wondered if it would happen. We had a lot to do in San José, too. We had to check on a lot we had bought three years earlier for which we still hadn't received the deed. The lawyer who had handled the sale for us had recently absconded with over a million dollars' worth of securities not long after he tried to get us to send him $750 to "pay our taxes" for us. We reported this to Albert Muller, who had been our agent and who also handled our tax payments for us—less than ten dollars per year. He had reported the attempted fraud to his real estate office and then informed us of what had happened. The attorney was gone, and no one knew if our lot had been registered in our name. Albert told us the name of the lawyer who had been hired to straighten out the mess. We had been in contact with him since January trying to get our deed located. That was foremost in our minds as we thought about our forthcoming trip to San José, so it was hard to concentrate on George's kind offer of an evening out at a mountainside bar.

We all thanked George for the luscious dessert and the invitation, then returned to Casa de las Flores. Skip delivered a footlocker full of bed sheets and other items to Simona's house down in the village and a few other items to Antonio and Chini. He had already given most of his tools and fishing supplies to Antonio, except for those items Martha might need, which he placed in her bodega. He also organized and marked all Martha's keys, including a set for Paulina, who was authorized to sell the property if she could. (The off-season is a poor time to do any business in Nosara.) Then we asked Martha if she was ready for a last trip to the beach. She had told us that she wanted to go once more, even if she had to carry a wet swimsuit to San José with her. Her reply was, "Oh, I can't go; I have too much to think about. You two go ahead."

We told her she might miss seeing Robin Williams. It was rumored that he was soon to visit our neighbors at the big house across the road, but nothing definite. She just smiled at that and said, "Well, you can tell me about it."

Skip and I enjoyed a long, peaceful, thoughtful walk on the beach, all the way beyond Guiones Village. We had turned and started back when we heard a voice on top of the cliff calling down to us. It was Simona. She had already received word here, where she worked part-time, that Skip had delivered the footlocker to her house and even what was in it. She called her thanks down to us "for the beautiful things" and wished us a good trip home, along with conveying (all in Spanish) her sorrow that we were leaving. That gave us a warm feeling and added to our regrets about leaving.

The sun was lowering as we walked back toward the tide pools. We could see several people at the smaller pool, the one we call Mary's pool. We decided to take a dip there in case Robin Williams might be among the few figures we could see ahead, chuckling at the idea.

Sure enough, the first person we walked by in order to enter the water was Robin Williams. We smiled at him and Skip said, "Hello, neighbor," receiving a shy smile and, "Hello," in return. We proceeded on into the pool to enjoy the low swells coming over the rocks—and to surreptitiously peep at the famous actor without seeming obvious.

Skip said quietly, "I just can't make myself impose on his privacy. He comes here to escape the press of crowds and the inane adulation of his worshipers. I think I'd want to be left alone if I were him."

I fully agreed with that. We could also see two young children we supposed to be his. Our neighbors, who operate a yoga retreat, seemed to be baby-sitting as Robin and a woman we didn't recognize slowly strolled the shoreline and studied shells. It was a very quiet and peaceful scene.

After twenty minutes or so, we decided we had better get back to Martha, since we were going out to eat tonight. Being in the presence of someone famous wears off pretty quickly if there's no interaction. We were delighted to see Robin, but it was not really a very fulfilling moment. We quietly left, walked to the jeep, and drove back to report to Martha.

After quick showers we dressed and walked over to Martha's. As we climbed the steps to her front porch, she hopped up from her rocker and asked, "Well, did you get to see Robin Williams?" She was obviously not expecting a positive response.

I replied enthusiastically, "Yes! He was at the lower tide pool, right where we were swimming! You missed it, Martha. We were as close to him as from here to that lounge chair!"

Martha could only say, her eyes wide, "Holy Heaven! Now I wish I had gone along."

Skip interjected, "You know, he seemed almost bashful, not at all like he acts when he's under the spotlight. He was very quiet and subdued. I liked him better this way, although I've enjoyed some of the roles he's played, like in *Dead Poet's Society*. He's a fine actor."

We had happy hour on the back deck as usual, chatting about our day and our forthcoming trip to San José. We had a lot to think about. Around six, just as the sun was setting, we rinsed our glasses and headed for the jeep. We were headed to La Dolce Vita, the little Italian restaurant just down the road from us, next to Esperanza. We climbed the hill between the rows of lovely hibiscus flowers and crotons, many of which came from Casa de las Flores, and walked on into the crude but quaint *ranchito* structure Jerry and Jane had built for their business. Jerry came out to greet us, looking somehow like the cat that swallowed the canary. Martha whispered, "I bet Robin Williams was here to eat."

Jerry seated us at our favorite table, still grinning broadly. Skip said, "You look extra happy, Jerry. Was Robin Williams here? We saw him on the beach today."

Jerry replied, "Yes, he was here for dinner last night. He signed our menu. Isn't that something?" We all smiled and agreed as we sat down and looked at the menu chalked on a slate in the corner.

After discussing the menu and making those important decisions, we chatted and looked around the room. Skip said, "Hey, don't stare, but I think that's Kurt Russell at the other table, over near the kitchen."

Martha and I took measured peeks in that direction. I said, "It sure looks like him." There were two preteen boys and a young woman with him who bore a striking resemblance to Goldie Hawn. *Too much coincidence,* I thought.

Martha put her two cents in; "I'm not sure. I don't know Kurt Russell that well."

We puzzled some more over that as we waited for our dinners to arrive. Jane, a trim, blond, and beautiful Englishwoman, brought out some fresh Italian bread with garlic-flavored olive oil to dip it in. We commented about how well her plantings were doing, and she thanked Martha again for the cuttings she had provided. Jane mentioned that she was planning a visit to her mother during the off-season. Then she went back to work before we could ask her if that was Kurt Russell at the other table.

Dinner was great, and as we were leaving, Skip said good-bye to the folks at the other table. The man smiled a big, toothy smile through a very masculine "five o'clock shadow" with a little wave and nod. It had to be him! I guess that was his family with him. Costa Rica is a hot place right now for the Hollywood set, and they tend to bring their families, since it is a relatively safe, restful setting, without much nightlife.

We had read in the *Tico Times* that more movie stars were visiting this country. Charlie Sheen, a friend of Woody Harrelson, had visited down at Quepos. Demi Moore and Bruce Willis had bought property up at Playa Grande where a new golf course was nearing completion. Also mentioned as visitors were Arnold Schwarzenegger, Don Johnson, Kevin Costner, and Jack Nicholson. We had seen an interview with Dean Kane (*Superman*) on TV and heard him say he wanted to surf at Costa Rica because he had heard the waves there were the best. Whatever the truth, all this attention will probably change this pleasant little country even more than the tourist boom of recent years has affected it.

Skip commented as we drove back to Casa de las Flores, "That had to be Kurt Russell. Nobody else looks like that, with the strong jaw line and cleft chin. And that must have been Goldie Hawn's daughter; she was a young Goldie, no doubt about it."

I agreed; it had to be.

Martha said, "Well, we'll find out. Somebody'll talk about it sooner or later. Oh, well . . . let's play some games before we go to bed. There's nothing left to do; we're all ready to leave in the morning."

More games . . . oh, jeez! But what the heck, this is our last night here. We played with Martha until nine-thirty and then headed off to bed.

Up at five-thirty, happy anniversary! April 3 was our forty-second year together, not counting three years of steady companionship before that. We would celebrate it with a long, hot, dirty drive to San José. It's one of those trips we always feel fortunate to survive, what with Tico traffic, loose steering, slow brakes, and such hazards to contend with. Still, it was another step forward in life, part of that great adventure of living and never knowing what's coming next.

We carried our bags to the jeep with Antonio's help, gave a last few items to Antonio, and locked the house. Skip handed Martha the last of the keys we had used during the past seven years. That was that; we were on our way again.

We got Martha's stuff nicely packed into the jeep along with ours and were ready to leave when Chini arrived with a bicycle. She wanted to go with us as far as Nicoya, where she was going to exchange her little girl's bicycle; there was something wrong with it. Rats. Skip had to repack things so there would be a seat for Chini in the rear of the jeep. Oh well, we still hit the road by 6:05 A.M., not far from our target time. We wanted to be on our way ahead of the bus, and this would still do it.

We dropped Chini off in Nicoya and then stopped for diesel fuel where Chet had begun patronizing twenty years ago. The attendants there recognized the jeep and gave us good service as usual, flashing big smiles in the process.

Next stop, the Tempisque Ferry—George Miller and Boli appeared beside us to chat during the crossing. The ferry engine was out of commission, so we were towed by a tugboat. That gave us smug Americans something to discuss, something to reinforce our superiority, all in good fun, of course (?).

The roads on either side of the ferry were still terrible, none of the promised repairs having been consummated. We kept reminding ourselves that this is a poor country, reciting that old reminder, "If you want everything to be like it is back home, then stay home." So we picked our way between potholes as fast as we could, trying to keep our grumbling to a minimum and praying that the old jeep would hold together.

Martha said, "Holy Heaven!" as Skip hit a deep, bone-jarring pothole.

He responded, "Wow, that was a bad one! I try, but I can't miss them all. I'm doing my best."

Martha said soothingly, "I know; you're doing a good job. Won't they look at us when we walk into the hotel lobby covered with dust and these rust flakes in our hair?"

We all laughed, imagining the beautiful lobby of the Villa Tournon with its colorful wall hangings and polished floors and woodwork.

We proceeded along some better roads, through several construction projects, a couple of radar speed check stations (yes, they use radar regularly, and people speed in spite of the potholes), then up the long, dragging slopes of the mountain crossing. Overall we made good time, entering San José just about noon, right on schedule for the crazy noon traffic. Martha kept up a steady flow of instructions as we wove our way through the maze of vehicles, street vendors, parked trucks making deliveries, and pedestrians. The word *teeming* fits the scene nicely; teeming streets of a teeming city—especially the teeming traffic.

What a relief to arrive safely at the hotel and take a shower! We took the time to clean our suitcases as well; they were filthy, just as we had been. We immediately made reservations to ride the aerial tram through the rain forest the next morning. It was the hottest new eco-attraction in the country at the moment, and we had decided to give it top priority before departing the country.

Actually, we took care of our top priority right away. After our showers, Francisco arrived to drive Martha to see her lawyer, since she needed to take care of some taxes and property requirements. But before she went there, she graciously had Francisco drive Skip and me to the office of the attorney who was searching for the deed to our lot. It was located in an area with which we weren't familiar, but Francisco, the old taxi man, zigzagged around a maze of back streets, asked directions a couple of times, and soon dropped us at the appropriate door. Martha offered to return for us, but we declined, thanking her and Francisco for their kindness.

We had expected a hole-in-the-wall office with a Tico lawyer and perhaps a secretary. Instead, we found a large, well-staffed organization. An attractive receptionist seated us and offered coffee. After twenty minutes or so we were led into a large, well-appointed office and intro-duced to Senor Juan de Dios Alvarez, senior partner in the firm. He was obviously of East Indian extraction, despite his Tico speech. He seated us and told us, to our great relief, that an aide was on her way with our documents. They had only just located them that morning. He explained that the deeds had been entered into the national computer file and that no matter who holds deeds or other papers, it is this computer file that is the official word. He told us never to buy land from someone on the basis of paper documents; they must be confirmed on the national computer file.

Attorney Alvarez also explained that there was a deed filed in each of our names. There is no allowance for joint ownership except through incorporation, so Skip and I would each have a deed for half the property. It seemed strange to us; we had never been told that.

Worse yet, the deeds, in true Spanish tradition, would have been filed in our mothers' maiden names! No wonder they had been difficult to locate. We were feeling fortunate that they had been able to find our documents at all.

During some minutes of waiting, after Juan had explained business matters to us, we chatted of inconsequential things. We mentioned seeing

Robin Williams on the beach back in Nosara. Juan de Dios (John of God) grinned and said, "Just a few days ago Mr. Williams was sitting in the very chair you are sitting in," as he pointed at Skip. We all chuckled about that.

Soon Senor Alvarez's aide knocked and entered, placing a folder on his desk. He ran a practiced eye over the papers, checking their accuracy, it seemed. He found a minor error having to do with lot dimensions but said he would notarize the documents and give them to us, then send us corrected copies the following week.

We paid Juan for his services and thanked him profusely, leaving his office feeling tremendously relieved and happy. We had been afraid that we would never hold the deeds to our lot in our hands, and now we had them! We felt like dancing and celebrating, as we found our way back to the hotel.

Our celebration amounted to a nice dinner of *corvina tartar*, white sea bass with tartar sauce, a specialty of the hotel dining room. We even splurged with dessert, ice cream with chocolate sauce, at Martha's suggestion. Martha's trip to the lawyer had been successful as well, so she joined us in our mellow mood enjoying the nice dinner. We retired early and slept easily.

Martha met us for breakfast the next morning with, "I've been up since five-thirty; what time did you get up?"

Too early for such challenges. I just responded, "We slept well. How did you sleep?"

The tour bus picked us up after nine to take us over the mountain to the aerial tram. The bus was nearly filled, and this was getting into the off-season. "The tourism business mustn't be too bad," I commented as we boarded. A guide lectured to us about the ecosystems we would be seeing as we crossed the mountain highway through Braulio Carrillo National Park. It took about an hour, most of it through steep rain forest, with large trees, some loaded with air plants such as bromeliads and orchids. The trees were usually surrounded with large ferns. Things looked damp at the higher elevations, drier farther down. The guide said it was exceptionally dry in the area of the tram.

As our guide pointed out a waterfall called the Horse's Tail, the bus slowed. I looked out the window on the opposite side of the bus and saw George and Boli looking for plants to add to George's collection. Apart from the unusual coincidence of crossing paths like this, I said to Skip, "Imagine, right here in a national park, collecting plants!"

Skip grinned. "Yeah, the rules must be different here, or they're having good luck escaping the law. Back home they would be arrested and fined for taking plants from a public area. George sure does love his plants, and . . . well, maybe his collection will help save some of them."

We crossed the divide, passing through Zurqui Tunnel, the only highway tunnel in Costa Rica. The aerial tram concession soon appeared on the right. It didn't look like much. I guess having been to such places as Disney World and Busch Gardens makes us difficult to impress, especially when all the hoopla had us expecting something impressive.

We were told where to wait while our guide picked up our tickets. In ten or fifteen minutes a farm tractor pulled a wagon outfitted with seats up to the loading platform where we waited. We were hauled down a steep, narrow dirt road through the jungle to a stream where we got off and walked across a footbridge. A guide pointed out a bird that was standing half-hidden in the water, and we trudged a short distance farther to board another wagon for the final passage to the tram terminal.

We boarded cable cars, each of which carried about six people, including a guide who told us what to look for and answered questions. Our guide was a pretty, young, bright biology major from the University of Costa Rica. If we asked a question she couldn't answer, she relayed the question by two-way radio to her more knowledgeable and experienced supervisor and then passed on the answer.

On our outward-bound pass in the tram we viewed the lower story of the forest, while the return loop carried us through the canopy. It was an intelligent arrangement, installed with great effort aimed at minimizing disturbance to the natural surroundings. No roads had been constructed to install foundations and support piers. All that concrete and steel had been hauled in by helicopter, they told us. The workers who installed it had hiked in on foot. That part impressed us.

Lack of rain for the past five days, however, left the "rain" forest kind of blah. We could see many plants wilting; a few of the more vulnerable appeared dead. The plant life here was accustomed to having rain virtually every day, and this drought, even though of short duration, was hurting things. We saw some birds and a few blossoms and butterflies, but nothing spectacular.

Arriving back at the terminal, we exited the tram and had a quick lunch, then were sorted into groups for a short hike on a nature trail through the jungle. Our first stop was to inspect a line of leaf cutter ants, each carrying a large piece of leaf across the dirt road. The leaf fragments they carried were many times their size and held nearly straight up above their backs. I commented to Skip, "Don't they remind you of a line of tiny sailboats following each other across a muddy ocean?"

He grinned and nodded, replying, "Yes they do, but their sail makers must have been drunk." The leaves had been cut into all sorts of shapes and were carried at various angles.

There had been so many ants on their little path that they had worn it smooth, or maybe they had a road crew that moved pebbles and such obstacles out of the way. However it had been accomplished, their path was quite visible as it crossed the road. They were certainly industrious little creatures, worthy of all the photographic attention they were getting. Yellow signs lettered in black had been posted: ANT CROSSING.

We learned more about rain forest plants, insects, and bird life on the nature walk, then rode the wagons back out to the highway where our bus waited. We arrived back at San José after five, quite a bit later than we had expected.

Martha was concerned about missing contact with George Miller for our trip to the mountainside bar, but when we entered the hotel there was a message waiting. George would wait until we arrived; just let him know when. Martha got off a quick call. In just over half an hour we were showered, dressed, and climbing into a taxi.

It was a busy time for traffic in the city, so the ride to the suburb of Sabanilla tended to the wild side. We puzzled over why we never saw many wrecks under such conditions, failing to come to a good conclusion. Upon reaching Sabanilla Square, which surrounded a pretty church, as is typical, we gave our driver 500 colones, about $2.50 at the time, including a tip, which he was happy to receive. (Tipping is not required, so even small tips are appreciated.) We couldn't spot George and Boli, so Skip said he would walk around the square to make sure they weren't waiting on the other side.

By the time Skip returned, Martha and I were struggling into sweaters, which George had thoughtfully brought for us. He told us it would be cold up on the mountainside and as we had just come from the coastal jungle he didn't expect that we would think of such exotic items as sweaters. He was right. Skip shrugged on a sweater, too, and Boli soon had us zipping through traffic nearly as fast as the taxi driver had. In about fifteen minutes we were out of the city, zigzagging up a narrow mountain road.

The steepness increased and we got glimpses of wonderful views of city and mountains off to our left. The area had become quite rural, the air clean and cool. Not being used to such crispness, we rolled up our windows.

Boli soon made a steep, abrupt right turn into what could well have been a farmyard, it was so rustic. There was a long, low building made of rough lumber. We parked in a lot that had probably once been a pasture and walked over to one of the shacklike outbuildings that was surrounded by a cloud of smoke and steam. The smell was delicious! A boy was tending a pair of large cast-iron kettles full of pork strips simmering in pork fat. Shades of childhood on the farm! I remembered such scenes, and so did Skip.

George laughed at our reaction; he had expected it and was obviously pleased. He said, "That's why I brought you up here. There aren't many places like this in the States anymore. I think it's pretty special."

He led us on down to the main building bearing a crude signboard over the entrance, which read: PIZOTE CHICHARRONERA. *Chicharrones* are fried pork fat or, more precisely, what is left after the oil or lard has been rendered out of a piece of fatback. I know this doesn't sound very appetizing, and I largely agree. But in Costa Rica they often leave some meat with the fat, or at least leave the skins with the strips of fatback, and when fried crisp and munched along with plenty of *cerveza* (beer) to wash it down, it kind of grows on you. Back home we would probably call them French-fried pork rinds or something like that.

The other part of the name of this bar was *Pizote,* which was earlier explained as the Tico name for the coatimundi, the smart ring-tailed animal that looks like a long-legged raccoon. So in English the name of this bar would be something like the Coatimundi Fried Pork Rind Maker. I liked it.

By the time George shepherded us into the dark, low-ceilinged barroom, Boli had secured us seats on short-legged stools around a table, all rough and handmade. Soon we were sipping Imperial beer and munching on *chicharrones* as if we had been born to it. Mexican music with an insistent Latin beat seemed to vibrate the numerous beer signs and banners that adorned the walls of the large room. Several animal heads, including a few boars' heads, stared vacantly out over the revelry.

One of the most interesting features of the place was that it had several freshly butchered hog carcasses hanging from the ceiling just in front of the bar. Of course Martha had to walk over to inspect them, and

291

Skip was only too ready to accompany her. They were very clean, gleaming white on the skin side. They hung in halves, so you could look inside the body cavity and see the muscle and ribs. The skins had been scraped, following a dunking in scalding water. The heads had been removed and the bodies sawed in half lengthwise, feet and legs still intact. They seemed to belong here, and no one appeared to be revolted by them.

Back at the table, George recommended the *mondongo* (tripe) soup, perhaps just for effect, but that's all it took to entice Skip. He ordered it on the first round, before even downing a single beer. Martha and I ordered the ham and bean soup, being entirely disinterested in the tripe soup. Along with the fresh bread they served with the soups, it made a mouth-watering meal. George and Skip had seconds on soup. Our waiter brought some more pork to our table, this time strips of lean meat done in the same kettles as the pork rinds. They were excellent, being less fatty, but soon we had enjoyed all the fried meat we could hold.

We chatted, told jokes, and laughed, trying not to think of the amount of cholesterol we had consumed. We were impressed by the number of people who crowded into the place and by the affluent look of many of them. Apparently the smart set from the city had discovered the Pizote Chicharronera and made it a part of their nightlife. We were happy that George had persisted in getting us to join him in coming here. It truly was a special place.

The city lights were beautiful to see as we drove back down the mountain. We noticed some rather large gatherings of people at the overlooks, at first thinking that they were just viewing the city at night. But George commented, "Maybe they're watching for that new comet . . . what's its name?"

Skip replied enthusiastically, "Oh, yeah! What is it? Hale-Bopp or something like that." But Boli didn't stop and we couldn't spot it from the moving car, so we didn't see Hale-Bopp. (We saw it after we returned home. It was a wonderful sight.)

Boli took us to George's house in Sabanilla, since George wanted us to see it. None of us had been there before. It was rather typical of the houses in that area, small and neat, just a few rooms. It was a place for George and his guests to stop over while doing business in the city or waiting for travel connections.

We said our grateful good-byes to George, and then Boli drove us back to the Villa Tournon, very tired but very happy.

It wasn't late when we arrived back at the hotel, just past nine, but we had to arise at 4:30 the next morning to be at the airport in time for our 8:00 A.M. flight to Miami. We had it down pat by now: pay our bill before retiring, arise at 4:30, have our bags out front for the taxi at 5:00, be at the airport before 6:00, board about 7:40, hope to take off on time, at 8:00. Everything clicked except the takeoff; that was delayed until about 8:30 for some reason unknown to us.

Things went smoothly at Miami. We hugged Martha good-bye, being reminded once again that she wished we would return again next year. Then off we went to locate the "Super Shuttle" to Fort Lauderdale Airport. That's what we got for taking the cheapest ticket deal we could find—an extra step in the process of getting home. The shuttle van wasn't hard to find, but once we got rolling, our driver kept dozing off. I stayed awake just to yell at him in case he swerved too far off the highway. We were traveling at about seventy on I-95, and I wasn't about to let him crash if I could help it.

We grabbed a bite to eat at Fort Lauderdale and then hopped our commuter flight to Jacksonville. From there we flew to Charlotte and then to Baltimore, where Glenn and Louise Lytle picked us up. We had happy greetings and hugs from them and began chatting so rapidly that Glenn missed an interchange and we wound up taking a long way home. It was midnight when we arrived, after a long, long day of travel, and we were grateful to be safely home.

I flipped the kitchen light on and saw a note on the table. It said: "Dear Mom and Dad, Welcome home. I moved some of my things into the spare bedroom. It's a long story. I am OK. Will see you tomorrow. Love, Bud." Reality sets in.

We puzzled about the note as we prepared to retire, though its meaning was pretty clear: a marriage on the rocks. Well, we were bone weary, too tired to worry. We flopped into our bed, our wonderful number one bed. We were out of Costa Rica for good.

Epilogue

Within the month after returning home in April 1997, we received our corrected deeds from Attorney Alvarez. We were pleased that he kept his word. It also gave us faith in his services, should we get a buyer for our lot. We did. With Mr. Alvarez' help, we sold our lot before the year was out. It was purchased by a lovely Canadian couple who are bound to be good citizens and make a contribution to the area.

Martha returned to Nosara without us in 1998, but she still had several friends visit her there and keep her company for parts of her stay. When no one was visiting her, she told us, she was lonely, and we felt bad about that. But we still felt we had to do some different things now, as we've explained.

Skip and I toured South America from late January to mid-February, then visited friends in Florida and participated in an Elderhostel program about South Georgia and the Okeefenokee Swamp. While in Florida we purchased a modest winter residence in Largo, between Tampa and St. Petersburg.

Skip and I still read the *Tico Times* when Martha passes them on to us, which helps us keep abreast of what's going on in Costa Rica, but the juiciest information is still obtained through the grapevine, i.e., straight from Martha. When she returned after her '98 season in Nosara, she couldn't wait to fill us in on the year's happenings, and we couldn't wait to hear about them.

Martha had difficulty getting her guests in and out of Nosara due to the closing of the airport there. The locals wouldn't stop using the runway as a quick route to town, and they wouldn't keep their cows and pigs off it, so the authorities closed it for the whole season pending some better fencing and some kind of agreement. The alternate airstrip was still Carrillo, a rough fifty-minute drive from the development in the opposite direction from Nosara.

Martha's first guest of the season was Kevin, a young man from Shippensburg whose floral shop she patronizes. She had told him so much about Nosara during her visits to his shop that he accompanied her on the trip down and then stayed with her for two weeks. He enjoyed his visit, but had become so sick during the second week that he passed out. She made some calls in a state of near-panic, finally getting the local doctor to meet her off-hours at his office. The medicine he provided worked an overnight cure, much to everyone's relief. Word is that Kevin was so delighted with his trip that he's ready to return next year.

One of Martha's guests was her travel agent, Vickie, from the AAA Agency in Shippensburg, along with her son, her sister, and a friend. They arrived in Carrillo early one morning expecting to be met by Bolivar. But Boli happened to be busy that morning, so he had asked his brother, Juan, to make the trip. Juan forgot. Vickie waited awhile, then asked the airport guard for help. He took her to a telephone where she called Martha. With the help of the guard, Vickie found a taxi and along with her companions was delivered to Casa de las Flores safe and sound.

Water bills may now be paid at the grocery store, La Paloma, an important bit of progress for Nosara. This, along with the rehiring of Michael Sandweg as development manager, has things looking up. The prior manager, Hugh, had his hand in the till, according to Martha's sources. That is such a common thing there.

George Miller had asked Skip to take pictures of his house before we left last year, since he had planned to renovate it and wanted "before and after" photos. Martha reported that the result was beautiful. He'd added a new bedroom and bath for his lady, LaRue, plus an attractive entrance, which dressed the old place up quite a bit.

George had some guests down from Pennsylvania to be married on the beach at Garza, then had a big reception at his newly renovated house. Later, Boli and LaRue had a huge party for George's eightieth birthday, including many Ticos. I asked Martha if George had gotten the facelift he had claimed he would get when he turned eighty. Martha had forgotten about that and figured he had been kidding.

Pablo, the Tico fisherman who had taken Skip, Mel, and Chet out in the boat in 1981, was still living in Nosara at last report. We had heard a few years ago that he had sired a child with his daughter or granddaughter. I hope this is only a rumor, but . . .

Antonio's woman, Chini, had found steady work at Robertson's, the place where Franco had worked and had committed suicide. Chini had even arranged some part-time work for Antonio there, although this takes him away from Martha at unforeseen times.

We asked Martha how reliable Antonio had been for her this season, and she said he was just fine. But she went on to say that besides working for Mr. Robertson on occasion, he had asked for time off to go fishing quite often, and she, of course, acceded quite easily to his requests. It sounded like business as usual for Antonio. He gets to have his cake and eat it, too, "working" for Martha. She paid him for four hours per day, five days per week, and he may have worked an average of fifteen out of that twenty hours from the sound of things, and knowing his past history. Still, Martha loves him, and was proud that he caught eight kilos of lobsters on one of his fishing forays.

Bill and Pam Lancaster, who had operated the Bamboo Bar in Nosara, opened another restaurant called "Marlin Bill's" where Renata's German restaurant had closed, next to the Hotel Taype. The managers of the Hotel Taype, which was generally known as "the German hotel," tried to change its name to "Star of the Pacific," but it failed to catch on. We're not sure what the official name is now; certainly the latter name seems pretty pretentious.

Martha went on to tell us that the beaches had been quite eroded due to *El Niño*. Things didn't look the same at all. Rocks were showing where they had never been seen before and sand was piled at odd places. But by the end of the season things were back to normal; the ocean had healed the scars caused by those earlier storms.

And yes, that was Kurt Russell with Goldie Hawn's lookalike daughter at the restaurant the night before we left last year. Martha had told us we would hear the truth of it sooner or later, and here it was. Skip's instincts had been correct.

Ralph and Liz Webster celebrated their fiftieth wedding anniversary at the Estancia, the place where the first fashion show had been held. Ralph had even worn a suit (in that heat!) and Liz a gown. They had come to Nosara from Fargo, North Dakota, after retirement, and Ralph had regularly practiced his long jump technique on the beach in preparation for the Senior Games back home. I believe he had been a judge before retirement.

The Kennedys sold the big place they had built on the mountain above Nosara and moved into a vacant house on top of the hill above Casa de las Flores, near the Baumunks'. Dianne Kennedy's two kittens escaped while she was away and wandered down through the jungle to Martha's. She heard them crying in the night and lured them in with milk. Next day she called around until she learned they belonged to Dianne, who gratefully reclaimed them.

Martha showed us an article in the *Tico Times* about the Costa Rican equivalent of our EPA, which vowed to remove all houses built within the Maritime Zone. This zone includes everything less than 150 meters from the high tide line. They vowed to bulldoze all such properties.

We thought of Mary and Jim Rasmussen's lovely house where the wedding was held (Chapter 14) along with numerous other properties we knew of. Some say it could never happen; others say it will.

Bananas were few this year due to *El Niño*, and while there had been loads of mangoes, the monkeys had eaten or ruined most of those. Antonio had to haul away wheelbarrow loads of half-eaten mangoes and dump them in the jungle. So, between *El Niño* and the monkeys, Martha had to buy most of her fruit this year. But she said it was worth it to be able to watch the monkeys so regularly.

The beautiful Hotel Playas de Nosara was out of business for the most part this year, since John Frazier had the place torn up for further reconstruction. Even the kitchen was closed. The stockholders were very displeased, as usual, condemning John's management.

I asked Martha if it was difficult for her when she was alone. She replied, "Well . . . I wasn't afraid of being alone, but I got awfully tired of just reading . . . no one to play games with. George had me down for dinner a lot, and LaRue went to the beach with me most of the time. The Baumunks would stop for me when they went out to eat if I didn't have company. And the telephone helped a lot. I could just dial up Beverly or LaRue when I needed someone to talk with, and without everyone listening in like they did on the old CB. The phone was clear, too, just like at home. That was wonderful. But I didn't like being alone very long. I read so many books!"

Skip said sympathetically, "Sure, no one likes to be alone too much, and that would be real bad, no one to play games with." We all chuckled at that, knowing what each other was thinking.

"I'd like to sign up for one of the old condos," she continued. "I know so many of the people there, and one condo is open for January, February and March. It would just suit me fine, but I don't have my place sold yet and I don't want to do anything until I get it sold, so I guess I'll just have to wait."

I said, "That would be just perfect for you, Martha. Mary is there, and the Websters, and they have that nice pool now. It would be closer to the store and everything."

298

Later we received a letter from Mary Yost. She was suffering a serious bout with cancer and would not return to Nosara. It is so sad to see the "old guard" decimated. We will miss them and their wonderful tales of old Nosara.

Then during winter '98–'99 we learned from Martha that Mary Yost had succumbed to cancer. We mourn her passing, and are glad to have known her.

In the spring of 1999 we received word from Martha that she had sold Casa de las Flores. George Miller, always looking out for her, took it off her hands. We know she was relieved, as were we. The old place had become a burden to her. It is the end of another chapter of our connection with Nosara and Costa Rica.

When Martha returned from Costa Rica, she was eager to update us on the season's happenings. We delayed the reunion for a week or so because Skip had a bad cold. Just when he began to mend, Martha called to ask if it would be OK to visit us and give her report. She arrived about twenty minutes later to give us a detailed account over iced tea at the kitchen table. She looked healthy and tan, energetic as usual, and hugged us both.

She rehashed the selling of Casa de las Flores, saying how she appreciated George Miller taking it off her hands. Bolivar handled the details, making it a hassle-free transaction. He already had one of his construction workmen living in the house we built, the "new house."

She had really missed Mary Yost and decried the passing of the old guard. Ilona Biddington seemed to be surviving her bout with breast cancer. The Baumunks were back, and George was still playing tennis in his mid-eighties. Dos Elston had her house up for sale. Property values were still rising.

Since LaRue hadn't returned this year, Martha found a new friend to accompany her to the beach. Stephanie Donatelli, also rather lonely since her husband Phil was busy overseeing construction of their new house, became quite a fine beach companion. We were pleased that she found someone so compatible.

Martha arranged to swap the old "jeep" for a stay in one of the condominiums next year. And she has been promised that she can use it when she visits. But meanwhile she has it rented for more than the value of its sale. What a gal!

While in San José, Martha stayed at the new Bougainvillea Hotel, north of town. The owner, Hans, an old acquaintance, had flowers waiting in her room when she arrived. Of course, she was delighted.

When Martha had finished relating her season's story, I looked at Skip and asked, "Well, are you going to tell Martha what we've been up to?"

Skip said, "Yeah, Martha, we've been writing a book."

She looked puzzled, asking, "About what?"

I volunteered, "Its title is *Jungle Paradise, Almost: Our Adventures in Costa Rica.* You remember I told you I was keeping a diary to write a book? Well, we really did it."

Skip added, "Yes, and we dedicated it to Chet. It will even have a picture of the plaque in the church."

As her tears flowed, Martha stammered, "Well my goodness . . . isn't that something . . . !"

I added, "But you're the main character, Martha."

"Well . . . , I'll buy a copy!"